A DECADE

ARMAGEDDON

New Geography Essays

By

Susanne Trimbath

First published January 2024

by

Spiramus Press Ltd
102 Blandford Street
London W1U 8AG

www.spiramus.com

© Spiramus Press

ISBN
9781913507619 Hardback
9781910151587 Paperback
9781913507084 Digital

British Library Cataloguing-in-Publication Data.

A catalogue record for this book is available from the British Library.

Printed and bound in Great Britain by Grosvenor Group (Print Services) Ltd

A DECADE OF ARMAGEDDON

Contents

A DECADE OF ARMAGEDDON

Foreword

Susanne Trimbath's essays on the 2008 financial crisis represent a critical element in the continuing discussion of inequality and the growing power of a small financial elite. Although perhaps lost to many over time, the great financial crisis presaged our current reality by showing, in a definitive way, how inside power players can manipulate crises to their own advantage.

Her tracing of the role of Treasury officials in kowtowing to the financial giants shows that both President George W. Bush and Barack Obama did not differ in terms of deference. The results of a light touch, rather than punishment for clear malfeasance, could be seen in contributions to political leaders on both sides, and a refusal to confront the stark injustice of bailing out the ultra-rich while tossing working- and middle-class people out of their homes.

This has left a legacy with unfortunate characteristics. As conservative economist John Michaelson put it succinctly in 2018, "The economic legacy of the last decade is excessive corporate consolidation, a massive transfer of wealth to the top 1 percent from the middle class." In the United States, an affluent class of roughly 1.35 million people—the top 1 percent—is doing fine, but wealth gains have been especially concentrated among the top 0.1 percent, roughly 150,000 people. Since the mid-1980s, the share of national wealth held by those below the top 10 percent has fallen by 12 percentage points, the same proportion that the top 0.1 percent gained.

Our politics today are downstream from these realities. The whole tenor of contemporary politics has been how to cope with a popular rebellion against the privileges of the elites, however malicious their actions. This was evident in both parties: the rise of Vermont Senator Bernie Sanders among Democrats and Donald Trump on the Republican side. These politicians are derided for being divisive, which is clearly true, but they would not thrive if the legacy of the Great Financial Crisis did not so shape our political realities.

As a daughter of working-class Pennsylvanians, Susanne perhaps was more attuned to these sentiments, and perhaps more sympathetic, than many financial analysts, particularly those associated with elite universities and financial companies. They want to play with theories and come up with projections; Susanne wants to show how real people, ordinary people, are impacted by both the greed of financial elites as well as the inability of government to rein it in.

A DECADE OF ARMAGEDDON

Readers of this volume will be schooled in these developments, and perhaps may be inspired to think about how our society and economy can be structured in a way that is more equitable and just. This does not mean socialism; Susanne, as far as I know, still embraces capitalism as the most effective economic system. But she is also no market fundamentalist, particularly when market power, in finance as well as other areas, has become ever more concentrated in ever fewer hands.

Systems can and should change, as they did after the Great Depression and as well during the Reagan revolution. It's when they don't that we need to worry about our own future and that of future generations.

Joel Kotkin is an internationally-recognized authority on global, economic, political and social trend. He is the author of ten previously published books, including the highly praised **The New Class Conflict** *(Telos Press), which describes the changing dynamics of class in America. He is Executive Editor of the widely read website NewGeography.com.*

Introduction

This as-it-happened review of the causes, consequences, and repercussions of the 2008 Global Financial Crisis ("GFC") is more than a history lesson – it's a look into the future. The GFC was the result of a rigged Washington-Wall Street game. Politicians placated you, telling you they really knew what was happening and what to do about it. "Pay no attention to that man behind the curtain", they said, telling you everything is under control. It wasn't. All the signs of the impending collapse were there at least five years before it happened. Washington regulators ignored the signs, the lessons not learned after all the previous crises. Wall Street always finds a way to profit from the problems it creates. I take no pride or pleasure in being right about predictions that devastate the economy and its people. But it is going to happen again.

The 2008 GFC was like all the financial crises that happened before it, and it will be the same for those that come after it. The regulators and bankers who cause financial crises love to think that *their* crisis is different; but they never are.[1] They just never learn the lessons. So, they make up excuses about how this crisis was so different that it was unavoidable.

The articles are arranged in seven parts that outline the overall event:

1) The US government bailed out the banks first, then

2) Congress held a bunch of hearings and wrote some legislation.

3) The failure of homeowners to pay their mortgages was initially pointed to as the culprit that caused the GFC but,

4) The actions of the Federal Reserve and Treasury tell a different story.

5) Eventually, everyone figured out that banker and broker behavior in the years leading up to the crisis was the real culprit.

6) The Treasury and Federal Reserve, along with other regulators and Congress, repeated behaviors that had by now become embedded in the way government works with financial markets.

7) Sadly, the public accepted the initial narrative of the irresponsible homeowner as the cause of the GFC. By the time the general media reported on the role of banks and regulators in creating and sustaining the GFC, it was too late. The public had grown weary of hearing about it and generally stopped listening.

---

[1] I discuss this in great detail in *Lessons Not Learned,* Spiramus Press, 2015 (LNL).

The first part of this collection has articles on the "Bailouts." The GFC bailouts provide evidence of the revolving door between Wall Street and Washington. For example, Jill Considine was the Chair and CEO who merged two SEC-registered self-regulatory organizations – National Securities Clearing Corporation and Depository Trust Company – to form Depository Trust and Clearing Corporation (DTCC), a holding company that is not registered with the SEC. That means they don't have as many regulatory requirements as their subsidiaries. After leaving DTCC, Ms. Considine was involved with a Bermuda company that provides services to hedge funds. Despite objections from members of Congress, she was named a Trustee for the American International Group bailout that cost $180 billion. Although repaid to Treasury, the investment yield was less than the interest rate Treasury paid to borrow money during the same period.

Fifteen years later, the Federal Deposit Insurance Corporation (FDIC) still owns some of the banks that failed during the GFC. That means FDIC is responsible for the assets and liabilities of the failed banks (they are in "receivership").[2] Some of the bank bailouts[3] were accomplished by special programs, made up by Treasury and the Federal Reserve. At that time, virtually every major broker converted their charter to become a bank to gain access to the Federal Reserve's financial largess. Overnight they were granted the new 'systemically important financial institution' moniker, which basically gave them 'too big to fail' status.

The government picked winners and losers without consideration for the cross-eyed incentive to fail that they created. The second part of the collection is "Congressional Hearings and Legislation" which often accomplish nothing more than create a public narrative that suits the purposes of politicians. Some banks/brokers were left to fail on their own in the GFC while others were bailed out or took part in mergers that were arranged by the Federal Reserve and Treasury.

During the GFC, homeowners were stuck between a rock and a hard place. Most homes were "under water" – the mortgage balance was higher than the market value of the home. If borrowers defaulted, it ruined their credit record. That's mostly what you heard about, that the owners gave up on the properties. If you are 50 feet underwater, why would you stay and bail it out? The banks and government told you there was no choice. During the GFC, the government

---

[2] https://www.fdic.gov/about/strategic-plans/strategic/receivership.html
[3] Available in LNL, Chapter 8.

A DECADE OF ARMAGEDDON

made it easier for you to default on your mortgage than to sell or pay off the mortgage. Lehman Brothers even refused to accept mortgage payments in Florida after purchasing multiples of the mortgage value in credit default swaps. Those swaps meant they could make more money if you defaulted than if you made your mortgage payment. If you listened to the news, you thought irresponsible homeowners caused the GFC. In reality, it was the bankers. Banks sold mortgages into bonds but never changed the lien on the property with the county recorders – so the bondholders couldn't prove ownership of the house if you defaulted on an underlying mortgage. All this is covered in the third part of this book, "Homeowners and Mortgages".

"Federal Reserve and Treasury Actions" are next. A lot of what the Treasury and Federal Reserve did to bailout Wall Street from the GFC required bending the rules. Neither entity, for example, was permitted by law to make loans to private companies; that was only for registered financial firms. Yet companies like Harley Davidson were recipients of the government's largess after the GFC. They did it again in 2023 to bail out Silicon Valley Bank and Signature Bank.

The fifth part of this book includes the articles about "Bank/Broker Behavior" in the years leading up to and following the GFC. Of course, fraud, cheating and other problems among banks and brokers were not unique to the GFC. In the years after 2008, they took bailout money and then decorated offices, threw lavish parties, and even paid for prostitutes. Although they were called to Capitol Hill to explain themselves, there were no further repercussions for that behavior. In 2018, Wells Fargo agreed to a $2.09 billion settlement over charges of selling mortgages it knew were based on inaccurate income information between 2005 and 2007.[4] Banks never admit liability when they make settlements and these banks were no different. There are many obvious examples of the US government helping large financial institutions without consideration for limiting the adverse incentive effects. Without repercussions, they just repeat the behavior *ad nauseam*.

The articles in the sixth part, "Systemic Issues", are probably the most technical, although still written in plain business language. These articles describe the lack of enforcement for existing rules.[5] The people who work at the Washington regulators and the Wall Street firms are recycled over and over. Each time they

---

[4] https://money.cnn.com/2018/08/01/investing/wells-fargo-settlement-mortgage-loans/index.html

[5] The necessity of **enforcement** and **discipline** for stable financial markets is the topic of *LNL*, Chapter 7

bring their own agenda, owing favors to the place they just left and creating obligations for the next place they want to get hired. Hundreds of people are recycled through the revolving door. Just as members of congress who lose their seat get jobs as lobbyists, the same is true for financial regulators.

The lack of enforcement for financial regulations is only surpassed by the lack of discipline when rule breakers are caught (or confess). The Dodd-Frank Act of 2010 was expected to make all the changes necessary to prevent another GFC. But most of it only required regulators to do studies and propose their own rules. Some of the required work still wasn't completed by 2023. For example, the SEC had 67 mandatory rulemaking provisions in Dodd-Frank; eight of them are still in the proposal stage and three haven't even been started.[6] Some of the new rules, like ones requiring broader applications of fiduciary duty across financial institutions, were eliminated by the next administration that moved into the White House.

"Public Reaction" to the GFC is the topic of the articles in the final part. At the time, "Occupy" movements started in lower Manhattan (New York City) and spread globally to major cities in about 70 countries by October 2011. Occupy movements protested the social and economic inequality created by large corporations and the global financial system. They were initially installed near stock exchanges. In 2012, a member of the Bank of England's financial policy committee, stated publicly that the Occupy movement in London was correct in its attack on the international financial system.

Fast forward a decade and Bloomberg news dubbed 2020 "The Year of the Meme Stock" as Reddit chat rooms touted various stocks as the next big money-makers. Where the Occupy movement decried the 1% for taking more than their share from global wealth, the Meme Stock movement declared "We Are the 99%". According to the documentary *Apes Together Strong* (2023, Finley and Quinn Mulligan), many household investors used their COVID-19 stimulus checks to invest in the stock market based on "tips" they got in Reddit chat rooms. By February 2021, I started getting Twitter messages, phone calls and emails from various Reddit users and moderators seeking an explanation of "what the heck just happened to me!?!". When I heard about the "GameStop Short Squeeze" on the news and started seeing social media posts about the "Mother of All Short Squeezes" (MOASS), I shook my head, closed my eyes, and muttered "here we go again". I'll save the rest of that story for the Epilogue.

---

[6] https://www.sec.gov/securities-topics/dodd-frank-act

A DECADE OF ARMAGEDDON

As I prepared this collection, I was both pleased and dismayed at finding that much of what I predicted about the aftermath of the GFC came to pass. There are several places where I was able to include updated website links, more current data, or updates on the consequences – and often repetition – of actions that led to the GFC and the Great Recession. My overall feeling is one of increasing dismay. I see evidence of the same problems building up in today's headlines. The names have changed, but the problems of capital market self-regulation and the Washington-Wall Street Revolving Door remain. As long as the foxes are in charge of the henhouse, no nest egg can be safe.

A Note to Readers

I hope the business language presentation in this collection will help you understand the causes and consequences of financial services run amok. The title of this book could easily have been *Wall Street Gone Wild*. We can trace the origins back to deregulation in the Reagan, Bush, and Clinton administrations. What pushed it over the edge was Washington's incompetence and inaction in the form of both regulators choosing to look the other way and the Federal Reserve dropping interest rates and keeping them low enough to give Wall Street cheap borrowing costs. We should have expected nothing less than the global financial crisis that we experienced because the regulatory ineptitude took place in the US, home to the world's largest financial markets.

For those readers who already have a viewpoint, who had direct experience with the Global Financial Crisis ("GFC") and the subsequent recession, you may find a slightly different take here than that generally reported in the media at the time. If you didn't experience the GFC, you may be shocked and amazed by what did – and didn't – happen. When I left consulting and started teaching economics full-time at a community college in 2016, I found that very few students knew anything about what happened just eight years earlier. Most were too young: more than half of community college students are less than 22 years old, so they were young teenagers when it happened. Some remembered the financial morass it caused for their parents and their parents' businesses. Those students who had experienced the GFC and recession directly were amazed to learn that US financial regulators had seen all this before and yet played a major role – again – in causing another financial crisis. Regulators failed to learn the lessons of previous crises, lessons about prudent regulation, strict enforcement and the disciplinary actions that remove the incentive for Wall Street to do it all again.

This collection of articles provides an "as-it-happened" look at the causes, consequences, and repercussions of the GFC. It contains 72 of more than 100 of my articles and blogs published on NewGeo from 2008 to 2015. I selected the ones that are relevant to the GFC that developed during the Great Recession of 2007 to 2008. I was drafting *Lessons Not Learned* while I wrote these articles. Some of them are business language versions of chapters that ended up in that book. Where the subject matter is very similar, I include references to LNL as footnotes for anyone interested in taking a deeper dive. In fact, the cover for LNL was inspired by the same photo used on NewGeography.com for the article "The Swaps of Damocles" (see p138). The articles and blogs are presented here in chronological order within each of the seven parts. Each part includes a brief introduction to the collection of articles in that category.

There were no footnotes on NewGeo, though I sometimes included "notes" at the end of articles. In this collection, those were moved to footnotes for this book. Hyperlinks are available in-text for the PDF version; for readers of the printed editions, they are in footnotes. There is also a resources tab on the webpage with these hyperlinks, the QR code at the back of this book also links to this.[7] Where I could make a brief update to the content of an article, those are in footnotes; longer updates are in the Epilogue. All long tables have been moved to appendices for ease of reading.

---

[7] https://spiramus.com/decade-of-armageddon-links-and-references

Acknowledgements

I met Joel Kotkin when we both worked with Milken Institute in California. He was already a prolific author, and I was a newly minted economics Ph.D. I remember asking him for advice about writing and getting published. He told me two things that stay with me to this day. First, whatever your subject or field, there is a public dialog taking place in print, TV, radio, and all forms of media. Your goal as a writer is to enter that dialog. Thinking about writing that way helped me understand the approach I needed to take to get more of my work published more often. The second thing he told me is that no one gets rich writing books that stem from academic research. Joel told me to think about my books as very expensive business cards. They are a way for people to find out about your work, your research, your ideas, and your capabilities. Remembering that helped me to get past watching the sales count and instead focus on how my ideas are received.

Joel started NewGeography.com (NewGeo) in early 2008 as a joint venture with Praxis Strategy Group. The battery of contributors aligned with NewGeo included specialists in global, economic, political, and social trends – but none in economics or finance. Joel approached me shortly after the financial crisis came to a head in 2008. From October of that year through early 2017, he published more than 100 of my articles and blogs on the website. Joel personally edited each piece. The most frequent feedback he gave me was to "stop burying the lead!" I tended to write as if telling a story where I didn't want to give away the ending. As he explained to me, it is the economic and financial conclusion that captures the audience's attention and makes them want to read the rest of the article. I am a tremendously better writer today than I was before working with Joel. For that, I will always be grateful.

This collection never would have been published without encouragement from Carl Upsall at Spiramus Press. Cecilia Hallpike was instrumental in getting the online articles arranged and formatted for publication as a book. My thanks also to my sister, Rebecca Hillebrand, who helped me see that the publisher thought I could sell more books than I thought I could – her on-going support for my work is a constant source of encouragement. PJ Buchanan helped to keep my writing from sounding like an academic paper; she read an early version of the Introduction and made valuable suggestions for improvements.

Finally, I am grateful to the more than 78,000 users who follow me on X-Twitter. Their questions often spur me to take a closer look at current events. They regularly remind me that there are more than 500,000 users on Reddit, mainly household investors, who draw inspiration from my work. Many had never heard about direct registration of stock shares before I talked about it in podcasts, X-Tweets and documentaries. They claim that in the eighteen months after they first contacted me, I inspired them to put over 5 million shares of GameStop into direct registration, where they are beyond the reach of Wall Street. The movement of GameStop shares to direct registration was so noticeable – about 25 percent of all GameStop shares are held by household investors through direct registration – that the company started reporting the total number of shares in direct registration in their routine SEC reports. To those "Apes" I can only say: "ook ook"!

1. Bailouts

The bank and broker bailouts came in a wide variety of flavors. The specific legislation is covered in chapter 2 (Congressional Hearings and Legislations). Here we present the articles and blogs that are all about who, what, when, where, and why there were bailouts in 2008-9 for Wall Street and not for Main Street. Much of what was being done required new laws or at least the bending of some existing laws. This chapter includes articles on who got the money and how the true cost, which was to be borne by US taxpayers, was hard to calculate and often purposefully hidden from public view.

Should we bailout Geithner too?

January 22, 2009

This morning the Senate Finance Committee approved the nomination for treasury secretary of Timothy F. Geithner, head of the Federal Reserve Bank of New York. Geithner is a Wall Street darling, but taxpayers may have a different take. Senator Jim Bunning (R-KY) reminded us at the Senate confirmation hearing January 20 that Geithner was part of every bailout and every failed policy put forth by the current Treasury Secretary [Henry "Hank" Paulson Jr.]. After you read this, you should begin to see why I'm so opposed to Geithner's appointment – I don't want the fox any closer to the hen house than he already is.

For starters, look at what the Fed has admittedly been up to – this is from a recent speech by the President of the San Francisco Fed,[1] Janet Yellen. The Federal Reserve Act authorizes the Fed to lend to "individuals, partnerships, or corporations" in extraordinary times. For the first time since the Great Depression, the Fed is invoking this authority to make direct loans to subprime borrowers – that is, those who can't get credit from a bank.

Basically, the New York Fed, under Geithner's direction, created a couple of special companies so they could print money to get around restrictions on what the Fed can do directly. Now, be perfectly clear on this first point – this is not Treasury or TARP or Congress that's spending this money. It's the Federal Reserve. They don't have to ask Congress for money, they just print it. The Fed is providing "credit to a broad range of private borrowers." And by-and-large, they don't have to tell you who they give the money to, either. Here's how Yellen put it:

---

[1] https://www.frbsf.org/our-district/press/presidents-speeches/yellen-speeches/2009/january/yellen-us-monetary-policy-objectives/

"It is worth noting that, as the nation's central bank, the Fed can issue as much currency and bank reserves as required to finance these asset purchases and restore functioning to these markets. Indeed, the Federal Reserve's balance sheet has already ballooned from about $900 billion at the beginning of 2008 to more than $2.2 trillion currently—and is rising."

Average Federal Reserve balance sheet

Year	Reserves	% change
2000	$625,822,500,000	
2001	$653,774,500,500	4.5%
2002	$740,502,000,000	13.3%
2003	$762,853,509,434	3.0%
2004	$803,004,846,154	5.3%
2005	$843,397,519,231	5.0%
2006	$877,922,692,308	4.1%
2007	$907,023,643,846	3.3%
2008	$1,228,848,679,245	35.5%
2009	$2,175,364,000,000	77.0%

2000-2002 are for the last two weeks only of the year; 2009 is for the first two weeks only. Data available from https://www.federalreserve.gov/releases/h41/. [As of 10 May 2023, the Fed's balance sheet was $8.5 trillion, nearly ten times its value in 2008.]

Notice how easy it is to double our money – they just keep the printing presses running. In fact, the recent expansion is extraordinary. Since 2003 the Fed's balance sheet averaged only $838 billion. So, this doubling has all taken place in the past year. In the last recession, around 2002, the Fed's balance sheet increased by only 13%. If the current recession started in 2007, and if the Fed's balance sheet is any gauge, then we're in for much worse.

Where are they spending all this cash? You probably didn't hear that the Fed started buying commercial paper through these "private-sector vehicle[s]" created to sidestep an act of Congress. (Commercial paper is the short-term debt of corporations.) Another thing you aren't hearing about is that back in

November 2008, the Fed bought $600 billion of mortgage-backed securities from AIG. This action, if taken without subterfuge, would not be legal. The Federal Reserve Act limits the Fed to buying securities that were issued or guaranteed by the US Treasury or US agencies. In order for the Executive Branch to get around a limit placed by the Legislative Branch, the Fed got help from the Treasury.

Yellen laid it out unabashedly: "Cooperation with the Treasury is necessary because the program entails some risk of loss and, under the Federal Reserve Act, all Fed lending must be appropriately secured. The Treasury has committed $20 billion of TARP funds to protect the Fed against losses on the Fed's lending commitment of up to $200 billion." Don't kid yourself: this is a credit default swap on a national level.

On June 26, 2008, the Fed used this scheme to buy the assets of Bear Stearns. That money went to JP Morgan.[2] On November 25, 2008, Geithner's New York Fed bought out the underlying assets for which American International Group (AIG) had written credit default swaps, saving AIG from having to pay off the swaps when the assets failed. On December 12, 2008, they bought more residential mortgage-backed securities from AIG. Those two bailout packages currently stand at about $73 billion. The big ones are those where the recipients are not being named. On October 27, 2008, they bought commercial paper from "eligible issuers." On November 24, 2008, they bought "certificates of deposit, bank notes, and commercial paper from eligible issuers."

In an odd twist of democracy, you can read all about Geithner's personal income tax problem[3] but you won't find anywhere information on who is benefiting from this particular bailout money which Geithner is in charge of passing out. The commercial paper bailout from the Fed (this doesn't include anything that Treasury is doing or that Congress has authorized) stands at $333 billion.[4]

They aren't done, either. According to Yellen, there are plans in place to substantially expand this spree of lending, buying, and guaranteeing to include

---

[2] https://www.federalreserve.gov/BoardDocs/LegalInt/FederalReserveAct/2008/20080626/20080626.pdf

[3] https://www.finance.senate.gov/release/baucus-grassley-comment-regarding-treasury-nominee-geithner

[4] https://www.federalreserve.gov/releases/H41/Current/h41.pdf (Link is to current report. For records going back to June 1997, see https://www.federalreserve.gov/releases/H41/)

more kinds of assets issued by more kinds of institutions, like commercial loans and non-agency mortgage-backed securities.

Senator Chuck Grassley (R-IA) referred to this as Geithner's participation in "a monstrous act of government intervention and ownership over our financial markets." While TARP has a Special Inspector General and various congressional oversight duties, similar transparency and oversight does not exist for the bailouts conducted by Geithner in New York. Geithner may be, as Grassley asked him, "the general, drawing on your financial sector expertise, who will marshal the financial troops and assets of the Treasury Department." But he can't "lead our nation to prosperity."

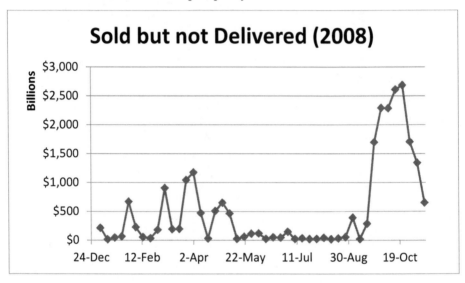

Figure 1
Source: Public data, available from the Federal Reserve Bank of New York.

He couldn't, in six years, stop the primary dealers in US Treasuries from selling more bonds than Treasury issued (Figure 1). The only way this could go on to the extent that it did, with an average of $2.1 trillion of Treasuries sold but undelivered for seven weeks from September 24 to November 5, is because Geithner did not have the support of the "financial troops" to stop it. In fact, I will suggest to you that this level of abuse, in what amounts to massive naked short selling of US Treasury securities,[5] could only be done with complicity.

---

[5] https://www.ipsnews.net/2009/01/finance-us-treasury-nominee-failed-to-halt-bond-scam/

A DECADE OF ARMAGEDDON

Finally, it is a simple matter to compare Geithner's activities at the Fed to those of Ken Lay at Enron. Remember all those "partnerships" with cool names derived from Star Wars movies? Geithner's New York Fed created Delaware Limited Liability Companies with the name "Maiden Lane" which is the Fed's street address in New York. They are using unregulated companies to make loans and to buy and sell assets completely outside the view of the public. The Senate Finance Committee approved Geithner's nomination on January 22, 2009 in an Open Executive Session. Geithner has proven he can hide the ball; let's not let this scheme move to Treasury.

The bailouts payments mount, the budget expands, the deficit widens, the national debt increases. How high is up?

March 4, 2009

How far can the totals go? Federal Reserve Chairman Ben Bernanke testified before the Senate Budget Committee[6] on March 3, 2009. He believes that the markets will be "quite able" to absorb the debt issued by the US government over the next couple of years to cover all the bailout and stimulus payments "if there is confidence that the US will get it [the economy] under control." When Senator Lindsey Graham (R-SC) suggested an "outer limit" at which the national debt was three times gross domestic product, Bernanke said that "it wouldn't happen because things would break down before that." They'll be lending to homeowners who have higher debt ratios than that. Frankly, I'd rather lend to the US government at that ratio, and I suspect a lot of investors – both domestic and foreign – feel the same way.

On the one hand, Bernanke spoke like a "Master of the Universe" when he told the Senators that he wasn't worried that printing all this extra money would generate future inflation. He said that when the economy begins to grow again, the Federal Reserve is "very comfortable" they will be able to deflate their bloated balance sheet. On the other hand, he did not sound like a Federal Reserve Chairman when Bernanke said, "We don't know for sure what the future will bring." Of the two Bernankes I like the second one better: no one knows exactly what the future will bring. Why pretend that you know what the

---

[6] https://www.federalreserve.gov/newsevents/testimony/bernanke20090303a.htm

best action to take three years from now will be – or what impact it will have. I find it disconcerting, to say the least.

There are a few things we can watch for in the coming weeks and months. The President's budget came out yesterday and will go through Congress now for approval. Don't get too distracted by it though – virtually everything in it can change. Instead, work with what you know. The stimulus package was passed, and the states are getting details now on how much and for what they can expect money from Washington. Focus on where that money is going. The best way to minimize the damage being done by the Federal Reserve's printing presses is to be sure that money is spent in the real economy. That means roads, bridges, schools, sewer systems – and not research and development on sources of alternative fuel or studies on global warming. We are in the middle of a crisis. This is not the time to spend on wishes and dreams. If the money is spent on real infrastructure projects, it can help to mitigate the potential inflationary effects later.

The Treasury and the Federal Reserve have no choice but to keep their foot planted fully on the accelerator. Setting infrastructure in place now means we'll get good traction later when the economy starts moving forward.

Digging into AIG bonuses and other aid recipients

March 18, 2009

On Sunday March 15, 2009, American International Group, Inc. (AIG) revealed the identities of some of the beneficiaries of about half of the nearly $180 billion the US government has committed ($173 billion actually paid out so far) to support the ailing international financial giant. As we now know, AIG sold credit default swaps (CDS) that paid off if the market value of some bonds fell. (I use the term "bond" here generally to refer to the alphabet soup of CDO, CLO, MBS, etc. – all of which are debt that is sold to the public.) (See Appendix 1 for MBS diagram and explanation). Most CDS only pay off if the borrower fails to make payments – something that hasn't happened in the case where AIG is making payments. The geniuses at AIG – and we know they are geniuses because they earned $165 million in bonuses for the effort – took on completely unknown risks for, apparently, insufficient premiums, resulting in the need for an emergency $85 billion loan last September from the Federal Reserve Bank of New York (courtesy of my buddy Tim Geithner) to "avoid severe financial disruptions"… as if **that** worked!

Whatever. So, now AIG is letting us know who got our money: $22.4 billion for payouts on the CDS and $27.1 billion to buy the bonds underlying the CDS (so some of the CDS could be cancelled). That's about $50 billion so far for derivatives – no one knows how much more they'll need. Here's a summary by the country where the recipients are based:

Country	CDS Payout
US	$16.0
France	$13.3
German	$8.1
Switzerland	$3.3
UK	$2.0
Canada	$1.1
Netherlands	$0.8
Scotland	$0.5
Spain	$0.3
Denmark	$0.2

Numbers in billions. $4.1 billion paid to "other" not included here. Numbers won't total to $49.5 billion due to rounding.

There was also $12.1 billion paid to US municipalities (states, cities, school districts, etc.) – where states invested, for example, bond proceeds prior to expenditure. In those cases, the municipalities invested in assets with guaranteed rates of return (another genius idea at AIG!). The bigger numbers belong to the states that had recent large bond issues – for example, $1.02 billion to California which has yet to distribute a dime of the bond money raised for stem cell research (due to on-going litigation).

AIG took $2.5 billion for their own business needs – like the bonuses? The $165 million bonuses were just for the London-office that specialized in selling those very special CDS. Total bonuses paid were $450 million for all the geniuses at AIG[7] – the AIG who made $6.2 billion in 2007 and lost $37.6 billion in the first nine months of 2008![8]

The most interesting bit, perhaps, are payments of $43.7 billion to securities lenders – those stock and bond holders who lend out their shares to enable short sellers. This means that AIG borrowed stocks so they could short sell them –

[7] https://www.marketwatch.com/story/aig-details-105-billion-payouts-banks?dist=FSQ
[8] https://www.marketwatch.com/investing/stock/AIG/financials/income/quarter

make an investment that paid off only if the prices fell. (If you don't know what short selling is, here's a five minute video that explains it in a light-hearted way.)[9] Bottom line – it gave AIG incentives to push down market prices. And their announcements and actions at the end of 2008 certainly achieved that goal. Way to go, geniuses!

The continuing debate on AIG

March 19, 2009

The House of Representatives is debating a 90 percent tax on executive bonus payments made to companies receiving bailout funds. Anything they pass will still have to get through the Senate and past the President's desk. They are "upset about something they already did," according to Dan Lungren (R-CA). Congress ignored the opportunity to deal with this[10] back when you and me and 100,000 other voters were telling them not to pass the bailout legislation.[11]

Executive compensation schemes at American International Group (AIG) have been under investigation by the New York State Attorney General, Andrew Cuomo since last fall. He is ramping up the investigation now, given the news over the weekend of new bonus disbursements, to determine if the bonus contracts are unenforceable for fraud under New York law. AIG agreed with Cuomo last October not to use their own "deferred compensation pool" to pay bonuses – and then bargained with executives to make the payments anyway! AIG execs got contracts in early 2008 that guaranteed their bonuses[12] – information that former Treasury Secretary Paulson and current Treasury Secretary Geithner (former President of the New York Federal Reserve Bank) had when they initiated the original bailout.

It's pretty amazing 1) that taxpayers are bailing out a company that's under criminal investigation; 2) that Treasury didn't negotiate compensation schemes before they wrote the first check (like they do with auto workers?); and 3) that the bonuses are a bigger story than the fact that more than one-third of the bailout money was shipped overseas.

---

[9] https://www.cc.com/video/7pous8/the-daily-show-with-jon-stewart-the-money-honey-bee

[10] http://edition.cnn.com/2009/POLITICS/03/19/aig.bonuses.congress/index.html

[11] H.R.1586 - FAA Air Transportation Modernization and Safety Improvement Act 111th Congress (2009-2010) was signed by the President on 08/10/2010 and became Public Law No: 111-226 without mention of TARP

[12] https://abcnews.go.com/images/Business/EdLiddy03_14_09_letter.pdf

Layout for the bailout: $3.8 trillion and counting

March 21, 2009

Bloomberg.com reporters Mark Pittman and Bob Ivry are reporting a running total of the money the US government has pledged and spent for bailouts and economic stimulus payments.[13] The total disbursed through February 24, 2009 stands at $3.8 trillion; the total commitment is $11.6 trillion. The Federal Reserve is providing the largest share at $7.6 billion, followed by the US Treasury at $2.2 trillion and Federal Deposit Insurance Corporation (FDIC) at $1.6 trillion. The Department of Housing and Urban Development (HUD) and support for Fannie Mae and Freddie Mac, combined with purchases of student loans – bailout money that comes closest to directly bailing out Main Street – total only $760 billion – less than 7 percent of the total.

The national debt currently stands at $10.8 trillion[14] — versus an authorized limit of $12.1 trillion.

Last week, US Treasury Secretary Timothy Geithner got into a tiff with the rest of the world (denied by President Obama) by telling them that they should spend at least 2 percent of their GDP on their own stimulus packages.

The US commitment of $11.6 trillion equals 81 percent of US 2008 gross domestic product (GDP, $14.3 trillion). The $787 billion fiscal stimulus is 5.4 percent of GDP. Just the two-thirds of the stimulus that represents new spending (one-third is tax cuts) is 3.6 percent of GDP. Here's what financial institutions in various countries got from US taxpayers by way of the AIG bailout:

Country	Bailout Benefit (billions)
US	$ 31.1
France	$ 19.1
German	$ 16.7
UK	$ 12.8
Switzerland	$ 5.4
Netherlands	$ 2.3
Canada	$ 1.1

---

[13] The Bloomberg article is no longer available free online. ProPublica has a Bailout Tracker updated through 2022. It is available at https://projects.propublica.org/bailout/.
[14] https://fiscaldata.treasury.gov/americas-finance-guide/national-debt/. As of 2 February 2023, it is $31.5 trillion.

Country	Bailout Benefit (billions)
Spain	$ 0.3
Denmark	$ 0.2
Italy	$ 0.2
Serbia	$ 0.2

Mortgage-backed securities: 1/3 not backed!

April 11, 2009

On April 3, 2009, (Formerly Hon.) R. Glen Ayers spoke at the American Bankruptcy Institute in Washington, D.C. Ayers is a former bankruptcy judge, now with the law firm Langley & Banack in San Antonio, Texas. He spoke on a subject I covered on March 4 (see p59) – not all mortgage backed securities are actually backed by mortgages. The rush to write more mortgages and to issue more bonds meant that mistakes were made in the paperwork.

The Ayers speech is connected to an article he wrote with Judge Samuel L. Bufford, who had the California case I mentioned last month where the mortgage note disappeared after being transferred to Freddie Mac. In the article, "Where's the Note, Who's the Holder",[15] they drop this bombshell:

> "A lawyer sophisticated in this area has speculated to one of the authors that perhaps a third of the notes 'securitized' have been lost or destroyed."

Meaning that 1/3 of the mortgage-backed securities are not backed by mortgages!

This is the junk that Treasury Secretary Geithner wants to finance the hedge funds to purchase. As of the end of 2008, there was $6,838.7 billion worth of government-backed mortgage bonds outstanding. An additional $178 billion were issued in the first two months of 2009.[16]

Scary stuff. No wonder the hedge funds are giving Geithner's Public-Private Investment Partnership "two thumbs-down."

According to an article in the July 9-23 issue of Rolling Stone magazine, for a 2006 mortgage-backed security (MBS) issued by Goldman Sachs,

---

[15]https://livinglies.me/2009/02/19/this-is-it-where%e2%80%99s-the-note-who%e2%80%99s-the-holder-enforcement-of-promissory-note-secured-by-real-estate/
[16] Data from SIFMA.org.

"58 percent of the loans included little or no documentation – no names of the borrowers, no addresses of the homes, just zip codes."

In he article ("The Great American Bubble Machine"[17]), Taibbi confirms a lot of what I've been writing about Wall Street's involvement in the financial crisis – and more.

And don't forget: these MBS are what the government is putting our money into with the new toxic asset "Legacy" program. A July 8, 2009 Press Release from the U.S. Treasury lists the firms who will be buying what the government is selling.[18] You'll notice that Goldman Sachs isn't putting up any money. Now we know why – there's no "M" in their "BS".

Who's watching AIG?

May 16, 2009

The House Committee on Oversight and Government Reform held a hearing on Wednesday – "AIG: Where is the Taxpayer Money Going?"[19] Questions are being raised about whether the bailout better serves the interests of AIG's customers and trading partners or the interests of US taxpayers.

The highlight of the Committee's questioning of Chairman and CEO Edward Liddy came when Chairman Town (D-NY) asked the blunt question: "Why would you give retention bonuses to AIG employees who failed? Plus, the economy is so messed up, where would they go?" On the minds of many committee members were the facts that AIG got $70 billion in TARP money, $50 billion through the Federal Reserve Bank of New York's Maiden Lane LLC and another $60 billion directly from the Federal Reserve Bank of New York (the FRB-NY's AIG Credit Facility). When compared to the fact that AIG is currently worth just $5 billion, the repeated question became: "How will taxpayers be repaid?" Mr. Liddy pointed to the value of some subsidiaries and other assets that can be sold off, but he had to admit that the timing and possibility of AIG repaying taxpayers really "depends on the economy and the capital markets."

The Trustees of the AIG Credit Facility Trust testified in the second panel. The Trustees were named by the Federal Reserve Bank of New York, under then-

---

[17] This article originally appeared in the July 9-23, 2009 of Rolling Stone; posted online April 5, 2010.

[18] https://home.treasury.gov/news/press-releases/tg200

[19] https://oversightdemocrats.house.gov/legislation/hearings/aig-where-is-the-taxpayer-money-going

President Timothy Geithner, in September 2008. The panel included one non-Trustee – Professor J.W. Verret of George Mason University School of Law. Professor Verret expressed concern over the form of the AIG trust agreement: "I am concerned by the AIG trust because of the precedent it sets. Secretary Geithner has announced his intention to create another trust to manage the Treasury's investment in Citigroup as well as other TARP participants. If the AIG trust, crafted during the Secretary's tenure as President of the New York Fed, is used as a model for these new entities, the risk to taxpayers will be multiplied many times over." Professor Verret raised three specific problems with the agreement: 1) the agreement specifically expects the Trustees to act in the best interest of the US Treasury, not the US taxpayers; 2) the Trustees cannot be held liable for their actions; and 3) the Trustees can invest on information they gain in the course of their duties.

At the end of the hearing, the final question went to Representative Kaptur (D-OH). Too many of the AIG Trustees also serve or have served as directors and officers to other TARP recipients. Ms. Kaptur noted that all of the witnesses are connected to Wall Street and all know each other. Evidently, one of the Trustees, Jill Considine[20], is involved with a Bermuda company that provides services to hedge funds. Ms. Considine was uncomfortable naming the hedge funds that benefit from her advice because the Bermuda company is private – it is also foreign. Considine took Kaptur aside when the hearing ended, engaging her in an animated conversation – off the record, of course.[21]

It seems evident that some of the Trustees didn't recognize the risks AIG was taking when they were in a position to have close contact with not only AIG but their counterparties – those final recipients of the bailout money. If the Trustees missed the AIG risk then, when they were regulators in the self-regulatory industry and serving on Boards at the Federal Reserve Banks, then what can we expect from them now?

---

[20] Ms. Considine was named Chairman & CEO of Depository Trust Company in 1999. The same year, she orchestrated the merger with National Securities Clearing Corporation and three other clearing organizations to form the holding company Depository Trust and Clearing Corporation (DTCC). She remained Chairman & CEO of DTCC until 2007.

[21] Politico later reported: 'Standing just a foot or two from Considine, Kaptur said, "You are defending the worst-behaving corporations that are too big and too irresponsible." "They hire outside people to come in and rape us," Kaptur said, her voice rising.' https://www.politico.com/story/2009/05/kaptur-explodes-at-aig-trustee-022494

$12.8 trillion committed to bailout

June 2, 2009

Shortly after I told you that Bloomberg.com is reporting a running total of the money the US government has pledged and spent for bailouts and economic stimulus, reporters Mark Pittman and Bob Ivry updated the totals: So far, $12.8 trillion has been pledged – an additional $1.2 trillion over the earlier report. The total disbursed through March 31, 2009, stands at $4.2 trillion. The Federal Reserve is still committed to providing the largest share at $7.8 trillion, followed by the US Treasury $2.7 trillion and FDIC $2.0 trillion.[22]

The national debt currently stands at $11.3 trillion[23] — versus an authorized limit of $12.1 trillion. Spending, lending and bailouts by the Federal Reserve are not counted toward the limit.

This week, US Treasury Secretary Timothy Geithner is in China. Mainland China holds $767.9 billion of Treasury securities at the end of March 2009, about 7 percent of the total national debt. Japan, the second largest major foreign holder, has $686.7 billion.

---

[22] The Bloomberg article is no longer available free online. ProPublica has a Bailout Tracker updated through August 2022 that includes taxpayer money that went to bailout the financial system. It is available at https://projects.propublica.org/bailout/. According to ProPublica, Treasury earned $109 billion over 6 years on $635 billion disbursed. That's an annual yield of 1.2%. Over the same period, Treasury paid an average of 3.1% to borrow money through the sale of public debt.

[23] https://fiscaldata.treasury.gov/americas-finance-guide/national-debt/ As of 2 February 2023, it is $31.5 trillion.

Figure 2

Notes: Data from Department of the Treasury. Caribbean Banking Centers (Carib Bnkng Ctrs) include Bahamas, Bermuda, Cayman Islands, Netherlands Antilles, Panama, and British Virgin Islands. Oil exporters include Ecuador, Venezuela, Indonesia, Bahrain, Iran, Iraq, Kuwait, Oman, Qatar, Saudi Arabia, the United Arab Emirates, Algeria, Gabon, Libya, and Nigeria.

The US bailout commitment of $11.6 trillion equals 89 percent of US 2008 gross domestic product (GDP).

No bailout of small businesses

July 17, 2009

CIT Group Inc. acknowledged today that "policy makers" turned down their request for aid. It's always sad when a company fails and goes into bankruptcy – people lose their jobs, all the vendor companies that sell them products suffer from the loss of business, etc. But what makes this one especially sad is that CIT, according to Bloomberg News, "specializes in loans to smaller firms, counting 1 million enterprises, including 300,000 retailers, among its customers."

This news comes on the heels of an appearance by former Secretary of Treasury Hank Paulson before the House Committee on Oversight and Government Reform. Summing up after the hearing, Chairman Edolphus Towns (D-NY) admitted that Congress turned over complete authority to Paulson in the Bailout last fall (Troubled Assets Relief Program, TARP): "with no accountability, no checks and balances." The result is "seemingly arbitrary decision-making."

Representatives at the hearing repeatedly accused Paulson of deceiving Congress by telling them (and everyone else) that the bailout money would be used to help homeowners. In the end, it was as if the previous administration pillaged the US Treasury on their way out of town.

In the third of a series of hearings designed around the Bank of America merger with Merrill Lynch, Paulson told the Committee that he had the authority[24] to remove Ken Lewis as head of the bank if he didn't go through with the merger.

Rep. Jim Jordan (R-OH) said there was "a pattern of deception." He asked specifically, when did Paulson know that he was going to give the money to the banks – which he did on October 13 – after telling Congress on October 3 that he was going to use it to buy up bad mortgages? Paulson's response was that he believed Congress knew they were giving him flexibility to do whatever he wanted – so he did.

The question now is this: did Paulson pick and choose among his friends to decide who got a bailout? Special Inspector General Neil Barofsky will report to the House Oversight Committee next week with the release of his quarterly report to Congress on the use of TARP funds. Recall that Barofsky's office is the only one with the authority to initiate criminal prosecutions. Maybe Paulson is still on his list.

Bailout success!!

July 18, 2009

"I guess the bailouts are working…for Goldman Sachs!"

The Daily Show With Jon Stewart, July 16, 2009, "Pyramid Economy"

Goldman Sachs reported $3.4 billion second quarter earnings. Mises Economics Blogger Peter Klein says[25] these earnings are the result of political capitalism – earned in the "nebulous world of public-private interactions." Klein points to an interesting perspective offered by The Streetwise Professor[26] (Craig Pirrong at University of Houston): Moral Hazard. Goldman Sachs' status as "too big to fail," conferred on them by the United States Government, has allowed them to increase the money they put at risk of loss in one day's trading by 33 percent

---

[24] https://oversight.house.gov/wp-content/uploads/2012/01/20090716Paulson.pdf

[25] https://mises.org/wire/goldman-sachs-best-business

[26] https://streetwiseprofessor.com/moral-hazard-goldman-edition/

since last May. Goldman received $10 billion in the TARP bailout on October 28, 2008; they returned the money on June 9, 2009.[27] By April 2009, they had paid about $149 million in dividends on the Treasury's investment – a negligible return. Goldman Sachs also will be receiving transaction fees for managing Treasury programs under contracts awarded to them during the Bailout and beyond. When Goldman Sachs changed its status to "bank" last year they also gained access to the FDIC safety net, which perversely provides incentives for banks to take risks by absorbing the consequences of losses.

To underscore the importance of cronies in capitalism, Goldman Sachs is on track to dole out bonuses equal to about $700,000 per employee[28] – a 17 percent increase over 2006, when bonuses were sufficient to "immunize 40,000 impoverished children for a year ... throw a birthday party for your daughter and one million of her closest friends ... and still have enough left over to buy a different color Rolls Royce for each day of the week."[29]

Since employees of Goldman Sachs will one day be in charge of the US Treasury, it only makes sense that the company has to keep them happy now – how else can they be assured of future access to capital?[30] The House Oversight and Government Reform Committee seems to think that former Treasury Secretary Hank Paulson – himself a former Goldman Sachs bonus recipient – gave bailout money to his cronies after telling Congress the money was for Main Street homeowners.

If it isn't clear by now that the United States Government is picking the winners and losers[31] in this economy, the experience of CIT Group Inc. – a century old lender to hundreds of thousands and small and medium-sized businesses that is being allowed to fail – should remove any doubts you may have had until now.

The United States Government passed an additional $12.1 billion to Goldman Sachs through the AIG bailout – money that won't be returned unless AIG succeeds. To assure *their* success, AIG is preparing to pay millions of dollars more in bonuses to their executives this year under the premise that a contract

---

[27] https://projects.propublica.org/bailout/

[28] https://caffertyfile.blogs.cnn.com/2009/06/22/goldman-sachs-may-make-its-largest-bonus-payouts-ever/

[29] https://abcnews.go.com/Business/FunMoney/story?id=2723990

[30] https://www.huffpost.com/entry/goldman-sachs-in-talks-to_b_235153

[31] https://oversight.house.gov/wp-content/uploads/2012/02/20090716Paulson.pdf

is a contract and must be honored (unless it's a UAW contract,[32] of course.) JP Morgan Chase reported better than expected earnings; even Bank of America, still reeling from the Merrill Lynch merger and extensive mortgage losses in California, earned $3.2 billion in the second quarter of 2009. Citigroup reported $4.28 billion profit in the second quarter.

With government money and government protection coming at them from all sides, it's a wonder *all* the big banks and big bank employees aren't rolling in dollar bills by now.

Follow the money: Special Inspector General for the bailout

July 24, 2009

The House Committee on Oversight and Government Reform held a critically important hearing on July 21 titled "Following the Money:[33] Report of the Special Inspector General for the Troubled Asset Relief Program (SIGTARP)." Sadly, the mainstream media underreported the meeting. They focused on Federal Reserve Chairman Ben Bernanke telling the House Financial Services Committee "don't worry," but missed Special Inspector General (SIG) Neil Barofsky telling the Oversight Committee all the really sexy stuff: Conflicts of Interest, Collusion, and Money Laundering.

Bernanke likes to tell us his Federal Reserve could take on a Super-Cop role,[34] but the truth is quite the opposite. Reviewing the SIG report, Oversight Committee Chairman Edolphus Towns (D-NY) described it as "a wake-up call to the Treasury and the Fed that our financial system cannot be run behind closed doors."

Back in October 2008, Congress passed a bill to relieve the suffering caused by the Subprime Crisis. The Troubled Asset Relief Program (TARP) gave Treasury the authority to "purchase, manage and sale $700 billion of toxic assets, primarily troubled mortgages and mortgage-backed securities." Within days, then Treasury Secretary (and former head of Goldman Sachs (NYSE: GS)) Hank

---

[32] https://www.cnbc.com/2013/12/11/retired-gm-workers-just-lost-450m-in-benefits-judge-rules-against-united-auto-workers-uaw.html

[33] https://oversight.house.gov/hearing/following-the-money-report-of-the-special-inspector-general-for-the-troubled-assets-relief-program/

[34] https://www.cbsnews.com/news/bernanke-fed-can-handle-supercop-role/

Paulson unilaterally decided to take the money but to do something completely different with it – that is bail out his good-old friends on Wall Street.

Representative John J. Duncan, Jr. (R-TN) noted that the banks that got TARP bailout money didn't use it to help homeowners but to buy other banks, increase investments in China, improve their balance sheets and, now, report huge profits. This is not merely something that bothers grousing Republicans. Representative Dennis J. Kucinich (D-OH), one of the house's most radical left members, called the TARP bailout program "one bait-and-switch after another... This is an ongoing fraud and deception on the American people."

We are committed to neither political party but agree that TARP has done precious little to help homeowners or the Main Street economy while performing wonders for Wall Street. There should be no surprise now that only 325,000 homeowners have been helped[35] instead of the 4,000,000 we were promised (see p53).

Since the October 2008 switcheroo, our elected officials in Congress have not been trying to stop Treasury or even rein in the TARP beneficiaries. Real-Life Super Cop SIG Barofsky told the House Oversight Committee, "Treasury takes the position that it will not even ask TARP recipients what they are doing with the taxpayers' money." In some bizarre logic that only a Washington-insider could understand, they seem to think that if they don't ask, they don't have to tell.

Not surprisingly Treasury is left trying to discredit SIG Barofsky's report. According to Chairman Towns, the *Rogue Treasury* has "requested legal opinion from the Department of Justice challenging the Special Inspector General's independence."[36] Representative Jason Chaffetz (R-UT) discretely pointed out that there is a distinct danger that the Secretary of the Treasury will try to stop Barofsky's request for additional allocations to keep SIGTARP operations running past mid-2010. Representative Dan Burton (R-IN) called Treasury's actions "blatant attempts to intimidate Barofsky to keep this information from the public."

Early news reports focused on just one number[37] from the report: the potential for the government to spend $23 trillion to fix the financial system. Sadly the

---

[35] https://www.politico.com/story/2009/07/wh-foreclosure-plan-a-bust-so-far-025095
[36] The current SIGTARP website does not provide any testimony before March 30, 2011. https://www.sigtarp.gov/Testimony Barofsky resigned effective March 20, 2011.
[37] https://abcnews.go.com/Business/Politics/story?id=8127005&page=1

media ignored the most sinister issues – and more obvious to anyone who read even the summary of the report or merely watched SIG Barofsky's testimony – raised in the report.[38] Here are the ones that give me indigestion:

- Treasury refuses to follow recommendations requiring fund managers to gather the information necessary to screen their investors for organized crime syndicates or terrorists (p183 of report). In my 20+ years in financial services, one rule sticks in my mind: "Know Your Customer." It means that you never do business with anyone you can't vouch for, because financial intermediaries, like banks and brokers, must stand behind every transaction they put in the system – even if their customer defaults. So why is it that we are now funneling trillions of dollars through financial intermediaries who are not required to gather enough information from their investors so we can be sure we aren't funding terrorism?

- SIG Barofsky said that "Blackrock (NYSE: BLK) may have incredible profits under contracts with both Federal Reserve and Treasury." Representative Marcy Kaptur (D-OH) suggested that SIG Barofsky "look at the people involved, not just companies like Blackrock" because the same people who created the subprime crisis are now working for the Federal Reserve on the bailout. They have the same staff investing government programs and private money without any "separating wall" to prevent conflicts of interest.

- It appears that Treasury, the New York Federal Reserve and even Presidential Economic Advisor Larry Summers may be passing information to their friends that can be used for financial gain, giving positions in bailout programs to business associates, and engaging in "too cordial relationships" with bailout recipients, according to Representative Darrell Issa (R-CA), Ranking Minority Member of the Oversight Committee.

- Treasury is "picking winners and losers" in the public/private partnership programs in a completely opaque process. SIG Barofsky calls this potentially "devastating to the public's view of government." People are hungry for information, too: The SIG's website has received 12 million hits by people interested in getting copies of testimony and reports.

- TARP is no longer a $700 billion bailout. "Treasury has created 12 separate programs involving Government and private funds of up to almost $3

---

[38] https://www.sigtarp.gov/sites/sigtarp/files/Quarterly_Reports/July2009_Quarterly_Report _to_Congress.pdf

trillion... a program of unprecedented scope, scale, and complexity" according to SIGTARP's quarterly report to Congress.

- Treasury and the Federal Reserve have ignored recommendations to stop relying on rating agency determinations (p184 of report). They continue to rely on rating agencies – the same ones who made tragic misjudgments over the past two years – in making determinations about the prices we will pay for the purchase of "troubled assets" or "legacy assets" or whatever name they decide to apply to the junk bonds in the hands of private banks. By relying on the rating agencies (who played a role in the crisis by rating junk bonds as triple-A credits), the bailout programs run the risk of being "unduly influenced by improper incentives to overrate."

- Representative Dan Burton (R-IN) suggested that Treasury Secretary Geithner is deliberately attempting to keep information from the public. SIG Barofsky has been unable to get more than one meeting with Treasury Secretary Geithner since January 2009 – and then only for a few minutes. This arrogance is not new to the current Administration's Treasury. Representative Issa says the Oversight Committee was twice promised data on the value of TARP assets from former Treasury employee (and former Goldman Sachs employee) Neel Kashkari. That data was "never forthcoming."

- Treasury has "repeatedly failed to adopt recommendations essential to providing basic transparency and accountability."

Representative Issa concluded that SIG Barofsky has given us the facts; now it's up to Congress to take action. In closing Chairman Towns said that if Treasury doesn't turn over information voluntarily, Secretary Geithner will be brought before the Committee to answer. "I can now understand why the Treasury Department would like to rein in the SIGTARP. But we are not going to let that happen."

I can think of 23 trillion reasons why the Treasury Department will fight him all the way. And just as many why we taxpayers should not like Tim Geithner and the rest of the insider crowd getting away with the murder of the American economy.

More money for bailout CEOs

December 30, 2009

The day before leaving town to vacation in an opulent $9 million, 5-bedroom home in Hawaii, the Obama administration pledged unlimited financial support[39] for Fannie Mae and Freddie Mac. The mortgage giants are already beneficiaries of $200 billion in taxpayer aid. On Christmas Eve, regulatory filings reported that the CEOs of the two firms are in line for $6 million in compensation.[40] Merry Christmas!

Executive compensation is the subject of many academic studies, but one focused on Fannie Mae from two Harvard Law School professors is especially well-named: "Perverse Incentives, Nonperformance Pay and Camouflage".[41] Executives are able to take unlimited risks and reap unlimited upside rewards knowing that US taxpayers will foot the bill on the downside. The mortgage-backed securities issued by the two firms remain at the center of the causes-and-effects of the financial meltdown.

The compensation for Fannie Mae's senior managers is recommended by the Compensation Committee "in consultation and with the approval of the Conservator",[42] which is the US Federal Housing Finance Agency (FHFA). The FHFA was created in July 2008 when Bush signed the Housing and Economic Recovery Act. At the time, the Congressional Budget Office estimated that the $200 billion Act would save 4 million homeowners. In the first six months, exactly one homeowner was able to refinance under the program. The Act also was supposed to clean up the subprime mortgage crisis – which it did not do as evidenced by the collapse of the global financial markets a few months later.

Back to the current problem of paying CEOs $6 million to run a bankrupt company whose every financial obligation is guaranteed by taxpayer money. Who is on the compensation committee that recommended this pay day? Dennis Beresford from Ernst & Young (E&Y); Brenda Gaines, recently from Citigroup; Jonathan Plutzik, from Credit Suisse First Boston; and David Sidwell, from Morgan Stanley.

---

[39] https://www.washingtonpost.com/wp-dyn/content/article/2009/12/24/AR2009122401588.html

[40] https://www.reuters.com/article/us-fanniemae-idUSTRE5BN1JB20091224

[41] https://papers.ssrn.com/sol3/papers.cfm?abstract_id=653125

[42] https://www.fhfa.gov/

Back in 2004, Ernst & Young was engaged as a consultant to Fannie Mae[43] – right after the Securities and Exchange Commission banned E&Y from taking on new clients. Citigroup took $25 billion in TARP bailout money[44] and Morgan Stanley took $10 billion.[45] Credit Suisse benefited by a mere $400 million as their share of the AIG Financial Products group bailout. Needless to say, this Compensation Committee knows a thing or two about controversies and federal aid!

Enjoy your luxury Christmas vacation, Mr. President, while 45 out of 50 US states are enjoying statistically significant decreases in employment[46] in the face of rising prices.[47] Please take some time to contemplate the words GE Chairman and CEO Jeff Immelt used in describing the leadership traits that need to change in America: "The richest people made the worst mistakes with the least accountability."[48]

And to the rest of you out there reading this, take some time to contemplate the words of Bill Moyers as he concluded a rather shocking essay on the role of lobbyists in the recent "healthcare reform" legislation: "Outrageous? You bet. But don't just get mad. Get busy."[49]

---

[43] https://www.nytimes.com/2004/04/24/business/company-news-fannie-mae-adds-ernst-young-despite-suspension.html

[44] https://projects.propublica.org/bailout/

[45] https://projects.propublica.org/bailout/#payments_table

[46] https://www.bls.gov/news.release/archives/laus_12182009.pdf

[47] https://www.bls.gov/news.release/archives/cpi_12162009.pdf

[48] The text of this speech is no longer available online. Details of the appearance are available in the GE Press Release https://www.ge.com/news/press-releases/jeffrey-r-immelt-chief-executive-officer-ge-will-address-united-states-military. Here's some context for the quote included in this article: "We are at the end of a difficult generation of business leadership, and maybe leadership in general. Tough-mindedness, a good trait, was replaced by meanness and greed, both terrible traits. As a result, the bottom 25% of Americans is poorer than they were 25 years ago. That is just plain wrong. Rewards became perverted. The richest people made the most mistakes with the least accountability. In too many situations, leaders divided us instead of bringing us together."

[49] https://www.pbs.org/moyers/journal/10092009/watch2.html

Suppressing the news: the real cost of the Wall Street bailout

December 29, 2011

No one really knows what a politician will do once elected. George "No New Taxes" Bush (George I to us commoners) was neither the first nor will he be the last politician to lie to the public in order to get elected. It takes increasing amounts of money to get elected. Total spending by Presidential candidates in 1988 was $210.7 million; in 2000 it was $343.1 million and in 2008, presidential candidates spent $1.3 billion. Even without adjusting for inflation, it's pretty obvious that it takes A LOT MORE MONEY now. For those readers who are from the Show Me state, $210.7 million in 1988 is equivalent to roughly one-third of the buying power used by Presidential Candidates in 2008.

When Texas Governor and presidential hopeful Rick Perry told Iowan voters in early November, "I happen to think Wall Street and Washington, D.C., have been in bed together way too long," it made headlines for Reuters and ABC.[50] But that's not news; that's advertising. News, according to Sir Harold Evans, is what somebody somewhere wants to suppress. News Flash: The average member of Congress who voted in favor of the 2008 Bank Bailout received 51 percent more campaign money from Wall Street than those who voted no – Republicans and Democrats alike.[51] That's according to research by the Center for Responsive Politics and it was reported as news by the OpenSecrets.org blog on September 29, 2008.

In other news fit to be suppressed, the Federal Reserve "provided more than $16 trillion in total financial assistance to some of the largest financial institutions and corporations in the United States and throughout the world." This was revealed in an audit of the Federal Reserve released in July 2011 by the Government Accountability Office.[52] All the goods and services produced in the United States in the last twelve months are worth about $14 trillion – Ben Bernanke and Timothy Geithner spent more than that to bailout Wall Street in twelve months! This is news, news that Bloomberg and Fox Business Network

---

[50] https://abcnews.go.com/blogs/politics/2011/11/rick-perry-harps-on-cozy-ties-between-washington-and-wall-street/

[51] https://www.opensecrets.org/news/2008/09/finance-sector-gave-50-percent.html

[52] https://www.sanders.senate.gov/press-releases/news-11-senators-back-house-progressives-in-demand-for-passage-of-entire-biden-agenda/?id=9e2a4ea8-6e73-4be2-a753-62060dcbb3c3

had to file lawsuits to get access to and that Bernanke and Geithner want to suppress.

The answer to the differences in the value of the bailouts – it was *"only* $1.2 trillion"* according to Bernanke – can be found in the GAO's audits. The latest audit of the TARP, released November 10, 2011 makes it clear: "In valuing TARP …, [Office of Financial Stability] management considered and selected assumptions and data that it believed provided a reasonable basis for the estimated subsidy costs …. However, these *assumptions and estimates are inherently subject to substantial uncertainty* arising from the likelihood of future changes in general economic, regulatory, and market conditions." [emphasis added]. TARP is under Treasury – which is run by Geithner – and is headed up by Timothy Massad, formerly of Cravath, Swaine & Moore LLP in New York …[still following this?]…, who represents Goldman Sachs, Morgan Stanley, etc. as underwriters for (among other things) European public debt. Cravath, Swaine & Moore[53] advised Citigroup on their repayment of TARP funds and Merrill Lynch in their orchestrated takeover by Bank of America.

The dispute about the cost of the bailout is not the stuff of conspiracy theories. This is basic finance and economics, not accounting. In accounting, debits and credits balance at the end of the day; in finance, you get to assume rates of return, costs of capital, etc., etc. – a lot of stuff that has much room for judgment. It is in the area of judgment that Bernanke and Geithner are able to make their numbers look smaller than those added up by Bloomberg and Fox. The GAO, on the other hand, should have no dog in this fight and therefore should (we live and hope) give us the right stuff to work with. GAO says (in a nice way) that Geithner has been fiddling with the numbers.

The GAO had been recommending to Congress that they get audit authority over the Federal Reserve System at least since 1973.[54] They finally got that authority in the Wall Street Reform Act of 2010 – about the only piece of that legislation that has so far resulted in anything of substance. The Center for Responsive politics also did an analysis of the campaign contributions for Senators who opposed the financial regulatory reform bill in 2010. Those

---

[53] https://www.cravath.com/news/citi-s-repayment-of-tarp-funds.html
[54] http://archive.gao.gov/f0102/091279.pdf

opposing the reforms got 65 percent more money[55] from Wall Street banks than those voting for the bill.

For politicians, it doesn't matter who votes for them. They will figure out what they need to say to get the money to get the votes to get elected. What they need most – and what makes them Wall Streetwalkers[56] – is the money. The big donors don't care who they give to, as long as the one they give to gets elected. According to Federal Election Commission data, Warren Buffett gives money almost exclusively to Democrats; Donald Trump likes to spread it around between the parties, as do Goldman Sachs employees. But that's only the money that can be traced back to a source, unlike the opaque donations[57] given to PACs and SuperPACs.

The revolving door between Wall Street and Washington swings both ways. When John Corzine departed Goldman Sachs in 1999, he left Hank Paulson in charge. Investment Dealers' Digest reported that Corzine left Goldman "against a backdrop of fixed-income trading losses." Corzine won a Senate seat in 2000 (D-NJ). He was then elected Governor of New Jersey[58] in November 2005, where he put forth Bradley Abelow for state Treasurer. Abelow worked with Corzine at Goldman and was a former Board member at the Depository Trust and Clearing Corporation, the world's largest self-regulatory financial institution. Together, Corzine and Abelow later went on to run MF Global into bankruptcy.[59] Both have been invited back to Washington, the first time a former Congressman has been called to testify before a Congressional Committee.

---

[55] https://www.opensecrets.org/news/2010/05/senators-who-opposed-financial-refo.html

[56] https://vvstaging.villagevoice.com/2008/11/05/wall-streetwalkers-the-sleazy-lehman-brothers-subsidiary/

[57] https://www.opensecrets.org/political-action-committees-pacs/2010

[58] https://www.fec.gov/resources/record/2005/jun05.pdf#page=7

[59] https://en.wikipedia.org/wiki/MF_Global. While Corzine was CEO at MF Global, the company admitted to improper co-mingling of company and client funds in the days leading up to the bankruptcy filing; customers losses rose to $1.6 billion. In 2017, Corzine was ordered to pay a $5 million fine from his own funds (not to be covered by insurance) and received a lifetime ban from the Commodities Trading Future Commission (CFTC). Despite recommendations from the CFTC and prominent Wall Street critic Senator Elizabeth Warren (D-OH), the Department of Justice (under the Obama administration) refused to prosecute Corzine for his role in the collapse of MF Global. https://observer.com/2017/01/jon-corzine-gets-5-million-fine-and-lifetime-ban-for-tanking-mf-global/

Wherever they get started, Washington and Wall Street tend to end up in bed together.

It's this kind of knowledge that makes me question why I should vote at all. Congressmen from both parties are generally for sale. Even with self-described liberals in Congress, right-wing conservatives could get approval for everything they want – free-for-all-banking and the US military engaged in active combat. It's the taxpayers – the mothers, fathers and families of service men and women – who suffer. Sure, Barack Obama took more money from Wall Street than John McCain – but it was only $2 million more, hardly enough to run one ad campaign in a big state.

Then I pause and remember what my mentor, Rose Kaufman, from the League of Women Voters of Santa Monica told me: if you don't vote, you open the door for someone to take away your right to vote. The benefit of living in a democracy with freedom of the press is that you can find out all those things that Washington and Wall Street "want to suppress." Whether or not we have good choices among the presidential candidates, we have choices. It's better than nothing.

2. Congressional Hearings and Legislation

How can America bail you out? Let Congress count the ways! Once the full-blown global financial crisis hit, the world experienced bailouts but could not avoid a recession. Tens of thousands of pages of new rules and regulations were produced in the space of about three years. The legislation included the creation of new regulatory agencies.

The US government also did something it had avoided for decades: they did a 'taking' by assuming ownership and operation of American International Group (AIG). France did it in the 1980s when they nationalized companies in the banking, aerospace, and steel sectors. It is sometimes called 'lemon socialism' – taking industrial 'lemons' under the public wing. The US Government had a long history of bailouts – from Penn Central Railroad in the 1970s to Chrysler Corporation in the 1980s and the airline industry in the 2000s. But the last "taking" before 2008 was almost 20 years earlier in 1989, when the government took ownership of savings and loan institutions.[1]

In addition to AIG, at least two very large banks were seized: Washington Mutual failed and was seized on 25 September 2008 and W Holding's Westernbank failed and was seized 30 April 2010. From 2008 through 2012, 100 banks were placed in receivership (seized) and still remained under control of the FDIC in 2023.[2] In total, the FDIC closed 465 failed banks from 2008 to 2012. In contrast, in the five years prior to 2008, only 10 banks failed.

This list of legislation includes The Housing and Economic Recovery Act of 2008 that authorized placing Fannie and Freddie under federal conservatorship (nationalized), the Emergency Economic Stabilization Act of 2008 (lovingly known as the Wall Street Bailout Act of 2008) that created the Troubled Asset Relief Program (TARP) for the Federal Reserve to buy $700 billion of junk bonds from banks to keep them afloat.[3] The flood of legislation was capped on 21 July 2010 with the "Dodd-Frank" Wall Street Reform and Consumer Protection Act.[4]

---

[1] Amtrak and the Post Office have straddled the border between public and private, but neither has been "taken" by the federal government.

[2] https://receivership.fdic.gov/drripbal/

[3] For details, see Table 9, p158 of *LNL*

[4] Detailed in Appendix 5, p219-30 of *LNL*

This perp walk needs handcuffs

February 9, 2009

Do many of us truly understand the scale of one trillion dollars? The following executives have been called to Capitol Hill to explain what they did with their shares of the $750 billion bailout:

- Mr. Lloyd C. Blankfein, Chief Executive Officer and Chairman, Goldman Sachs & Co.
- Mr. James Dimon, Chief Executive Officer, JPMorgan Chase & Co.
- Mr. Robert P. Kelly, Chairman and Chief Executive Officer, Bank of New York Mellon
- Mr. Ken Lewis, Chairman and Chief Executive Officer, Bank of America
- Mr. Ronald E. Logue, Chairman and Chief Executive Officer, State Street Corporation
- Mr. John J. Mack, Chairman and Chief Executive Officer, Morgan Stanley
- Mr. Vikram Pandit, Chief Executive Officer, Citigroup
- Mr. John Stumpf, President and Chief Executive Officer, Wells Fargo & Co.

The panel was called in by the House Committee on Finance. The House events are more exciting than the Senate, whose members take decorum too seriously to ask direct questions and raise their voices when they don't get answers.

These guys (no women) are being called in to answer questions about what they did with the $750 billion bailout. Most people don't really understand what a billion dollars is, let alone a number of billions that equals three-quarters of a trillion dollars. Let me try to bring it home.

Most people know what a million dollars is – it's been popularized in TV programs like "Who Wants to be a Millionaire?" and "Joe Millionaire". Most state lotteries have minimum prizes of a few million dollars. Angelina Jolie and other very popular actors reportedly receive $20 million for making one movie. Blockbuster movies can have more than $100 million in ticket sales on a good opening weekend. There are about 130 million housing units (homes, condos, trailers, etc.) in the US. The population of the US is a little over 300 million. We're working our way up to $1 billion if we think of $3 or $4 per person. $1 billion is about equal to the annual income of 16,555 Americans. The entire population of Nebraska earns about $120 billion in a year. The population of California would earn about $150 billion in a month.

The US Treasury and Federal Reserve paid $150 billion for an 80 percent stake in American International Group (AIG) in a bailout announced on September

16, 2008. On September 22, just days after receiving this bailout, AIG spent $443,000 on a spa outing at the luxurious St. Regis Resort[5] in Monarch Beach, California, including $23,000 in spa treatments. AIG visited the Hill on October 7, 2008 where its CEO defended the spending[6] as "necessary to maintain business."

When they left the Hill, they threw a second party for themselves at another luxury hotel, this time spending $86,000 at a New England hunting retreat. They canceled 160 events after Congress and the press complained, but they still went on to spend $343,000 on a three-day event at Arizona's Pointe Hilton Squaw Peak Resort in November. This time they made sure there were no AIG signs on the premises – three months later I still can't figure out why no one is in jail for fraud.[7]

Treasury, so far, has refused to tell us where much of the money went, beyond paying for pricey canapés and comfy beds. Not surprisingly, Fox Business Network ran a half-page ad in USA Today on February 3 to announce that they "sued the Treasury and the Federal Reserve" to find out where the TARP and FRB-NY money went. The Senate is considering subpoenas to get Treasury to tell them where it all went. Talk about imperial government!

Let's keep going because the numbers get bigger. The Treasury passed out $750 billion in their bailout. Treasury Secretary Henry Paulson and Fed Chief Ben Bernanke said that "The initiative is aimed at removing the devalued mortgage-linked assets at the root of the worst credit crisis since the Great Depression." (Bloomberg, September 19, 2008.) There were about 3,000,000 homes in foreclosure at the end of 2008.

But who was really being bailed out? For $750 billion you could buy all of them outright and still have more than $100 billion left over to pay off car loans, student loans, small business loans – or pay bonuses to all the Wall Street and Bank executives in 2008. California had the most foreclosures of any state in 2008 – 523,624. $750 billion would have saved all of them – three times over.

---

[5] https://abcnews.go.com/Blotter/story?id=5973452&page=1
[6] https://abcnews.go.com/Blotter/story?id=5987363&page=1
[7] By 2018, only 1 US banker had gone to jail for their actions in 2008. Kareem Serageldin, a trader at Credit Suisse, pled guilty in 2013 to inflating prices of mortgage-backed bonds and was sentenced to 30 months. https://ig.ft.com/jailed-bankers/

For $750 billion you could buy 3,507,951 single-family homes in the US. That's equivalent to every home built in the US in 2006 and 2007. You could buy about 3% of all the homes standing today in the US.

$750 billion would buy you 1,524,390 single-family homes in LA County, or 83% of the total. With $750 billion you could buy all the land in private hands in Los Angeles County (but not the buildings on it) and still have enough left over ($185 billion) to buy all the buildings and structures in Los Angeles city.[8]

Now, Congress is working on a stimulus package that is approaching $1 trillion. Not to rush you through the math, but if you got this far, then you are already three-quarters of the way there. Apparently, Los Angeles real estate is worth $1 trillion: That's about the value of all the residential, commercial and industrial property in LA County. (Actually, $1.109 trillion, but what's a hundred billion among friends?)[9]

A stimulus package of $819 billion should give $6,306 to every household. It won't, of course. But it should.

So, what's my conclusion? This bailout plan has little to do with addressing the root problems of the housing crisis or helping hard-pressed Americans. It's about bailing out the big banks and financial institutions from the consequences of their own miscalculations.

Financial reform or con game?

April 20, 2010

The news that Goldman Sachs is facing civil fraud charges from the Securities and Exchange Commission[10] came just days before a Washington Examiner story reported that Goldman Sachs, in the company's annual letter to shareholders, reassured investors that the financial regulatory reform being voted on this week in Congress will "help Goldman's bottom line." Yikes!!

Since the autumn of 2008, all things concerning financial regulation have been moving very rapidly. I often find it impossible to stay in front of it. The legislation is barely made public before it is changed – they even change

---

[8] Calculations use median home prices and median incomes. Unless specified as "single-family homes" the housing numbers refer to all housing units which includes condominiums, manufactured housing, apartments, etc.

[9] See page 5 of the 2009 Annual Report available at https://res.cloudinary.com/los-angeles-county-assessor/image/upload/v1622759864/AnnualReport/Annual_Report_2009.pdf

[10] https://www.sec.gov/news/press/2010/2010-59.htm

legislation in the days after Bills are passed. This makes it really hard for the ordinary citizen or even an informed researcher to clearly see where the bill ends up.

Ultimately, this reminds me of a con game I've seen played on the streets in New York called Three-card Monte.[11] It requires very fast hands to effectively manipulate the cards. As the professional con artist rapidly moves three cards – two aces and the queen of hearts – around the table, he challenges you to keep your eye on the queen. You are encouraged by the con and his shill – the co-conspirator among the audience – to place a bet on your ability to keep up with the movements. Of course, you can't win because the game is fixed. But – and here's why Goldman's joy at the financial regulatory reform makes me nervous – you will think that you can win when you see the shill winning.

Everybody[12] and their brother[13] have gone on record with some argument for or against the current version of financial regulatory reform in Congress this week. The question most often asked is: Will it end "too big to fail?" In my view, it is not the size of the firms but the size of the risks that are the real problem. While I don't mind losing $5 on a street corner, all Americans mind losing $3.8 trillion in the Bailout.

Here's the heart of the problem. There is something going on back-stage at Wall Street called the centralized clearing and settlement system. I worked in it in the US and have studied and consulted corresponding systems in the rest of the world. The system we have in the US was exported around the world thanks to the United States Agency for International Development. The system is designed to let all the stocks and bonds traded on the stock exchanges be paid for electronically. To expedite the process – known as settling trades in stocks, bonds and all the other financial instruments – the system accepts an electronic "IOU" for the shares until the real financial papers can be delivered. It requires that the money be paid immediately. The problem is that the system permits dealers to sell more stocks and bonds than exist without any incentive to deliver on time. The centralized settlement system simply holds the "failed to deliver" open indefinitely in the form of an electronic IOU. The value of the IOUs in the system has risen dramatically since 2001.

---

[11] https://www.ny.com/scams/3CardMonty.html

[12] https://www.huffingtonpost.co.uk/entry/financial-regulatory-refo_n_542825

[13] https://www.pewtrusts.org/en/about/news-room/press-releases-and-statements/2010/04/19/pew-urges-senate-to-pass-meaningful-financial-regulatory-reform

Figure 3
Source: Public data, available in annual reports of Depository Trust and Clearing Corporation and its subsidiaries.

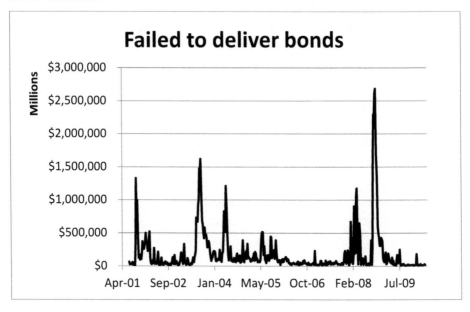

Figure 4
Source: Public data, available from the Federal Reserve Bank of New York.

A DECADE OF ARMAGEDDON

Notice the relationship of the timing of the spike in the bond failures to the financial crisis: the 17 primary dealers reporting to the New York Federal Reserve Bank failed to deliver about $2.5 trillion worth of US Treasury securities for seven weeks in late 2008 – no fines, no sanctions; worst of all, very little press coverage.[14]

This is the core of the problem – both in practice and in theory. This means supply is infinite – there is no limit to how many bonds can be sold because no one is enforcing delivery. In reality, no one should be able to sell more US Government bonds than the US Government has issued. That's a problem in the practices supported by the system. The theoretical problem is that all financial instruments, including the bonds issued by city and state governments, are being sold without any attachment to the real assets. This damages not only buyers in the stock market, but also the companies and governments who are trying to raise the money needed to keep delivering the services that we depend on them to provide.

The practice of allowing the delivery of electronic IOUs in place of shares of stock or Treasury bonds is a process that rewards financial manipulation instead of allocating resources to productive uses – the activity that capital markets *should* be doing. All the Congressional and the Administration talk about Wall Street reform is to centralize more trades into the existing settlement system[15] – the one with the trillion-dollar hole in it! Someone has convinced them that the centralized system can easily track and account for positions – the actual statistics present a very different picture.

Debt ceiling or spending limit?

February 16, 2011

We're seeing a lot of debate in Washington about what is commonly referred to as the "national debt ceiling." This post is an attempt to shed some light – and provide some good resources for further information – on what this really means. National debt is not the total of all future obligations the federal government is required to pay. It is basically all the public debt (like Treasury bills, notes and bonds) plus money we owe to other governments – in other

---

[14] https://www.investmentnews.com/unraveling-mystery-of-lump-sum-payments-54543

[15] https://abcnews.go.com/Politics/sen-christopher-dodd-banking-chairman-unveils-proposed-crackdown/story?id=10104732

words this ceiling only puts a limit on how much the federal government can borrow, not on how much they can spend.

The national debt number is available "to the penny" at the Treasury website.[16] There are only a few categories of debt that are not subject to the limit, mostly having to do with the way that Treasury Bills are issued to pay all the interest up front (discounted) and the way those payments are handled in accounting terms. Raising the National Debt Ceiling involves raising the limit on the public debt ceiling.

There is a bigger number that most other countries use to define "debt". The official definition for "debt" used in the European Union, for example, includes obligations that correspond to Social Security, Medicare, etc. at the national level, plus regional and local government debt. (Thanks to *Yannick* for initiating a discussion of the distinction with his comment to my 2009 piece on Public Debt Crisis, p124) In the US, the larger number is usually referred to as "total indebtedness". There is no limit set on the promises of the US government to spend money – for example, the almost $13 trillion committed to the post-crisis bailouts and stimulus was not subject to the debt limit despite that number being almost equal to the total national debt. The limit only applies to how much the Treasury can borrow to meet its obligations. So, if the question is "should the ceiling be raised?" then my answer is "it doesn't really matter." Congress can keep spending without it.

When politicians say they are against raising the debt ceiling[17] it's usually referred to as "Grandstanding"[18] – which Merriam-Webster explains is to act so as to impress onlookers.

This is your government on crack

February 12, 2013

Forget about a fiscal cliff[19] or the threat of sequestrations. Bernanke's use of the term "cliff" in 2012 is based on the erroneous analogy that fiscal policy had been moving along some level road for a period of time and was just now approaching an "end" or "falling-off" point. The reality is that federal spending has been rising rapidly since the federal government 1) absorbed the cost of repairing the damage done by the terrorist attacks of 2001, 2) decided to support

---

[16] https://fiscaldata.treasury.gov/datasets/debt-to-the-penny/debt-to-the-penny

[17] https://www.huffingtonpost.co.uk/entry/pawlenty-debt-ceiling_n_809633

[18] https://www.merriam-webster.com/dictionary/grandstand

[19] https://www.bbc.co.uk/news/magazine-20318326

wars on multiple fronts in the Middle East, 3) bailed out the Wall Street Banks, and 4) failed to pass a budget but 5) decided to continue spending as if nothing had happened. So called "sequestration" – which in this case basically means reducing spending and increasing revenue – would simply be a return to reality, coming down to earth, getting our feet back under us. Unfortunately, we the people appear co-dependents in this addiction.

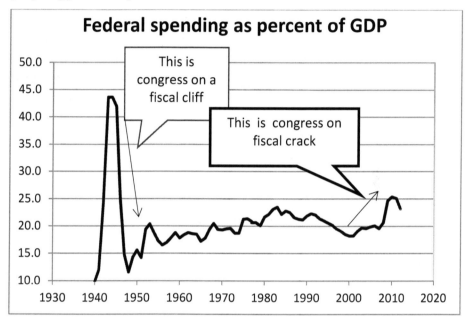

Figure 5
Source: Congressional Budget Office

This year started with Congress succeeding at its favorite athletic event: kicking the can down the road. The January inauguration of the President and installation of their new members provided the excuse. The fact remains that Congress has not passed a real federal budget since 1997 ("the first balanced budget in a generation".)[20] An "omnibus spending bill"[21] was passed in April of 2009 but that is not technically a budget.

Congressional inaction has left the federal government running on extensions ("Continuing Resolutions") of a budget that was passed when Bill Gates was still CEO of Microsoft, NASA landed the first spacecraft on Mars, and Google was working out of a garage. The last federal budget is from the time before iPods and iPads, before SPAM e-mail exceeded legitimate email, before

---

[20] https://www.washingtonpost.com/wp-srv/politics/special/budget/stories/080697.htm
[21] https://prospect.org/economy/congress-even-need-pass-budget/

Facebook, YouTube and Twitter – and before the global financial crisis that sent the world into recession and US federal spending into the stratosphere.

In lieu of doing anything meaningful, three senators – Kelly Ayotte (R-NH), Ron Johnson (R-WI) and Marco Rubio (R-FL), all in office since 2011 – took the time to write and introduce an amendment to the 1974 Budget Act that would require a macroeconomic analysis of the impact of new legislation.[22] This monumental act of denial[23] was such a complete waste of time that GovTrack.us gave it only a 9% chance of getting out of committee and a 1% chance of being enacted. In fact, from 2011 to 2013, while we were paying these three senators and hundreds more people in Congress, only 12% of the bills introduced in the Senate made it out of committee (11% in the House) and only 14% of those were enacted (24% in the House)! Having passed just a few more than 200 bills, the 112th Congress will go down in history as even less productive than President Harry Truman's "Do-Nothing Congress" (the 80th, 1947-1948) which nevertheless managed to get 906 bills enacted.

In the 2012 election, openings were available for one new president, 33 new senators and 435 new representatives. Instead, Americans re-elected the same President, 19 of the same senators (58%) and 351 of the same representatives (81%). As a result, the 113th congress looks a lot like the 112th.

Recently, President Obama signed an executive order to lift the 2009 freeze on federal employee salaries – including the salaries for all members of Congress. When Congress voted to rescind the executive order – they have to vote to prevent an automatic annual pay increase – they did it not just for themselves but for all federal employees. Then they kicked the can (of the "sequestration" spending cuts) down the road two more months.

Their final act in January was suspending the debt limit "at least until May 19". H.R. 325[24] may turn out to be the bright spot in this whole mess despite the fact that it gives Geithner's, now Lew's, Treasury carte blanche for financing profligate spending. The "No Budget, No Pay Act" was written on Thursday January 3, 2013; introduced in the House on January 21st by Rep. Dave Camp (R-MI since 1991) and cosponsor Rep. Candice S. Miller (R-MI since 2003);

---

[22] https://www.congress.gov/bill/113th-congress/senate-bill/184
[23] https://dictionary.apa.org/denial
[24] https://www.congress.gov/bill/113th-congress/house-bill/325

passed in the House on January 23rd by a vote of 285-144;[25] passed in the Senate on January 31st by a vote of 64 to 34.[26]

According to the bill,[27] if Congress does not pass a real budget by April 15, the salaries of the members of the chamber unable to agree to the budget will be held in escrow until either they pass a budget or the last day of the 113th Congress. All the new Democrat senators voted "aye"; all the new Republican senators voted "nay". The new House members were mixed. The bill goes to President Obama this week for signature.[28]

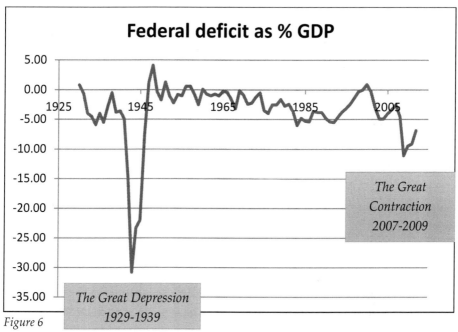

Figure 6

Source: Congressional Budget Office

Assuming he signs it, H.R. 325 allows the federal government to borrow money beyond the record $16.4 trillion debt we already owe. That debt is 104.5% of 2012's $15.7 trillion GDP. The budget deficit – which has to be covered by borrowing – is running over $1 trillion each year or about 7% of GDP. The deficit alone is 44% of federal receipts. In other words, the government is spending over 40% more than it earns! That's your government on crack.

[25] https://clerk.house.gov/evs/2013/roll030.xml

[26] https://www.senate.gov/legislative/LIS/roll_call_votes/vote1131/vote_113_1_00011.htm

[27] https://www.congress.gov/bill/113th-congress/house-bill/325/text

[28] The President signed the bill on 4 February 2013. It became Public Law No. 113-3.

It is like living with a drug addict: Waiting for the problem to resolve itself will get you nowhere. What you are seeing now, if it isn't already completely out of control, will get completely out of control.

The difference is that we, the taxpayers and our children and our children's children, have to shoulder the burden – something the families of addicts are advised not to do.[29] In a democracy, the majority rules and the majority decided to continue to live with these fiscal crack addicts. For the rest of us, our choice has to be to try to remain optimistic – take the good news where you can find it. There are no "fiscal therapists" or "family support groups" for disgruntled voters. We must seek out the venues where we can talk about the problem openly, don't be fooled when the fourth estate hides the crack vials[30] to gain favor with the Washington and Wall Street[31] elites and take care of ourselves.[32]

Our federal government: "There you go again!"

October 1, 2013

Remember this?

> The fact remains that Congress has not passed a real federal budget since 1997 ("the first balanced budget in a generation".)[33] An "omnibus spending bill"[34] was passed in April of 2009 but that is not technically a budget.

> Congressional inaction has left the federal government running on extensions ("Continuing Resolutions") of a budget that was passed when Bill Gates was still CEO of Microsoft, NASA landed the first spacecraft on Mars, and Google was working out of a garage. The last federal budget is from the time before iPods and iPads, before SPAM e-mail exceeded legitimate email, before Facebook, YouTube and Twitter – and before the global financial crisis that sent the world into recession and US federal spending into the stratosphere.[35]

---

[29] https://www.choosehelp.com/topics/living-with-an-addict/keep-family-healthy-living-with-alcoholic-drug-addict

[30] https://www.amazon.com/Lapdogs-Press-Rolled-Over-Bush/dp/0743289315

[31] https://www.washingtontimes.com/news/2012/sep/18/hurt-media-lap-dogs-in-hot-pursuit-of-the-wrong-st/

[32] https://www.flight93friends.org/

[33] https://www.washingtonpost.com/wp-srv/politics/special/budget/stories/080697.htm

[34] https://prospect.org/economy/congress-even-need-pass-budget/

[35] See p35

As one very famous Republican President said (repeatedly in his defeat of Jimmy Carter): "There you go again!"

And, sure, this isn't the first time the federal government has shut down for lack of spending authorization. I remember when my elderly mother and her sisters – first generation Americans eager to see the place where their parents disembarked after their long ocean voyage from Sicily – were so disappointed to find Ellis Island and the Statue of Liberty closed that October of 1996.

The big difference this time is the way the government is spending – which I discuss in detail in the article quoted above. *USAToday* has an article that summarizes just how different the government operates today[36] than it did 17 years ago. There is a big reason Republicans might want to re-think shutting down the government. According to *USAToday*, gun permits cannot be issued while the federal government is closed.

Let's hope one thing is the same in 2013 as it was in 1996 – when they re-opened the government Congress passed a real budget.

Update posted 27 Oct 2013: Unfortunately, Congress just kicked the can again – no new budget, no real action. They simply pushed the deadlines into January and February 2014 so we can do this all over again.

The "new" plan is to have a bi-partisan panel come up with a budget that everyone can live with while reducing the deficit – but that, my friends, is the very definition of insanity! The 2011 bi-partisan panel couldn't come up with a budget. Their failure is why we have sequestration.

Lobbying pays off 500-to-1

March 27, 2015

I suppose we should not be shocked: businesses that spend money on lobbying and campaign contributions get more favors from government than those that do not. I spent the weekend at Creighton University in a seminar sponsored by the Institute for Humane Studies.[37] I asked Creighton Associate Professor of Economics Diana Thomas about her research on the unintended consequences of regulation. One thing led to another and the next day I downloaded her 2013 paper "Corporate Lobbying, Political Connections, and the Bailout of Banks."[38]

---

[36] https://eu.usatoday.com/story/news/politics/2013/09/29/questions-and-answers-about-the-shutdown/2888419/

[37] https://www.theihs.org/

[38] https://papers.ssrn.com/sol3/papers.cfm?abstract_id=1878653

Here is a summary of what can be supported with scientific (statistical) evidence about the influence of big money on big government:

- Campaign contributions and lobbying influence the voting behavior of politicians.
- Campaign contributions and lobbying have a positive effect on wealth for the shareholders of the companies that spend.
- Businesses that pay lobbyists before committing fraud are 38% less likely to get caught; even when they get caught, they are able to evade detection almost four months longer than those that do not pay for lobbying.
- Firms with political connections are more likely to receive government bailouts in times of economic distress.

The US government has a long history of bailing out private industry. In 1970, the Federal Reserve provided financial support to commercial banks after Penn Central Railroad declared bankruptcy. Throughout that decade federal financial support was provided to private companies, banks and municipal governments: Lockheed, ($1.4 billion) Franklin National Bank ($7.8 billion) and New York City ($9.4 billion) were all recipients of Uncle Sam's largess. In the 1980s, it was Chrysler Motors ($4.0 billion), Continental Illinois National Bank ($9.5 billion) and the savings and loan industry ($293.3 billion). The data available at OpenSecrets.org doesn't go back further than 1990, but last year the finance industry spent nearly half a billion dollars[39] on lobbying and campaigns – the most of any industry sector.[40] Just after the terrorist attacks of September 11, 2001, the airline industry received $5 billion in compensation and $10 billion in federal credit. For these favors, the airlines spent barely $15 million in 1996-2000.[41]

These are all pittances in comparison to the money handed out in 2008 and 2009. *NewGeography* readers know that the average member of Congress who voted in favor of the $700 billion Bank Bailout received 51% more campaign money from Wall Street than those who voted no – Republicans and Democrats alike. The main finding in Dr. Thomas' paper is that banks that paid lobbyists and made political campaign contributions were more likely to receive TARP money. To put a fine point on it, for every $1 spent lobbying in the five years before the bailout, banks averaged $535.71 in TARP bailout money! We knew

---

[39] https://www.opensecrets.org/industries/totals.php?cycle=2014&ind=F
[40] https://www.opensecrets.org/industries/
[41] These bailouts and more are detailed in *LNL*

the bank bailout was rigged, but that is a better rate of return than even Warren Buffett got for his contribution to the bailout of Goldman Sachs.

The only good news is that spending – at least the spending that can be tracked – was down in 2014 from 2013. Spending by most industry categories has been in general decline since 2010. Between Congress and the Federal Reserve, businesses benefited from an estimated $16 trillion in government assistance since 2008. They are either having a "why bother" moment or the 2016 Presidential election will be another record breaking year for campaign spending.[42]

---

[42] House and Senate candidates spent $1,647 million in the 2014 election. In 2016, they spent $1,634 million. In 2020, spending had risen to $3,797.7; presidential candidates that year spent an additional $4,058.7 million.)
Source: https://www.fec.gov/data/spending-bythenumbers/.
To explore campaign contributions by interest groups, see:
https://www.opensecrets.org/industries/.

3. Homeowners and Mortgages

When I first wrote about the housing market, in the years leading up to the financial crisis and the Great Recession, I made a comparison to gold. The sub-title of my first article, "A New Kind of Gold," was widely misunderstood as a suggestion that houses were a safe investment. The true meaning was that people were treating houses like investments and not as places to live. It's fine to treat them as both, but it was never OK to treat your housing like a casino wager. As interest rates fell ever lower leading into 2008, too many buyers asked themselves "can I afford the mortgage" rather than "is this a fair price for the property". Meanwhile, bankers only asked "can I sell this mortgage in a package to Wall Street?" The same bankers who were lending money for mortgages and collecting fees from borrowers were then turning around and earning more fees for collateralizing the mortgages into bonds. The massive accumulation of fees came with an even bigger accumulation of risk. When the bonds came due, the tide went out and many bankers were not wearing trunks.

Surprise! For fiscally responsible, housing remains good as gold

November 14, 2008

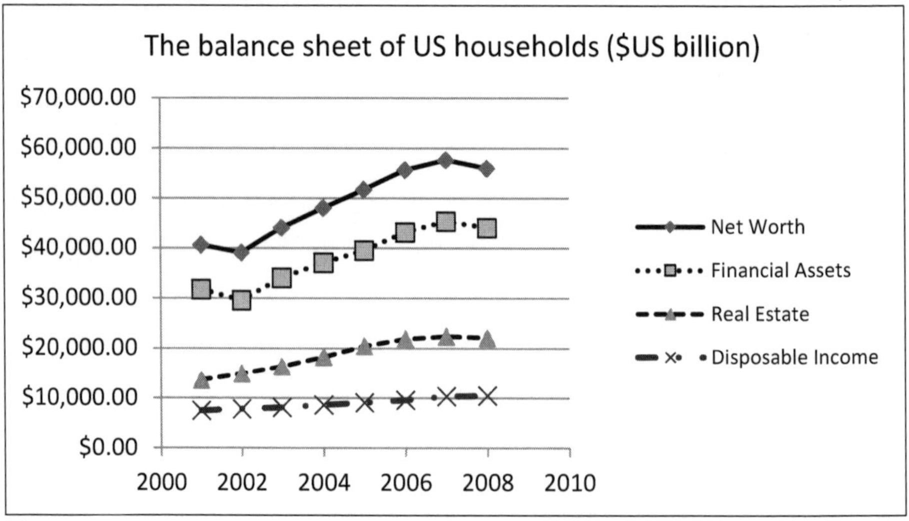

Figure 7

Source: FRB Flow of Funds data, author's calculations. 2008 is as of March 31, all other years are as of December 31.

Back in 2002, I compared housing to gold.[1] The surge in home buying in the 2000s looked like the 1970s rush to buy gold. Like the current times, the 1970s

---

[1] https://papers.ssrn.com/sol3/papers.cfm?abstract_id=316704

were a time of great economic uncertainty, followed by the rapid inflation of prices in the 1980s. Regardless of the actual return on investment, many people bought gold as a hedge against financial and economic turmoil. When Americans bought houses in the 2000s, they believed homes would provide some of that same protection, in addition to being a place to live.

Today it is fashionable to believe that this shift to housing was a tremendous mistake. Yet our research suggests that, if done responsibly, investments in real estate have continued – even amidst the severe bubble in certain locales – to serve as a decent hedge against hard times. Real estate may have taken a dive, but, over time, the stock market has remained even further under water. The reality is that the percentage of regular (conventional and prime) mortgages past due and 90 days past due were higher in 1984 to 1989 (average 0.59%) than they were in 2007 (0.49%). The fact that foreclosures in regular mortgages spiked upward in 2007 and 2008 may have more to do with the Failure of Financial Innovation than with the behavior of homeowners. (Notice that the past due rate is historically much higher than the foreclosure rate. They are now merging; and regular mortgage interest rates remain at historically low levels.)

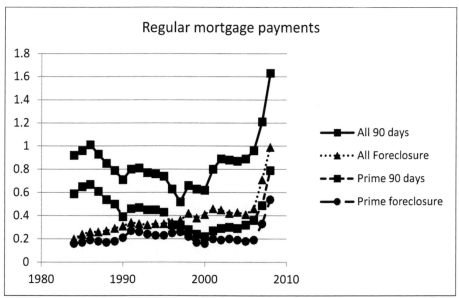

Figure 8

Source: Department of Housing and Urban Development, U.S. Housing Conditions, various issues. All conventional mortgages from 1984 to 1997, then "prime" conventional mortgages from 1998 to 2008 (first quarter). Prior to 1998, mortgages were not distinguished by borrower credit ratings. "90 days" is the percent of mortgage payments that are 90 days late. "Foreclosure" are those actually in foreclosure.

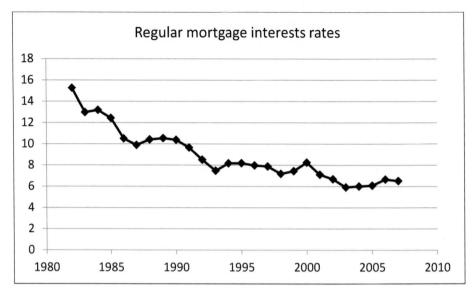

Figure 9
Source: Department of Housing and Urban Development, U.S. Housing Conditions, various issues. All conventional mortgages from 1984 to 1997, then "prime" conventional mortgages from 1998 to 2008 (first quarter). Prior to 1998, mortgages were not distinguished by borrower credit ratings.

Let's look at the record. Since the turn of the 21st century, the net worth of Americans grew six times faster than disposable income. Initially this was more the result of the increase in the value of financial assets than real estate. However, while financial assets dipped in value in 2002, real estate did not, hence the perception that houses could be a better "investment" than stocks and bonds. Real estate values continued to grow at a rate more than twice as fast as income. Last year the value of financial assets dropped 2.9%, but real estate assets dropped by only 1.4%.

The relationship between real estate shares and stock values has changed direction and become more volatile. From 1945 through 1980, the DJIA moved with household investment in real estate and then in the opposite direction through about 2002. In 2003, 2004 and 2005, the values of the DJIA and household real estate moved in the same direction. Now, it seems to be shifting once more, ironically again in favor of real estate.

A DECADE OF ARMAGEDDON

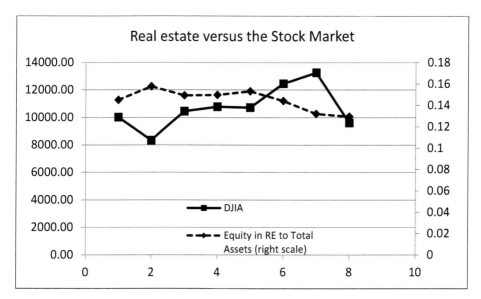

Figure 10
Source: Equity is measured as residential real estate holdings less mortgages, as a percent of total assets. DJIA is the Down Jones Industrial Average, a common measure of the stock market.

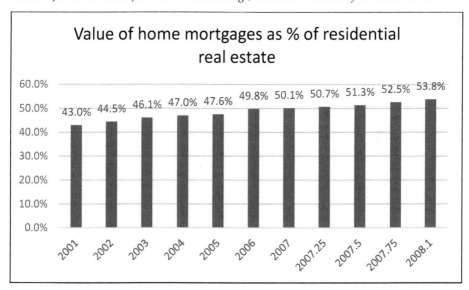

Figure 11
Source: FRB Flow of Funds data, author's calculations.

The stock market was never the "safe" investment. You could have invested in about 400 shares of General Motors stock at $83 a share in 2000; it closed at $3 today (with an analyst's target price of $0). Or you could have made a down payment on a $315,000 condo in Santa Monica; and sold it this year for $680,000.

When capital and productivity are again allowed to surge, we can expect the housing market to rebound first and more strongly than the stock market. Right now, even amidst the perilous economic news, we believe the turn back to real estate is just beginning, although the effects probably won't be fully felt until 2010. We see evidence of potential buyers sitting on the sidelines. There was already a surge in homes sales this summer as some buyers must have judged prices to have adjusted sufficiently in some regions.

So, then the question is: did the New Gold strategy work? Has homeownership shielded Americans from economic uncertainty? We think the answer is – surprisingly - "yes". As financial markets have become increasingly volatile, regular Americans were able to access the value of their homes. The aggregate value of mortgages increased from 44.4 percent of household real estate values in 2002 to 53.8 percent at the end of the first quarter of 2008. Note that this is not merely a result of falling real estate values. Aggregate real estate holdings increased every year except for the last one.

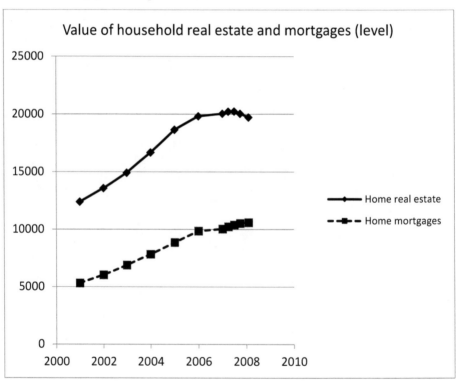

Figure 12
Source: FRB Flow of Funds data, author's calculations. Third quarter 2007 to third quarter 2008 are quarterly observations, all others are annual.

A DECADE OF ARMAGEDDON

When real estate values slowed down, mortgage values slowed down even more. And, obviously, it isn't because the bank reduced the value of the mortgage! It can only be because homeowners continued paying on existing balances.

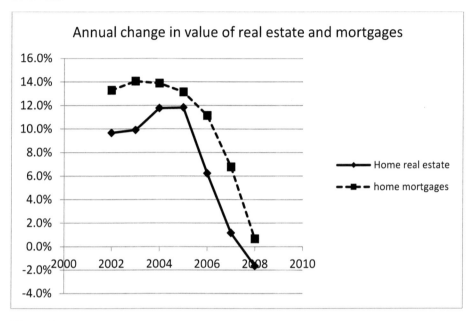

Figure 13
Source: FRB Flow of Funds data, author's calculations.

Before the "subprime crisis", household real estate values grew at an increasing rate – from 9.9% in 2003 to 11.8% in 2004. But the growth of mortgages slowed from 14.1% in 2003 to 13.9% in 2004 and to 13.1% in 2005 when the growth of household real estate remained constant. What was happening here? I think millions of responsible American households were paying into equity. And when things got tough in 2007, some of them dipped into that equity. Not to remodel the kitchen or to buy a boat; but to expand their small business or start their kids in college. These homeowners are "the rest of us who have been prudent and responsible" as Roger Randall called them in a Letter to the Editor of USA Today (November 11, 2008). Mr. Randall asks the question: "Where can the prudent sign up for rewards?" The answer is: Anyone who protected their credit score over the last eight years can still get a "no-doc" mortgage and bank credit for their small business. When a mortgage broker I know lamented that he couldn't write a mortgage for anyone with a credit score under 600, I asked: "If someone has a credit score of 585, should they be buying a house?" Of course, the answer is "no."

Sure, you can deride this activity as Americans "treating their homes like piggy banks." But the reality is that millions of Americans planned it this way. With a fiscally responsible approach to homeownership and financing, they have been and will continue to be able to insulate themselves from the worst of economic times. Good as Gold!

A housing boom, but for whom?

December 28, 2008

We just passed an era when the "American Dream" of home ownership was diminished as the growth of home prices outpaced income. From 2001 through 2006, home prices grew at an annual average of 6.85%, more than three times the growth rate for income.

This divergence between income and housing costs has turned out to be a disaster, particularly for buyers at the lower end of the spectrum. In contrast, for affluent buyers – those making over $120,000 – the bubble may still have been a boom, even if not quite as large as many had hoped for.

For middle- and working-class people, the pressure on affordability was offset by historically low mortgage interest rates which fell from over 11 percent around the time of the 1987 Stock Market Crash to 6 percent in 2002. Yet if stable interest rates were beneficial to overall affordability, the artificially low interest rates promoted by the Federal Reserve may have created instability. By allowing people to increase their purchasing power to an extraordinary level, low mortgage interest rates fueled a rapid escalation in housing prices.

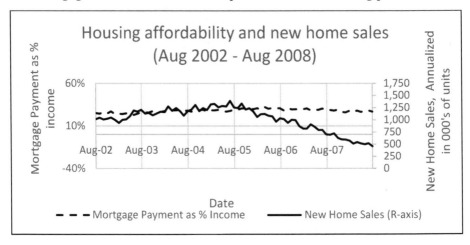

Figure 14
Source: Data from US Housing Market Conditions, U.S. Department of Housing and Urban Development, Office of Policy Development and Research, author's calculations.

A DECADE OF ARMAGEDDON

Now that prices are falling quicker than incomes, there should be a surge in new buyers. Since 1975, whenever the ratio of mortgage payments to income falls, home sales usually rise. The correlation coefficient indicates that for every 1% improvement in affordability there is a 2% *increase* in home sales. But now, something is wrong. In 2007, for every 1% improvement in affordability, home sales *fell* by 2%.

Part of the problem is that prices are still simply too high. Even as recently as August 2008, the median home price was still historically high in comparison to median income – about 4 times. It takes lower rates than in the past for a family with the median income to afford the median priced house. This means that homes are less affordable today than they were six years ago.

The last time that home sales fell as they became more affordable was in the 1990s at a time known as a "credit crunch." At that time, the ratio of home prices to income was actually lower – 3.8 times in September 1990 compared to 4.3 in September 2008. The difference was that between 1990 and 1992 mortgage interest rates averaged a hefty 9.26%. In the last 3 years, the average was 6.14% and while the words "credit crisis" bled in headlines around the world, the regular mortgage interest rate barely budged.

What we are clearly witnessing is a fundamental slow-down in the gains towards homeownership. Of course, most of the gains in homeownership in the US were made in the 20 years after World War II: owner-occupied housing went from 43% in 1940 to 62% in 1960. In the 40 years that followed ownership crept up a bit, from 62% to 68%.[2]

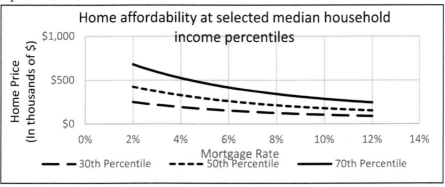

Figure 15
Source: Data from US Housing Market Conditions, U.S. Department of Housing and Urban Development, Office of Policy Development and Research, author's calculations.

---

[2] After retreating to 63% in 2016, recent data on homeownership in the US stood at 66% (first quarter 2023).

Boom, yes. But for whom?

One disturbing aspect of this slowdown has been its effects by class. Overall, ownership has gained only among households making $120,000 or more; for all other groups the ratio of owners to renters is lower today than it was in 1999. (About 80% of American households have income less than $100,000 per year. For Hispanics and African Americans, the number is closer to 90%.)

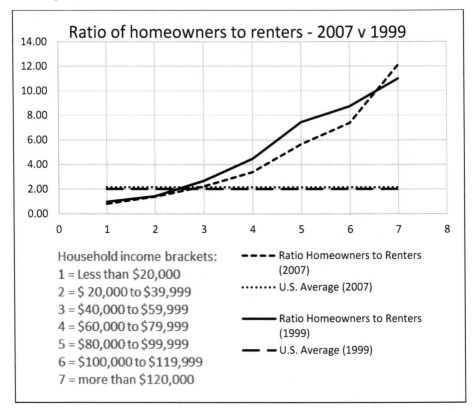

Figure 16
Source: *Data from US Housing Market Conditions, U.S. Department of Housing and Urban Development, Office of Policy Development and Research, author's calculations.*

There have been some exceptions, particularly among minorities targeted by national policy: expanding home ownership opportunities for minorities was a fundamental aim of President Bush's housing policy. In the early years of this decade Hispanics enjoyed a net 2.6 percentage point gain in home ownership. In the next four years, while most Americans were seeing a decrease in home ownership, the Hispanic population continued to see gains. Although African Americans initially gained more than Whites in home ownership, they gave back more of those gains in the housing collapse.

A DECADE OF ARMAGEDDON

The great irony is that exactly those programs aimed at improving affordability may have been responsible for this recent decline. We first wrote about Housing Affordability in 2002.[3] One of our concerns then proved to be true: buyers would focus on "can I afford this home" instead of "what is this home worth." Although there were some gains in overall home ownership rates in the US during the early part of the boom, about 40 percent of that was given back during the last four years as home prices surged out of reach.

The areas with the biggest losses in home ownership rates in the 2004-2008 period were outside the cities, particularly in the Midwest which encompasses Missouri, Iowa, Kansas, Nebraska, Minnesota and the Dakotas (west north central) plus Wisconsin, Illinois, Indiana, Michigan and Ohio (east north central). Of the geographic segments, non-metropolitan Americans gained the least in home ownership in the 1999-2004 housing boom; and only the Midwest geographic segment gave back more.

What about the future? The Obama-Biden Agenda Plan on Urban Policy mentions housing nine times, including a headline on "Housing" with plans for making the mortgage interest tax deduction available to all homeowners (it currently requires itemization) and an increase in the supply of affordable housing throughout Metropolitan Regions. The former should help middle-class households; the latter will help lower-income households. This is not a continuation of the Bush Administration policy which relied on stimulating the demand for housing by providing mechanisms to bring households into the market. The data shows that low-income households barely kept even on ownership (versus renting) under this policy, middle-class households suffered tremendous losses and only the wealthy, those making more than $120,000 in income, had a gain in home ownership.

The last President ignored our advice in 2002: "A more balanced effort to stimulate supply would equilibrate the potential adverse effect on prices" from over stimulating demand. Let's hope this new President gets the balance right.

---

[3] https://papers.ssrn.com/sol3/papers.cfm?abstract_id=349681

Changes in Homeownership Rates				
	Rate	**Change in rate**		
Location	*2008 Q2*	*1999-2004*	*2004-2008*	*1999-2008*
US	68.1	2.2	-0.9	1.3
Northeast	65.3	1.9	0.3	2.2
Midwest	71.7	2.1	-2.1	0
South	70.2	1.8	-0.7	1.1
West	63	3.3	-1.2	2.1
City	53.4	2.7	0.3	3
Suburb	75.5	2.1	-0.2	1.9
Non-metro*	74.9	0.9	-1.4	-0.5
White	75.2	2.8	-0.8	2
Black	48.4	3	-1.3	1.7
Other**	60.2	5.5	0.6	6.1
Multi	56.4	NA	-4	NA
Hispanic	49.6	2.6	1.5	4.1

Table based on historical data from US Housing Market Conditions, U.S. Department of Housing and Urban Development, Office of Policy Development and Research,

*Non-metro includes all areas outside metropolitan statistical areas (non-urban). Note from Census.gov: For Census 2000, the Census Bureau classifies as "urban" all territory, population, and housing units located within an urbanized area (UA) or an urban cluster (UC). It delineates UA and UC boundaries to encompass densely settled territory, which consists of: core census block groups or blocks that have a population density of at least 1,000 people per square mile and surrounding census blocks that have an overall density of at least 500 people per square mile.

**"Other" includes "Asian", which reports household incomes about 20% to 30% higher than the Racial/Ethnic category "All" regardless of income level category.

Responsible home buyers, why be frugal?

February 21, 2009

I was laying in bed this morning, listening to discussions of the Homeowner Affordability and Stability Plan, the 2009 version of a Homeowner Bailout. (The 2008 version was spent on the banks.) I listened closely because I had to decide if it was worth getting out of bed to earn the money to pay my mortgage or not. Like all those bankers that got a bailout, I was wondering if it might be worth more to me to default on my mortgage than to pay it. I mean, what if the only people getting bailed out are the ones who truly screwed up? Being right doesn't mean being rich and I didn't want to miss out.

I realized that I'd have to get out of bed and get to the office anyway if I was going to make sense of this Plan. Radio sound bites are no substitute for real research. Timmy Geithner put several documents up on his website.[4] Much like his plan to print $2.5 trillion, it's still more rhetoric than reality but at least this time they included lots of number, so I'm happy to rifle through it.

Step one in the Fact Sheet[5] is "Refinancing for Up to 4 to 5 Million Responsible Homeowners to Make Their Mortgages More Affordable." The Plan offers an example of a family with a $207,000 30-year fixed rate mortgage at 6.5%. The house value has fallen 15% to $221,000 so they have less than the 20% home equity needed to qualify for current mortgage rates (close to 5%). The lower interest rate would save this homeowner $2,300/year in mortgage payments.

First of all, this homeowner's monthly mortgage payment is $1,308 – about 8.6% of all mortgages fall into this range. About 60% of mortgages are below that level. If the mortgage is too much bigger than that, they are into "jumbo" territory in a lot of areas, so we'll say this plan is directed at the lower 60%. The example of a $260,000 home is a little pricey – the median new home in 2008 was $226,000 and the median existing home price was $202,000.

The lower price isn't just because home prices are falling. The US median home price has never been higher than $247,900 except in places like New York and California.[6] But the median home price has not skyrocketed in vast swaths of middle-class, middle-America. Finally, reducing your payments by $2,300 in a

---

[4] https://home.treasury.gov/data/troubled-assets-relief-program

[5] https://home.treasury.gov/news/press-releases/20092181117388144

[6] April 2023, the median sales price of existing homes in the US was $388,800 (FRED Economic Data, St. Louis Fed) or $275,939 in 2008-dollars.

year means a monthly savings of about $200 – enough to cover a northern winter utility bill.

If they reach the 4 million homeowners that they say they will, that's 5.3% of *all* homeowners. But only 1.19% of all mortgages are in foreclosure and only 1.83% are 90 days past due. Maybe they are going to help the slow-pays, because 6.41% of all mortgages have some past due payments. President Obama specifically said that he was doing this to help regular, middle-class homeowners. That should not mean those who have homes worth more than the national median.

Then there's this 15% drop in home value in Geithner's example. The national median fell 8.6% from $247,000 at the beginning of 2007 to $225,700 in the third quarter of 2008 (latest available from HUD). In the West, where California homes have a higher median price than middle-America, the median *new* home price rose from $320,200 in 2007 to $414,400 at the end of 2008. That's a whopping 29.4% increase in the median price for a new home! Eastern US median home prices did fall, but by 12.6% not 15%. Still, I wouldn't be hard pressed to find a city or two or three where home prices fell by 12%. But it doesn't appear that they will be middle-class homes in middle-America. Existing home prices have fallen across the board. But only in the West did these prices fall at an alarming rate. The average for the other regions was only 8.7%.

Median Existing Home Price					
Period*	US	Northeast	Midwest	South	West
2007	219,000	279,100	165,100	179,300	335,000
2008	191,600	246,800	152,500	167,200	253,600
% change	12.50%	11.60%	7.60%	6.70%	24.30%
* 2008 is for September, latest from HUD. 2007 is full year figure.					

Let's look at the rest of the bill: "A $75 Billion Homeowner Stability Initiative to Reach Up to 3 to 4 Million At-Risk Homeowners." This part is for those with adjustable-rate mortgages ("have seen their mortgage payments rise to 40 or even 50 percent of their monthly income") and excludes those slow-pays ("before a borrower misses a payment") that appear to be getting help from Part One. This Part is only available to those who have a high mortgage-to-income ratio and/or whose mortgage balance is higher than the current market value. Under the "Shared Effort to Reduce Monthly Payments" the federal government would step in to make some of your interest payments after the bank can't reduce your interest rate any further.

There's nothing here that says you'll have to pay the government back that money – ever. But if the interest rate reduction isn't enough, and having the government make some of your interest payments still doesn't get you down to a mortgage payment that is no more than 31% of your income (one of the definitions of affordable), then the government will even pay down some of your *principal.*

But wait, that's not all you get! If you and your bank can work out a deal here's what else Uncle Obama will throw in for you:

If you take this action	The government pays Your Bank	The government pays You
Do a loan modification	$1,000	Reduced interest costs and principal balance
Do it before you miss a payment	$500	$1,500
Stay current	$3,000 (over 3 years)	$5,000 (over 5 years)

Wow! I'm really beginning to regret being a responsible person. I comment on Part 3 of the plan in tomorrow's article. But this is really discouraging. I'm ineligible because I bought responsibly, before the Stimulus Bill gave out incentives to buy. I suspect there are about 70 million households out there just like me. Trillions of dollars running around the economy and all I can see is that the responsible majority will be paying for it while irresponsible bankers, brokers and home buyers benefit.

To tell you the truth, I need a tissue…

Housing bail out part deux: just another financial con job

February 22, 2009

Last night I wrote about the Obama Administration's housing bail out. But, I hate to say, there's more to tell you – and it's actually worse. In addition to the giveaways to mortgage holders, we also have to consider the federal government effectively offering to give a credit default swap (CDS, remember those?) to the banks. If one of the lucky homeowners that get a loan modification defaults on their mortgage because home prices fall again in the future, the federal government will make good to the bank for them. There are some differences between this and a real CDS, though – the banks won't have to pay a premium for the insurance. The federal government is selling CDS for $0. Nice. We taxpayers are putting up $10 billion for this piece.

Then there are the plans to "Support Low Mortgage Rates by Strengthening Confidence in Fannie Mae and Freddie Mac." There's that word again: confidence. In a con game, the con man isn't the one who is confident; he is the one who gives *you* confidence. You are so confident that you are making a good decision that you give him all your money to be part of his scheme. If you still have any questions about confidence schemes, watch "The Music Man" again.

The Treasury nationalized Fannie Mae and Freddie Mac (F&F) last year – they are now owned by the federal government. If you need more "confidence" than that in the strength of F&F, then you should consider moving to another country. Under the assumption that "too big to fail" makes sense, the new Bailout plan is increasing the size of F&F's mortgage portfolios by $50 billion – along with corresponding increases in their allowable debt outstanding. This part of the Homeowner Affordability and Stability Plan will cost $200 billion, an amount that goes beyond the $2.5 trillion cost of the Financial Stability Plan and the $700 billion in the Emergency Economic Stabilization Act/TARP and the $800 billion Stimulus Plan. The new $200 billion in funding, according to the Treasury's plan, is being made under the Housing and Economic Recovery Act.[7]

If you can remember back that far, the Housing and Economic Recovery Act was signed into law by the former and largely unmissed resident of the White House back in July 2008 to clean up the subprime mortgage crisis before any of the other bailout money was committed to clean up the subprime mortgage crisis. This legislation established the HOPE for Homeowners Act of 2008 which spent $300 billion to (1) insure refinanced loans for distressed borrowers, (2) reduce principle balances and interest charges to avoid foreclosure, (3) provide confidence in mortgage markets with greater transparency for home values, (4) be used for homeowners and not home flippers or speculators (5) increase the budget at the Federal Housing Administration so they can monitor that all this happens as legislated, (6) end when the housing market is stabilized and (7) provide banks with more ways and means to stop foreclosing on delinquent homeowners. Three million homes were foreclosed last year despite this legislation or any of the other bills that passed before and after it.

---

[7] https://www.govinfo.gov/content/pkg/PLAW-110publ289/html/PLAW-110publ289.htm

A DECADE OF ARMAGEDDON

Each new bill carries with it an increase in the limit on the national debt. The most recent Stimulus Package increased it from $11.315 trillion to $12.104 trillion effective February 17, 2009. The actual debt is currently at $10.8 trillion[8] and rising. With only $1.3 trillion between the actual debt and the limit, Timmy Geithner's pals back at the Federal Reserve will have to keep the printing presses running overtime.

The "new" Homeowner Affordability and Stability Plan is just a rehash of every old financial sector bailout plan. The definition of insanity, according to a quote attributed to Albert Einstein, is doing the same thing over and over again and expecting different results. Here we go again.

Why homeownership is falling – despite lower prices: look to the job market

February 27, 2009

There's something about "Housing Affordability" that makes it very popular: Presidents past and present set goals around it. The popularity of this perennial policy goal rests on the feel-good idea that everyone would live in a home that they own if only they could afford it. Owning your own home is declared near and far to be part and parcel of the American Dream.

Recently, however, it seems that Americans aren't all having the same dream. Despite improving conditions of affordability, home sales continue to decline. Affordability is balanced on a tripod of prices, incomes and interest rates. As incomes become unstable because of mounting job losses, housing falls further out of balance – no change in price or mortgage interest rates will be enough to rebalance the tripod within the next twelve to eighteen months.

In a new study on Homeownership Affordability[9] we identify two anomalies in the data: home sales are falling as housing affordability is rising; and the rate of homeownership since 2004 has fallen despite the apparent "boom" in housing.

Rising Affordability with Falling Sales

In the last three years, the average mortgage interest rate was 6.14%. Such historically low rates should improve affordability compared to, say, the time of the 1990s credit crunch when mortgage rates averaged 9.3%. Leading up to 2007, median income in the US rose by 0.6% and median home prices fell by

---

[8] https://fiscaldata.treasury.gov/americas-finance-guide/national-debt/ As of 2 February 2023, it is $31.5 trillion

[9] https://papers.ssrn.com/sol3/papers.cfm?abstract_id=1348143

3.1% – also a positive indicator for affordability. The mortgage payment to income ratio at the median has fallen to about 23%. Compared to 32% in 2002 and even 40% in 1988, just before the 1990s credit crunch, this should be a very positive indicator for homeowner affordability. Yet, new home sales have plummeted from a rate of about 1.4 million per year in the summer of 2005 to less than 500,000 by the end of 2008.

In 2007, for every 1% improvement in affordability, home prices *fell* by 2%. There clearly has been a breakdown in the fundamental relationship between supply and demand. Why? It appears potential buyers are concerned that homes are over-priced and, worse yet, that home price declines will increase in the future. There are indications that some households think that homes are overpriced regardless of affordability and, furthermore, not everyone who can afford a home is interested in buying one. Some communities, some jobs and some lifestyles are better suited to renting.

Ownership Policies with Falling Ownership

All this has occurred in the face of conscious federal policy. Expanding homeownership opportunities, especially for minorities, was a fundamental aim of the Bush Administration's housing policy – one strongly supported by Democrats in Congress. In June 2002, HUD announced a new goal to increase minority homeownership by 5.5 million by the end of 2010. Hispanics were the only minorities to have clear gains in homeownership through 2008: a 4.1 percentage point increase compared to the end of the last decade. The gains in homeownership for black Americans was about the same as for the nation as a whole. Yet the ownership rate for the nation as a whole declined by almost 1 percent during the more recent "housing bust" years.

Some regions saw bigger losses in homeownership than others, especially those outside the urban areas and particularly in the Midwest.

Where do we go from here?

We believe the analytical focus needs to shift to employment when analyzing housing for individual states, regions or cities. The accompanying table shows where, at the state level, the workforce is shrinking as unemployment is rising. (See Appendix 1 – State Change in Total Workforce and Number of Unemployed). These are the areas, much like Southern California at the end of the Cold War or Houston after the 1980s bust in oil prices, that will suffer potentially devastating drops in home prices as a result of forced sales by departing labor.

Supply, demand and pricing, the cost of financing, household income and home prices – all are critical factors in the equation of homeownership. But more than anything we believe that mounting job losses, in addition to a declining stock market, will now play the critical role. Over time, the current credit crisis will not only make funds more scarce – which must eventually drive up the price of credit – but also drive up the risk premium demanded by lenders. Growing job uncertainty will increase the price of credit even further.

These factors alone will negatively impact affordability in the future. Keeping mortgage rates artificially low (for example, as the Federal Reserve buys up mortgage-backed securities as proposed in Congress) will create upward pressure on prices, which in turn will hurt affordability. Additionally, we see continued imbalances in the supply-demand equation as foreclosures add inventory to the market.

In the coming 12 to 18 months, we believe that interest rates will rise, and incomes will, at best, remain flat in the face of the global recession. More importantly, as job losses mount, "affordability" will be less important and "maintainability" – the ability of homeowners to keep their homes in the face of unemployment – will emerge as a major factor. In the meantime, housing affordability will hang precariously out of balance due to falling incomes and decreasing jobs as well as surging real interest rates.

Want to foreclose? Show me the paper!

March 4, 2009

Since October 2008 I've been writing here about problems in mortgage-backed securities (MBS). There is more evidence surfacing in bankruptcy courts that the paperwork for the underlying mortgages wasn't provided correctly for the new bond holders, leading to delayed or denied foreclosure proceedings.

New York Times' Gretchen Morgenson is reporting new successes in cases[10] from Florida and California. A judgment on a home in Miami-Dade County (FL) was set aside on February 11 when the new mortgage holder could not produce evidence that the original mortgage lien (a financial claim on the property) had been assigned to the MBS holder. In one of the California cases, the lender tried for foreclose on a mortgage that had previously been transferred to Freddie Mac!

---

[10] https://www.nytimes.com/2009/03/01/business/01gret.html?_r=1&em

The earliest decision I've seen is from Judge Christopher A. Boyko in Cleveland. Plaintiff Deutsche Bank's attorney argued, "Judge, you just don't understand how things work." In his October 31, 2007 decision to dismiss a foreclosure complaint, Boyko responded that this "argument reveals a condescending mindset and quasi-monopolistic system" established by financial institutions to the disadvantage of homeowners. The Masters of the Universe were anxious to pump out mortgages into MBS so they could continue to earn fees – making money at any cost.

One element of the newest Homeowner Bailout program is to allow bankruptcy court judges to modify mortgage loans. If the types of cases decided in OH, FL and CA continue to spread, that may not be necessary. The first question in any foreclosure procedure will become: can you prove a lien?

This raises further questions about those "toxic assets" that Geithner and Bernanke are so anxious to buy up at taxpayer expense. According to the Morgenson article, some MBS holders are trying to force the mortgage originator to take back the paper. However, many of the worst offenders are already defunct.

Many investors have more to gain by letting your mortgage or company fail

March 5, 2009

I hate to say "I told you so" but… I told you so. The holders of the credit default swaps (CDS) have more to gain from the failure of the borrower than from accepting payments.

Bloomberg is reporting a strategy at Citigroup, Inc. to do just that. In one example, they can buy up Six Flags bonds at 20.5 cents on the dollar, pay a small premium to get the CDS and then collect the full face-value of the bonds when Six Flags files for bankruptcy – which the CDS holder can be sure happens.

Normally, before a company goes into bankruptcy, they would meet with the debt holders to try to re-negotiate their debt. Debt holders will usually do this because they have more to gain from the company remaining in operation than otherwise. Sometimes, the company may even get them to exchange their debt for equity, provided there is a good business model that has the potential for future earnings.

Now, as I've described repeatedly, the CDS holders have more to gain from the bankruptcy because they will get their entire investment paid back, with interest, not from the company that issued the debt but from another company that issued the CDS – some company like, for example, AIG!

Speaking of AIG, there was very little coverage of the Senate Committee hearing Thursday (3/5/2009):[11] "American International Group: Examining what went wrong, government intervention, and implications for future regulation." It was a stunner! Bottom line? Senator Jim Bunning (R-KY) told the panelists that if they asked for another dime for AIG, "You will get the biggest 'no'" ever heard. The entire committee was incredulous that Federal Reserve Vice Chairman Donald Kohn point-blank refused to tell them 1) who is benefiting from the AIG payouts on CDS and 2) how much more it is going to cost to bailout AIG.

Stand by, because home foreclosures are on the same course as Six Flags: homeowners attempting to re-negotiate their debt will find that somewhere in the background, a CDS holder has more to gain from the foreclosure because they will get their entire investment paid back, with interest, not from the homeowners but from some company that issued a CDS – some company like, for example, AIG!

One homeowner, two mortgage holders, no lien!

December 1, 2009

I've been following this for a while and writing about it on NewGeography.com since March – not all mortgage-backed securities (MBS) are actually backed by mortgages. So, when the homeowner goes into bankruptcy, there's no way for the MBS holder to prove a lien on the house and the judge awards the bondholder bupkus. In April, a bankruptcy judge in California wrote that as many as one-third of all MBS didn't have mortgages. No "M" in the "BS," as I like to put it!

Well, this story just gets better and better. It turns out that even when the MBS has an actual mortgage underneath it, the same mortgage is backing more than one security. Last week I talked to Matt Taibbi, who wrote in *Rolling Stone* magazine (The Great American Bubble Machine[12]) that 58 percent of an MBS issued by Goldman Sachs had nothing but a list of zip codes where the

---

[11] https://www.banking.senate.gov/hearings/american-international-group-examining-what-went-wrong-government-intervention-and-implications-for-future-regulation. Video requires Flash Player v9; majority (Senator Dodd) and witness statements available for download.

[12] https://www.rollingstone.com/politics/politics-news/the-great-american-bubble-machine-195229/

mortgages should have been. He told me about a lawyer in Florida who has a list of cases where two MBS holders showed up at the bankruptcy proceedings, both claiming that they owned the same mortgage. You can expect to read more on that here as the story develops.

Then it gets worse! Gretchen Morgenson reported in the New York Times[13] on Sunday that there are about 60 million mortgages registered with the Mortgage Electronic Registration System (MERS) to keep track of who owns which loans and which MBS. Problem was that MERS, created by Fannie Mae, Freddie Mac and the mortgage industry, thought they were too good to have to register liens against land at the county level – real estate 101 for any sober realtor. The Kansas Supreme Court has now ruled that changes in mortgage ownership registered with MERS – and not registered with the local land authority – have no legal standing.

Don't forget – MBS are the junk that Treasury Secretary Geithner wants to purchase with tax-payer dollars; and Federal Reserve Chairman Ben Bernanke committed $1.25 trillion[14] of freshly-printed dollars to buy up out of the marketplace this year. Here's the math made easy – the median house costs $177,000, figure an 80% mortgage, times 60 million mortgages: it looks like $8.5 trillion worth of mortgages could have no real estate underneath them! If the repo man comes knocking on your door, remember these four words: Show Me The Paper!

13

https://www.nytimes.com/2009/09/27/business/27gret.html?_r=2&scp=4&sq=gretchen&st=cse

[14] https://www.federalreserve.gov/newsevents/pressreleases/monetary20090318a.htm

4. Federal Reserve and Treasury Actions

The US monetized the impact of the 2008 crisis through the Federal Reserve's programs of quantitative easing whereby they expanded the money supply by an amount equal to about 25% of national output.[1] In 2009, then Treasury Secretary Timothy Geithner presented a 61-page proposal for legislation that would give the secretary the authority to make the final determination that a financial institution on the verge of default is systemically important. This is a prime example of regulation by revolution – an attempt to toss aside all previous practices. Regulation by revolution has been done before without successful outcomes. The Depository Institutions Deregulation and Monetary Control Act of 1980 set the stage for the Savings and Loan Crisis; the Financial Services Modernization Act of 1999 helped get global capital markets to the crisis of 2008. Essentially, Geithner's proposal would let the federal government nationalize a 'too big to fail' company. His idea was to codify and make permanent authority for the government to repeat what it did for AIG. The legislation was drafted at Davis, Polk & Wardwell, the New York lawyers for the Federal Reserve Bank and advisors to Federal Reserve and Treasury on AIG.[2]

Writing about the financial crisis in the US, former IMF chief economist Simon Johnson said, 'If you hid the name of the country and just showed them the numbers, there is no doubt what old IMF hands would say: nationalize troubled banks and break them up as necessary. (With James Kwak, 'The Quiet Coup,' The Atlantic, May 2009, published online on 26 March 2009), available at www.theatlantic.com/doc/200905/imf-advice.[3]

Fool me once, Geithner, shame on you, fool me twice...

February 21, 2009

Treasury Secretary Timothy Geithner revealed the new "Financial Stability Plan" on February 10, 2009. It's thick with "why we need it" and thin on "exactly what it is." He told Congress that he would open a website to disclose where all

---

[1] *LNL*, p. xvii, footnote 4.

[2] Ibid. p. 196. The initial version of the Dodd-Frank Wall Street Reform and Consumer Protection Act has a section that is virtually identical to Geithner's proposal: "Subtitle G – Enhanced Resolution Authority" (available at https://www.congress.gov/bill/111th-congress/house-bill/4173/text). The Dodd-Frank bill that passed into law required systemically important institutions to submit "resolution plans" for an orderly dissolution that did not include bailouts. Some of the Geithner's wording survived, but giving authority to the Fed or Treasury to take over financial institutions did not.

[3] Ibid. p. 37.

the bailout money was going. When asked if he would reveal where the first $350 billion went, he was a little vague on the details.

Senator Grassley (R-IA) asked him at the confirmation hearings about the Maiden Lane LLCs and the money he passed out to private, non-regulated companies. His written response then was "Confidentiality around the specific characteristics and performance of individual loans in the portfolio is maintained in order to allow the asset manager the flexibility to manage the assets in a way that maximizes the value of portfolio and mitigates risk of loss to the taxpayer." In other words, he wouldn't say. When asked "What specific additional disclosure would you support?" Tim's response was "If confirmed, I look forward to working with you and with Chairman Bernanke on ways to respond to your suggestions and concerns." Variations on the "If confirmed, I look forward to working on it" answer was cut and pasted into his 102-page written responses 104 times, or more than once per page.

Back in 2008 when the big bailout bucks were being passed around, we (and Congress) were led to believe that this was all being done to fix problems in housing and mortgage markets. Speaker of the House Nancy Pelosi (D-CA) said this in her speech on the floor before the vote: "We're putting up $700 billion; we want the American people to get some of the upside. ...[we] insisted that we would have forbearance on foreclosure. If we're now going to own that [mortgage-backed securities] paper, that we would then have forbearance to help responsible homeowners stay in their home." Three million homes went into foreclosure last year.

Speaker Pelosi went on to tell us that the bill would include "an end to the golden parachutes and a review and reform of the compensation for CEOs." Excuse my cynicism but Tim Geithner took a $500,000 walk-away bonus when he left the Federal Reserve Bank of New York, the maximum earnings allowed under President Obama's suggested compensation cap; but that was on top of his $400,000 salary which would put him over the limit. Obama appointee Deputy Secretary of State Jacob Lew took home just under $1.1 million last year as a managing director at Citi Alternative Investments, a unit of Citigroup, which so far took $45 billion in bailout money.

So, let's add this up. Tim hides $330 billion from us while he's at the Fed, refuses to tell Congress who it went to, refuses to tell Congress who Paulson gave the money to, and takes more than his share of compensation.

Now he wants us to believe that Treasury can "require all Financial Stability Plan recipients to participate in foreclosure mitigation plans." Fool me once, shame on you. Fool me twice, shame on me. I, personally, don't believe a word of it. And neither should you. It's all baloney, bogus, phantom. They are paying lip service to the American taxpayers, so you won't send those faxes to Congress or throw shoes at the new President. They are passing the money to the same Democratic big wigs that paid for their election campaigns – just as they did in the past to the Republicans. Tim is shoveling more money to the same private companies that he previously sent freshly-printed Federal Reserve notes. Now he can also pass out Congressionally-approved money. While Congress struggled with spending $800 billion to directly stimulate economic activity in the US, Tim thumbed his nose at them by presenting a plan to spread around more than $2.5 trillion that won't require their approval. That's the way it is, and I think it would be a very bad idea to stop him.

Yes, you read that right. I said it would be a bad idea to stop. I'm a fan of NASCAR racing. When a driver begins to lose control of the car and is sailing headfirst into a concrete wall at 190 miles per hour there is only one way to save it – stand on the gas. Your every instinct is to hit the brakes, to stop the car before you slam into the wall. But if you hit the brakes, you lose traction and control. By pressing down on the gas, you put power to the wheels which (hopefully) are still in contact with the track – with traction comes control and you can steer away from the wall. Oh, but it isn't easy! Every cell in your monkey-cousin brain will scream: "Slam on the brakes!"

So, it's like the economy is heading for the wall. And Tim has decided to hit the gas[4] – another $100 billion for the banks, $1 trillion for private capital to put in junk bonds, $1 trillion for private investors to spend on junk loans, $600 billion for Fannie and Freddie's debt – yet only $50 billion to reduce mortgage payments for "middle class homes" in foreclosure.

But even if we avoid hitting the wall, that doesn't mean we don't need to change course. For years (to continue the analogy) I have argued we need to fix the racetrack and improve the aerodynamics of the cars, so they won't head into the wall in the first place. I would insist that broker dealers have to deliver what they sell. I would prohibit the sale of derivatives in excess of the underlying assets. But that's technical stuff, like requiring roof flaps in NASCAR (little flaps that come up when the car spins backwards to keep it from going airborne). It

---

[4] https://home.treasury.gov/sites/default/files/initiatives/financial-stability/about/Documents/fact-sheet.pdf

would prevent the really bad wrecks, but then no one would tune in on Sunday if there weren't any wrecks, right?

Enjoy the show as Tim tries to keep from crashing into the wall. But don't be fooled that he is fixing anything. Even if he pulls the economy out this time, the track is still broken, and the cars are still not aerodynamically sound. They'll wreck it again – as they did in 1981 (inflation so high that Treasury bonds paid 19%), in 1987 (October stock market crash of 23% was worst of all time), in 1991 (junk bond collapse and credit crunch) and in 2000 (the dot.com bust).

This will keep happening until we take the time to understand the real causes and put in real solutions. The solution is not now and has never been to throw money at it. This is the "junkie cousin" approach that Amy Poehler (Saturday Night Live) compared to the Original Bailout package: "It's like you lend $100 to your junkie cousin to pay his rent. And when you run into him at the racetrack next week, you lend him another $50."

At what point do you "get it" that your cousin is gambling away the money you lent him for the rent, that this is not really helping your cousin to kick junk? The solution is not throwing money around but accounting for all the money already out there (including the stocks, bonds, and derivatives). It's not more regulation, it's enforcing rules that are already on the books. Real solutions take real work. I'm not hopeful that the US government and markets are willing to do the work. So, I'll make sure I'm wearing a helmet with my seat-belt buckled for the next crash, say just around 2017.[5]

Bernanke: Junkmeister hides the truth

March 4, 2009

Federal Reserve Chairman Ben Bernanke testified before the Senate Budget Committee[6] on Tuesday (March 3, 2009), the day after it was announced that AIG would be back at the federal teat for another $30 billion. The generally subdued Senate was nonetheless forceful in getting Bernanke to admit several things:

---

[5] In 2017, Donald J. Trump was inaugurated as the 45th president of the United States. The economy grew about 2.2% that year, but the federal budget deficit grew faster: 17.3%, or about 9% of GDP. The next official recession in the U.S. wasn't until the second quarter of 2020 (part of a worldwide recession caused by the COVID-19 lockdowns).

[6] https://www.federalreserve.gov/newsevents/testimony/bernanke20090303a.htm

- The Fed and Treasury are using the same three rating agencies to help them select triple-A collateral for bailout lending as were used to get triple-A credit ratings for junk mortgage bonds;
- Neither the Fed nor the Treasury will tell us all the companies that are getting bailout money;
- There is no "outer limit" to how much money the US government can print;
- No one knows the "outer limit" of how much money the US government can borrow;
- The "too big to fail" policy is a bigger problem than anyone thought it could be;
- No one was in charge of AIG – not bank regulators, insurance regulators or capital market regulators.

When asked about AIG several times, Bernanke replied that it's "uncomfortable for me, too." Through some hole in the regulations, the insurance regulators had no authority to monitor the financial products activities of AIG. Explained simply and bluntly, the world's largest insurance company sold credit default swaps (CDS, insurance against default) on the junk bonds issued from mortgages and consumer purchases. Many of those mortgages and consumer purchases were made foolishly – when the borrowers failed to repay the loans the bonds also failed. The people and companies that bought CDS on those bonds did not look too closely at AIG to see what would happen if the bonds failed. As it turns out, they didn't have to worry about AIG failing – AIG was deemed too big to fail.

When the bonds defaulted and the buyers of CDS protection ("counterparties") turned to AIG for payment, AIG turned to the federal government for help. The AIG bailout has cost $180 billion so far for which the US government owns 80 percent of a company that lost $61.7 billion in three months (for a total of $99.29 billion in 2008, an amount equal to all of their profits back to about 1990).[7]

Here's a tough question: Why won't the Fed disclose who is benefiting from the CDS payoffs? Bernanke made a comparison between your grandmother and AIG: like the owners of life insurance policies, the purchasers of financial insurance "made legal legitimate financial transactions. They have a right to privacy about their financial condition." In other words, no one should know how much life insurance your grandmother has. That's why the Fed won't tell us who bought the CDS insurance on junk bonds! Senator Ron Wyden (D-OR)

---

[7] https://www.reuters.com/article/ousiv/idUSN0134457520090302?pageNumber=1&
virtualBrandChannel=0

asked him to "come clean." Senator Bernard Sanders (I-VT) asked point blank: tell us who got the $2.2 trillion loaned by the Fed. He got a one-word response for his troubles: "no."

Bernanke said, "AIG made me angry... This was a hedge fund attached to an insurance company. We had to step in, we really had no choice. It's a terrible situation, but we aren't doing this to bailout AIG, we're doing it to protect the broader economy."

Here's how you connect the dots from AIG to main street: AIG is an insurance company and insurance companies are among the "safe" investments that money market mutual funds are allowed to invest their cash in – in fact most funds are required to keep some portion of their assets in these supposedly risk-free investments.

Basically, this requirement is there to make sure that cash will be available to meet the withdrawal requests from investors. Now, money market mutual funds and mutual funds are a favorite investment for retirement money, including the 401k plans that many people have through their employers. But also, your employer's retirement plan money is likely also invested in these funds. Pensions can hold stocks and bonds directly. But as the size of these plans gets bigger and bigger, it becomes increasingly difficult for one or a few investment managers to handle everything. The California State Teachers Retirement System and the California Public Employees Retirement System (Cal STRS and Cal PRS, for short), the largest pension funds in the world, have $160 billion and $180 billion in assets to invest. So, propping up AIG means that the investments made in the stocks, commercial paper, policies, etc. issued by AIG will not collapse and take with them the retirement assets of many millions of Americans.

In the final round of questions, Senators Warner (D-VA) and Wyden (D-OR) were especially clear on the point of finding out who is benefiting from the bailout of AIG. AIG was a good insurance company, Warner said, but their London-based financial products division started selling CDS in Europe. Now, American taxpayers are being asked to pick up the tab. Why does AIG continue to make the payouts when they require federal money to continue to exist? The Senators suggested that, at a minimum, Americans deserve to know who is benefiting from the CDS payouts. "It's time for some sunlight."

Geithner is Wall Street's lapdog

March 24, 2009

Treasury Secretary Tim Geithner is on the cover of the April 2009 issue of Bloomberg Markets magazine. In the lead article, "Man in the Middle," the authors refer to his time at the New York Federal Reserve Bank (FRB-NY) as "experience as a consensus builder." This overlooks the fact that it was easy for him to get everyone to agree, to build group solidarity, when he simply gave the banks and broker-dealers everything they wanted.

The Primary Dealers, those broker-dealers and banks who have a special arrangement with the FRB-NY for trading in treasury securities, agreed when Geithner let them fail to deliver $2.5 trillion of treasury securities for seven weeks in the fall; they agreed when he let them fail to deliver more than $1 trillion two years earlier; they agreed when he let them fail to deliver treasury securities even after Geithner's own economists told him it was dangerous. By the way, last year the FRB-NY's public information department prevented those economists from speaking on the record about their research on fails to deliver in Treasury securities with a Bloomberg reporter.

Now, at a hearing on March 24, 2009 before the House Financial Services Committee, Secretary Geithner and Federal Reserve Chairman Ben Bernanke lectured us on the awesome responsibilities of Treasury and Federal Reserve in the current crisis – without admitting that they had those same responsibilities while the crisis was being created.

In a joint statement from the Department of the Treasury and the Federal Reserve they offer no explanation for their failure to fulfil their "central role … in preventing and managing financial crises." Rather, they use the fact of that role to require that we accept whatever plan they put before us today as the best and wisest course. To convince us that their plan is the right one, they can all point to the fact that the stock markets rallied (gaining nearly 7% across the board) led by the shares of financial institutions (Goldman Sachs' shares went from $97.48 on Friday night to $111.93 on Monday – a gain of about 15%).

I criticized the "Public Private Partnership" when it was announced in February 2009. Calling Wall Street's bad investments "Legacy Assets" doesn't change the fact that they are "junk." They could call it "the hair of the dog" because they now want to invest taxpayer money into the same junk investments that started the financial snowball rolling downhill in the first place.

Just because the stock market rallied doesn't make this "consensus building" – I call it being Wall Street's lapdog.

Junk by any other name would smell

March 25, 2009

The Treasury this week disclosed details of their plan to pump $1 trillion into the financial system[8] by removing "Legacy Assets" from the balance sheets of banks. Wading through the multitude of documents and documents, I'm reminded of a remark by Michael Milken: "Complexity is not innovation."[9]

Since its inception, the plan has been sold to Congress and the media as one with potential positive payoffs for the public coffers. To support this idea, proponents point to the experience of the Resolution Trust Company (RTC) in resolving the Savings and Loan (S&L) Crisis.[10] Back then, RTC took over failing S&Ls – some of which were bankrupted by bad real estate loans made worse when they were forced to sell off below-investment grade bond assets – the by-now-well-known Junk Bonds.[11]

Selling off today's junk bonds will, I agree, clean up the balance sheets of the banks and make them more attractive to investors and depositors. But the investment in junk bonds now is not going to turn out like the investment in junk bonds then. For starters, the value of the junk bonds then declined as a result of the forced sell-off – Congress prohibited S&Ls from holding junk bonds on their balance sheets. When this supply was dumped on the market, the prices naturally dropped. Selling assets at depressed prices damaged a lot of S&Ls. RTC stepped in near the bottom of those prices to take control of the assets. When credit markets returned to normal, the prices of the junk bonds rose and the investments had positive returns.[12]

---

[8] https://home.treasury.gov/news/press-releases/tg65

[9] *Charlie Rose Conversations*, October 27, 2008 Episode

[10] https://www.amazon.com/gp/product/1402078714?ie=UTF8&tag=newgeogrcom-20&linkCode=as2&camp=1789&creative=390957&creativeASIN=1402078714

[11] https://www.amazon.com/gp/product/0195149238?ie=UTF8&tag=newgeogrcom-20&linkCode=as2&camp=1789&creative=390957&creativeASIN=0195149238

[12] For detailed examples of similar events that happened when California sold insurance assets to ex-Drexel managers, see "These Are the Plunderers" by Gretchen Morgenson & Joshua Rosner (Simon & Schuster, 2023).

Then, junk bonds paid extraordinary rates of return – 10 percentage points above Treasuries at the peak. At that time, a 30-year US Treasury bond could be paying more than 18% interest.

Now, we are talking about junk bonds that we all know are junk – no matter the fancy labels like "Legacy" that Treasury wants to apply to them. What rate of return could there be on a mortgage bond – no matter how you "slice-and-dice" it – created when mortgage interest rates were 5% to 6%?[13] Add to that our knowledge of the problems underlying these assets and it is increasingly unlikely that there will be any positive payoff for taxpayers in this plan.[14]

On March 25, 2009, Mirek Topolanek, President of the European Union, called the US economic plan "the way to hell." He said, "The path the United States has chosen is historically discredited", advising Americans to "read dusty history books" so as to avoid repeating "the errors of the 1930s" and the Great Depression. His concern is that we'll have to finance these trillion-dollar bailouts with borrowing and that will ultimately further undermine global financial markets. He's right, of course.[15] The public-private partnerships will finance the purchase of the "Legacy Assets" by issuing debt.[16] That debt will be guaranteed by the Federal Deposit Insurance Corporation (FDIC), the same agency that guarantees our savings accounts at the local bank. Our guarantee is backed by the payment of insurance premiums to FDIC. The guarantee on the debt used to purchase Legacy Assets will be secured by the Legacy Assets – which will be rated by the same credit rating agencies that gave us triple-A rated subprime mortgage bonds in the first place. How can this possibly turn out well? I'm sure Treasury, Federal Reserve and FDIC have good intentions, but as EU President Topolanek says, they may all end up as pavement on "the way to hell." As NYTimes columnist Paul Krugman said of the new plan, "What an awful mess."[17]

---

[13] See footnote 8. As of August 2022, Treasury earned about 1.2% on bailout "investments."

[14] http://www.newgeography.com/content/00679-story-financial-crisis-burnin%...

[15] The US debt ceiling (borrowing limit) rose almost 50% from May 2008 to March 2010.

[16] https://home.treasury.gov/system/files/136/archive-documents/legacy_loans_terms.pdf

[17] https://archive.nytimes.com/krugman.blogs.nytimes.com/2009/03/21/despair-over-financial-policy/?scp=1&sq=The%2520Geithner%2520plan%2520has%2520now%2520been%2520leaked%2520in%2520detail.&st=cse

Geithner's reforms: more power to the center may appeal to Europeans, but won't work for U.S.

April 1, 2009

There will be much talk in London about global financial regulation, particularly from the Europeans. But don't count on it ever coming into existence.

At a House Financial Services Committee on March 26 Treasury Secretary Geithner testified[18] that this particular subject "will be at the center of the agenda at the upcoming Leaders' Summit of the G-20 in London on April 2."

Secretary Geithner presented a 61-page proposal dealing with financial companies that pose systemic risk. Let me paraphrase the main points:

1. Create a Uni-regulator – This idea has been around a while; it won't hurt. We tried to do this in the US during the last round of sweeping financial reforms but couldn't make it happen, primarily due to protectionist politics among the existing regulators (SEC, FRB, Treasury, FDIC, etc.). The UK and others have done it. It didn't prevent the financial crisis from reaching them. Still, it wouldn't hurt to have at least one adult in charge of the financial markets when things get messy.

2. Make companies hold more cash to back up their riskier investments – The banks already have strict national and international capital requirements. It didn't prevent them from needing a bailout, but the big banks are still standing while the rest of the financial companies are gone. This is probably a good idea.

3. Set size limits on unregistered fund managers – I don't think there should be any size limits: if you provide financial services you should register. Don't plumbers have to be licensed? Why not bankers?

4. Figure out how to regulate derivatives – We've known for a long time that this was a problem. If they haven't figured it out by now, it's unlikely they'll get it right; the proposal is short on details. Geithner's plan is to bring derivatives into the same centralized system now used for stocks and bonds – consolidating the risk rather than dispersing it is definitely a bad idea. The

---

[18] https://media.npr.org/documents/2009/mar/geithner_032609.pdf

existing US centralized system has, as of December 31, 2007, only $4.9 billion to back up $5.8 billion in off-balance-sheet obligations.[19]

5. <u>Have the SEC set requirements for money market fund risk management</u> – I'm not sure why on earth anyone would want the SEC to assume this responsibility. The SEC has failed miserably at protecting investors[20] from basic short selling schemes and even more blatant schemes like Madoff's Ponzi. Risk management at financial institutions should be the job of the central bank – that means the Federal Reserve, not the SEC.

6. <u>Let the government nationalize "too big to fail" companies</u> – They just did this with AIG. In essence, the proposed legislation would codify and make permanent authority for the government to lather, rinse and repeat. Government ownership of financial institutions inevitably leads to inefficiency and worse.

We've tried creating "revolutionary" financial laws before: the Depository Institutions Deregulation and Monetary Control Act of 1980 set the stage for the Savings and Loan Crisis; the Financial Services Modernization Act of 1999 helped get us where we are now. Better laws come about in "evolutionary" ways. It starts with a generally accepted good business practice, which all market participants follow. Eventually, one or more participants find a way to advance their position by cheating, by not following that good practice. When they get caught, new laws are created to codify the original "good business practice" and some punishment is put in place for those who don't. What was once considered just a good way to conduct business now becomes a legal business requirement.

Geithner's proposed legislation is law by revolution – an attempt to toss aside all previous practices. The legislation was drafted at Davis, Polk & Wardwell, the New York lawyers for the Federal Reserve Bank and advisors to Fed and Treasury on AIG, not the kind of experience I'd want on my resume this year. There is an embedded comment on page four in the pdf-document: "Can Congress write a federal statute trumping a State Constitution?" I'm not sure what frightens me more: that they want to take power away from the states or that they don't know if they can get away with it! Now is the time to give *more*

---

[19] Ten years later, as more bonds and derivatives moved into the centralized system, they had only $4.1 billion to back up $135 billion in off-balance-sheet obligations (31 Dec 2017).

[20] https://www.sec.gov/about/offices/oig/reports/investigations/2009/oig-509.pdf

authority to the states, not less. By their own admission, federal authorities have proven themselves incapable of protecting investors: Treasury Secretary Geithner told the House, "our system failed in basic fundamental ways."

Worse yet is the idea of proposing a global financial regulator, which will be high on the agenda at the G-20 Leaders' Summit. Designing one regulatory framework for financial services to serve the capital markets in every country is akin to looking for people in every country to "cheat" the same way. Capital markets can work anywhere in the world, but the social and cultural foundations of the system that supports these markets may be quite different. The laws and regulations will need to be quite different, too. When it comes to developing the financial institutions that provide the infrastructure for robust capital markets, there is no "one size fits all".

"Stable financial markets through reform" has been the theme of innumerable conferences, conventions and meetings of the leaders and finance ministers of country groups from G8 to the United Nations. Two decades of experience with the "Washington Consensus"[21] tells us that global regulation will not work any better than concentrating all the power in Washington.

Here's the primary problem with trying to design one set of financial reforms that will serve many nations: Financial services are global not multi-national. Most other products and services sold around the world are multinational, but not global. For example, salt is a multinational product. The salt sold in Cairo is basically the same product as salt sold in Paris or London. Perhaps the label contains the word "salt" in a different language; maybe the Danes use more salt than the Swedes and the Japanese combine it with sugar. But a package of salt contains the same product and is used for the same purpose – one product, used the same way in many nations.

Financial services are different.[22] A share of stock in Paris has different rights, a different meaning, than a share of stock issued in Buenos Aries. Bondholders play a prominent role in restructuring companies in bankruptcy in the US; in France, debtors are protected from bondholders completely. Yet anyone anywhere can buy a share of a French company or the bond of a US company – many products, used for different investments in one world. For reasons like this, there is no one solution for regulating the banks, brokers and stock exchanges in every country.

---

[21] https://en.wikipedia.org/wiki/Washington_Consensus
[22] https://papers.ssrn.com/sol3/papers.cfm?abstract_id=289426

Economists have known for a long time that global financial regulation – or even "sweeping" national changes – won't work. Perhaps the lesson from the current financial crisis will be that national regulation must be supplemented with more oversight in the States. Given Geithner's plan and his penchant for ever more consolidation of authority over financial services, it's unlikely we'll get the chance to find out.

Geithner's toxic recycling plan nixed by big fund

April 3, 2009

The success of Treasury Secretary Geithner's Public-Private Investment Partnership Program depends on getting private investors interested in buying junk bonds off the banks' balance sheets. Now it seems that at least one hedge fund is giving the plan "two thumbs-down."[23]

The New York Post is reporting that Bridgewater Associates, one of the few that might qualify for Treasury's program, decided that "the numbers just don't add up." Besides saying it would be a bad investment, the fund's founder raised questions about conflicts of interest – something we find surprising. Hedge fund managers are supposed to be those free-wheeling, unregulated, we'll-buy-anything investors – always willing to take a risk and suffer the consequences of market outcomes.

Bridgewater's concern is that Geithner's junk bond plan includes hiring asset managers – who will also be investors. There are clear conflicts of interest because these managers will "have both the government and the investors to please and because they will get their fees regardless of how these investments turn out," wrote Bridgewater founder Ray Dalio. Imagine, a hedge fund worried about collusion among asset managers? Maybe it takes one to know one?

The real question is why Geithner would set up a program putting US taxpayer money in the hands of unregulated hedge funds and then go to Europe a few days later and blame the global financial crisis (at least in part) on hedge funds and their lack of regulation? Dalio is right: it just doesn't add up.

The rogue treasury

April 8, 2009

The US Treasury took enormous powers for itself last fall by telling Congress they would use these new powers to "ensure the economic well-being of

---

[23] https://nypost.com/2009/04/02/no-private-hedge/

Americans." Six months after passage of the Emergency Economic Stabilization Act of 2008 Americans are worse off. Since it was signed into law on October 3, 2008, here are the changes in a few measures of our economic well-being:

	Before TARP	So far
National Unemployment	7%	8%
Lowest state unemployment	3.3% (WY)	3.9% (WY)
Highest state unemployment	9.3% (MI)	12% (MI)
National Foreclosure rate (per 5,000 homes)	11	11
Lowest state foreclosure rate	< 1 in 7 states	< 1 in 6 states
Highest state foreclosure rate	68 (NV)	71 (NV)
Dow Jones Industrial Average	10,325	7,762

"Before TARP" figures are as close to October 3, 2008 as possible; "So Far" figures are most recent available, which varies by category from February through April. Unemployment and foreclosure rates by state are from Stateline.org

The Troubled Asset Relief Program (TARP) was sold to Congress and the American public as an absolute necessity to save the American Dream of homeownership. Once the legislation was passed and the funds were released, however, Treasury decided to give the money to banks with no restrictions on its use – no monitoring, no reporting requirements, no nothing. We are worse off today than we were when the legislation was signed – and are likely to remain so when TARP has its first birthday later this year.

Yet, the US government has already paid out $2.9 trillion, with further commitments to raise the total to over $7 trillion – a number that Senator Max Baucus (D-MT) said "is mind-boggling, indeed it is surreal. It's like having a second government." The money Treasury is passing out is more than all government spending in 2008. The Senate Finance Committee, of which Baucus is chair, held a hearing on March 31 (TARP Oversight: A Six Month Update).[24] The three parties established as monitors in the 2008 legislation were there to testify. Without exception they "are deeply troubled by the direction in which Treasury has gone."

Senator Chuck Grassley (R-IA) suggested [referring to former-Secretary Paulson] that Congress "was awed by a person who comes off of Wall Street, making tens of millions of dollars. ... You think he knows all the answers and

---

[24] https://www.finance.senate.gov/hearings/tarp-oversight-a-six-month-update

A DECADE OF ARMAGEDDON

when it's all said and done you realize he didn't know anything more about it than you did."

As soon as Treasury got the money they decided to bailout big banks instead of helping homeowners with mortgages bigger than the market value of their homes. Since then, Paulson, Geithner, and Bernanke have refused to comply with demands to produce documents about the TARP recipients' use of funds.

Neil Barofsky, Special Inspector General and the one monitor with authority to pursue criminal investigations, directly solicited information from the recipients of TARP funds – all over Treasury's objections that it couldn't be done. Barofsky received responses from all 532 recipients. He will be summarizing the findings, but so far knows that some banks used TARP funds to pay off their own debt (including at least one bank that used TARP funds to pay off a loan to another bank that also received TARP funds); some banks made loans they couldn't otherwise have done. Some banks monitored the funds separately from their other assets; some co-mingled the money with no effort to separate, monitor or control what they did with the TARP bailout money.

Elizabeth Warren, Chair of the Congressional Oversight Panel, brought up the central issue: once Treasury decided not to bailout homeowners, what was the plan? "What is the strategy that Treasury is pursuing?" she asked. "We have asked this question over and over, with the notion that without a clearly articulated plan and methods to measure progress to goals, we cannot have good oversight." Warren is still waiting for an answer. She also added that there is no bank in this country that would lend with a policy of "take the money and do what you want with it" – which is exactly what Treasury has done.

Senator Debbie Stabenow (D-MI) put it bluntly: auto manufacturers get reorganization (through bankruptcy) while banks get subsidization. One side is being held accountable for their past bad decisions and the other side has a total lack of accountability. Her bottom line: "If we don't *make* things in this country, we won't *have* an economy."

Warren laid some of the blame with Congress, who "gave treasury significant discretion" but is unable to get real-time explanations for what is being done with the bailout money. There is no transparency when it comes to Treasury. "Without it, I'm afraid .... Congress and the American people have been cut out of the conversation", she says. One group in Michigan is being asked to bear enormous pain and another group in New York is not – that's the way Stabenow sees it and Warren agreed. The alternative offered by Warren is that either

Congress manages to "get Treasury to get some religion and put standards in place" or Congress has to step in with new legislation.

Geithner's collusive capitalism

April 29, 2009

Jo Becker and Gretchen Morgenson (she reported on the lack of mortgages behind mortgage-backed securities) did a long piece on Treasury Secretary Timothy F. Geithner[25] in the *New York Times*. They paint a stark picture of Secretary Geithner's brand of "Collusive Capitalism": lunch at the Four Seasons restaurant with execs from Citigroup, Goldman Sachs and Morgan Stanley; private dinners at home with the head of JPMorgan Chase.

Most importantly, Becker and Morgenson raise the question of why – with all that frequent contact – Geithner never sounded the alarm about these banks? Indeed, as I've pointed out before, Geithner took no steps to prevent $2 trillion in US Treasury bond trades go unsettled for seven months – until it was over, when he called a meeting of the same bankers that caused the problem to have them do a study, take a survey, make some suggestions, etc. The one action that needed to be taken – to enforce finality of settlement – was never on the table.

When the banks behaved recklessly in lending, trading, issuing derivatives and generally fueling the Bonfire of their Vanities, according to Becker and Morgenson, Geithner's idea was to have the federal government "guarantee all the debt in the banking system." As author Martin Weiss asks in his ads for *Money and Markets*, "Has US Treasury Chief Geithner LOST HIS MIND?"

Bernanke: For good or for ill

December 23, 2009

This week, *Time* magazine named Federal Reserve Chairman Ben Bernanke "Person of the Year 2009." CNBC's panel of experts gave Bernanke the "Man of the Year"[26] title (no misogynists there!) in 2008. And well they should since their sponsors are among the biggest recipients of the Paulson-Bernanke-Geithner bailout. As I select the link from their website to imbed in this story, an ad from Wells Fargo (NYSE: WFC) is displayed in the right half of the screen. Click on "home" and it's an ad from General Motors (OTC: MTLQQ), another bailout recipient.

---

[25] https://www.nytimes.com/2009/04/27/business/27geithner.html?_r=1&hp
[26] https://www.cnbc.com/id/28277448

I imagine Bernanke is quite embarrassed this holiday season as a result of the many, many less than flattering comparisons he is receiving. CNBC's sister network, MSNBC, took exception to anything flattering in the designation by reminding everyone that being named Person of the Year is not an honor. *Time's* definition, according to MSNBC, is: "The person or persons who most affected the news and our lives, for good or for ill..." They list a few of the previous winners, including Adolf Hitler (1938), Joseph Stalin (1939), and Ayatollah Khomeini (1979). One writer likened Bernanke receiving the award to "celebrating an arsonist for his heroics in putting out a fire that he set."[27]

Regardless of *Time* managing editor Rick Stengel's qualifying statements, the tone of the write-up suggests, to Charles Scaliger at *The New American* at least, that Bernanke has a "cult of personality" within the Washington, D.C. Beltway. If you've never met Bernanke, which I never have, it's hard to imagine he has the kind of personality that one could be cult-ish about. Former Federal Reserve Chairman Alan Greenspan, who I also never met, regardless of his other shortcomings had the ability to say what it took to get the economy to do what he wanted it to do – he didn't always pick the best things to get it to do, but he was able to get a message across. Bernanke, on the other hand, never seems quite comfortable in front of Congress the way Greenspan used to appear. A nervous central banker is very bad for the economy.

The designation – whether or not it is an honor – came the day before the Senate Banking Committee approved President Obama's nomination of Bernanke to four more years[28] as Chairman of the Federal Reserve. That nomination and approval represent further steps in what Rolling Stone writer Matt Taibbi calls "Obama's Big Sellout."[29] The President, and 16 out of 23 Senators on the Banking Committee, seem to hold the mistaken impression that those who got us into this mess are going to be able to get us out. Republican Senator Jim DeMint of South Carolina was among the dissenters: "We can't have a Federal Reserve that the majority of Americans no longer trust, and that's what we have today." Bernanke himself told Congress less than ten months ago that he didn't know what to do about the economy. Maybe the eventual good that will come from Bernanke's 2009 effect on our lives will be the demise of the Federal

---

[27] "Bernanke: Time's Man of the Year" by Robert Borosage, December 16, 2009, OurFuture.org blog

[28] https://www.banking.senate.gov/newsroom/minority/senate-banking-committee-approves-bernanke

[29] *Rolling Stone*, 14 December 2009.

Reserve system in the United States and an end to the mountains of fiat money that it produced in vain efforts to solve the financial crisis that will forever be linked to Ben Bernanke's name: Person of the Year "for good or for ill."

Buffett and Paulson: Part of the problem

February 10, 2010

Warren Buffett, CEO of Berkshire Hathaway, and Henry "Hank" Paulson, former Treasury Secretary, were guests of honor at the annual meeting of the Omaha Chamber of Commerce this week.

That the two of them are together should be no surprise: Paulson orchestrated the largest bailout of financial institutions in the history of the world – and Buffett is an owner of some of the largest financial institutions. To put it bluntly, Paulson helped bail out Buffett's financial institutions and now Buffett is helping Paulson tout his book.[30] It's not a pretty picture.

Yet, the event sold out well in advance. Granted, Buffett's contribution to Omaha's economy cannot be minimized. Warren Buffett keeps Omaha on the global map – travel anywhere in the world, tell them you're from Omaha and see whose name comes up first. He is also a regular contributor to charitable and social causes throughout the region. Berkshire Hathaway's (NYSE: BRK) companies employ about 246,000 people – though only 19 of them are at the Omaha headquarters.[31] None of BRK's companies are among the top 25 employers in greater Omaha. (Nebraska Furniture Mart, with just over 2,700, ranks 32nd and is the only one in the Top 100.)

We all have 20/20 vision in hindsight, including Senator Chuck Grassley (R-IA). In April 2009, seven months after the Bailout passed, Senator Grassley said of Paulson that Congress "was awed by a person who comes off of Wall Street, making tens of millions of dollars. … You think he knows all the answers and when it's all said and done you realize he didn't know anything more about it than you did."

The Troubled Asset Relief Program (TARP) was sold to Congress and the American public as an absolute necessity to save the American Dream of homeownership. It was supposed to be used to help homeowners with mortgages bigger than the market value of their homes. As soon as Paulson's

---

[30] *On the Brink: Inside the Race to Stop the Collapse of the Global Financial System*, Business Plus, February 2010. Business Plus was an imprint of Hachette Book Group. Hachette closed Business Plus in 2014 and the imprint's founder, Rick Wolff, was let go.
[31] https://www.berkshirehathaway.com/2008ar/2008ar.pdf

Treasury got the money they decided to bailout big banks instead. Since then, Paulson, along with current Treasury Secretary Timothy Geithner, and Federal Reserve Chairman Ben Bernanke have refused to comply with demands from Congress to produce documents about the TARP recipients' use of funds. The legislation was passed and the funds were released, and Treasury gave the money to banks with no restrictions on its use – no monitoring, no reporting requirements, no nothing.

So, why would Warren Buffett look so favorably on Paulson? Warren Buffett – our widely revered Oracle of Omaha – is one of those who built the boom in the capital markets and are benefiting from the bust. No surprise then that Buffett, whose primary business vehicle is a financial holding company, supported the bailout of financial institutions. BRK's businesses include, among others, property and casualty insurance and financial holding companies.

Of course Buffett was in favor of the bailout – his companies directly benefited as did the investments made by his companies. He put $5 billion into Goldman Sachs preferred stock with a 10 percent dividend – a substantially better rate of return than the US government got on our $10 billion bailout. Berkshire Hathaway was the largest shareholder in American Express Co. when they received $3.4 billion from Uncle Sam. Paulson is now insisting that US taxpayers will profit from the TARP bailout[32] – if we do, which I doubt,[33] I'm sure we won't profit as much as Buffett did.

Paulson claims, in his book, that he turned to Buffett for advice about saving Lehman Brothers from demise. This strikes me as a very odd story, considering that Buffett told the press in March 2009 that he couldn't understand the financial statements of the banks getting the bailout money. Add to this the fact that Senator Ben Nelson (D-NE) told me that he talked with Warren before voting for the first bailout package. (I button-holed him after lunch with the

---

[32] https://www.newsweek.com/how-government-profiting-tarp-78659 When TARP ended on 3 October 2010, $475 billion had been committed for disbursement.

[33] I was right to be skeptical. According to the US Treasury: "As of October 31, 2016, cumulative collections under TARP, together with Treasury's additional proceeds from the sale of non-TARP shares of AIG, exceed total disbursements by more than $7.9 billion."
https://home.treasury.gov/data/troubled-assets-relief-program. That's an annual return of about 0.3%. During the same period, the Treasury paid an average of 2.6% on interest bearing debt. The Treasury continues winding down TARP investments and disbursements.

Sarpy County Chamber of Commerce[34]) and you begin to get the real picture – the government was taking advice from financial institutions about bailing out financial institutions.

To bring the problem full circle, consider this. In January, a bi-partisan Financial Crisis Inquiry Commission was appointed to find the answers to the causes of the financial crisis.[35] They may not have to look any further than the nearest mirror. USA Today reported earlier this month that the members of the panel "have consulted for legal firms involved in lawsuits over the crisis."[36] A Commission composed of members who earn their livelihood from financial institutions is unlikely to solve the mystery of the causes of the greatest financial collapse in the history of the world.

Like the Commission, Hank Paulson and Warren Buffett are part of the problem – not the solution.

Catching up to the Fed

December 9, 2010

It's hard to believe that it's been nearly two years since we first wrote about the game of "hide the ball" that Junkmeister Ben Bernanke is playing. Finally, Congress is getting some admissions out of the Federal Reserve about the gusher of cash that was opened up when the insides fell out of Wall Street's Ponzi scheme. Remember, you read it here first! Trillions of dollars were funneled to private, non-regulated companies. According to the New York Times article,[37] the release of documents on 21,000 transactions came about as a result of a provision inserted by Senator Bernard Sanders (I-VT) into the Restoring American Financial Stability Act of 2010. I covered the hearing in March 2009 when Bernanke told Senator Sanders he would not reveal who got the money – but I wrote three months earlier about the deal brokered between the Treasury and the Federal Reserve to circumvent a Congressional prohibition on lending to non-regulated companies. Sanders called it a Jaw Dropper[38] by the time he saw the actual documents.

---

[34] https://www.sarpychamber.org/

[35] https://usatoday30.usatoday.com/money/companies/regulation/2010-01-10-commission_N.htm

[36] https://usatoday30.usatoday.com/news/washington/2010-01-31-conflict_N.htm

[37] https://www.nytimes.com/2010/12/02/business/economy/02fed.html?_r=2&ref=federal _reserve_system

[38] https://www.huffpost.com/entry/a-real-jaw-dropper-at-the_b_791091

Lest you think that all is hunky-dory because the money is being paid back, don't forget the old adage: "It takes money to make money." Everyone that borrowed had the opportunity to make money on the money they got at (virtually) no cost. In the interim, small businesses, homeowners, student borrowers, etc. are paying enormously high interest rates for the little credit they can get. The profits go to Brother Banker.

The Federal Reserve released papers on $12 trillion, about half of the $23 trillion distribution estimated by Special Inspector General Neil Barofsky. Despite admitting to pumping an amount equal to about the entire annual national output into the economy in the form of cash – belying the real decline in the output of goods and services – Ben Bernanke told 60 Minutes recently that he was "100% certain" that inflation is not going to be a problem. [39] Makes you wonder what else they're hiding.

---

[39] Bernanke was right on this point. Inflation remained relatively close to 2%. The reason? In 2008, the bailout money went to banks who held it as excess reserves. Instead of taking on the risk of lending it to businesses and households, banks earned interest from the Federal Reserve – a risk-free return for doing nothing. In contrast, the Economic Impact Payments during COVID-19 emergency went to households who spent more of it than they saved; inflation jumped to nearly 5% in 2021 and 8% in 2022.

5. Bank/Broker Behavior

There is no question that the actions of financial industry professionals led to the financial crisis that developed into the Great Recession. Criminal charges were brought against those who cheated their way into getting a share of the bailout money, but those responsible for creating the situation that required the extraordinary bailout measures were not called to discipline. Quite the contrary, many were paid elaborate bonuses at the same time their financial institutions were receiving bailout funds.[1]

Blame Wall Street's phantom bonds for the credit crisis
November 26, 2008

The "credit crisis" is largely a Wall Street disaster of its own making. From the sale of stocks and bonds that are never delivered, to the purchase of default insurance worth more than the buyer's assets, we no longer have investment strategies, but rather investment schemes. As long as everyone was making money, no one complained. But like any Ponzi Scheme, eventually the pyramid begins to collapse.

For the last couple of months trillions of dollars' worth of US Treasury bonds have been sold but not delivered to the buyers. Trades that go unsettled have become an event so common that the industry has an acronym for it: FTD, or fail to deliver.

What's the result? For the federal government, it's an unnecessarily high rate of interest to finance the national debt. For states, it's a massive loss of potential tax revenue. And for the bond buyers, brokerage houses, and banks, it's yet another crash-and-burn to come.

First, a primer: The Federal Government issues as many bonds as Congress authorizes (the total value is an amount that basically covers the national debt). Many are purchased by brokers and investors, who then re-sell them in "secondary" trades. The way the system is supposed to work is that the broker takes your bond order today and tomorrow takes the cash from your account and 'delivers' the bonds to you. The bonds remain in your broker's name (or the name of a central depository, if he uses one). If there is interest, the Treasury pays the interest to your broker and he credits your account for the amount.

What is happening today that strays from this model? Because the financial regulators do not require that the actual bonds be delivered to the buyer, your

---

[1] For more on this, see *LNL*, especially page 145.

broker credits you with an electronic IOU for them, and, eventually, with the interest payments as well. But the so-called "bonds" that you receive as an electronic IOU, called an "entitlement", are phantoms: there aren't any bonds delivered by your broker to you, or by the government to your broker, or by anyone.

The significant result of the IOU system is that brokers are able to sell many more bonds than the Congress has authorized. The transactions are called 'settlement failures' or 'failed to deliver' events, since the broker reported bond purchases beyond what the sellers delivered. Since all of this happens after the US Treasury originally issues the bonds, the broker's bookkeeping is separate from US Treasury records. That means there is no limit on the number of IOUs the broker can hand out...and there are usually more IOUs in circulation than there are bonds.

The ramifications are far reaching for the national budget. Wall Street, by selling bonds that it cannot deliver to the buyer — in selling more bonds than the government has issued — has been allowed to artificially inflate supply, thereby forcing bond prices down. As the price of bonds falls, the return on those existing bonds rises; and that means the US Treasury has to pay higher interest rates the next time it goes to issue bonds to cover deficit spending. Those undelivered Treasuries represent unfulfilled demand by investors willing to lend money to the US government. That money — the payment for the bonds — has been intercepted by the selling broker-dealers. The subsequently artificially low bond prices are forcing the US government to pay a higher rate of interest than it should in order to finance the national debt.

The market for US Treasury bonds has been in serious disarray since the days immediately following September 11, 2001. Despite reports, reviews, examinations, committee meetings, speeches, and advisory groups formed by the US Treasury, the Federal Reserve, and broker-dealer associations, massive failures to deliver recur and persist. Somehow, government, regulators and industry specialists alike believe that it's OK to sell more bonds than the government has issued. It shouldn't take a PhD-trained economist to tell you that prices are set where supply equals demand. If a dealer can sell an infinite supply of bonds (or stocks or anything else for that matter), then the price is, technically-speaking, baloney. And the resulting field of play cannot be called a "market".

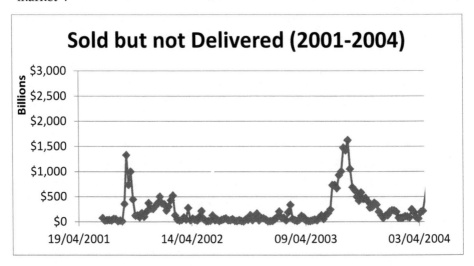

Figure 17
Source: Federal Reserve Bank of New York Primary Dealers only (all US Treasury Securities), author's calculations.

If regulators and the central clearing corporation would only enforce delivery of Treasury bonds for trade settlement — payment — at something approaching the promised, stated, contracted and agreed upon T+1 (one day after the trade), there would be an immediate surge in the price of US Treasury securities. As the prices of bonds rise, the yield falls. This falling yield then translates into a lower interest rate that the US government has to pay the next time it needs to borrow the money to fund the budget deficit and to refinance the existing national debt.

This week's drop in the yield on US Treasuries was accompanied by a spike in bond prices. The data won't be released until next week, but you can expect to see that a precipitous drop in fails-to-deliver occurred at the same time. Don't get your hopes up, though. One look at the chart above will tell you that the good news won't last until real changes are made to the system.

As a bonus insult to government, consider the $270 million in lost tax revenues to the states. This is because investors (unknowingly) report the phony interest

A DECADE OF ARMAGEDDON

payments made to them by their brokers as tax exempt; interest earned on US Treasury bonds is not taxed by the states.[2]

For the bond buyer, the situation poses other problems and risks. As an ordinary investor, you're not notified that the bonds were not delivered to you or to your broker. Of course, your broker knows, but doesn't share the information with you because he or she plans to make good on the trade only at some point in the future when you order the bond to be sold.

The electronic IOU you received can only be redeemed at your brokerage house, and no one knows what will happen if it goes under, although I suspect we'll find out in the coming quarters as more financial institutions get into deeper trouble. You're probably not aware that, in order to cash in that IOU when you're ready to sell, you depend not on the full faith and credit of the US government, but on your broker being in business next month (or next year) to make good on the trade. In other words, you're taking Lehman Brothers risk, and receiving only US Government risk-free rates of return on your investment.[3]

Your broker, meanwhile, enjoys the advantages of commission charges for the trade, maybe an account maintenance fee and – more importantly – the use of your money. Wall Street is not sharing any of this extra investment income with you. In my analysis of Trade Settlement Failures in US Bond Markets,[4] I calculated this "loss of use of funds" to investors at $7 billion per year, conservatively.

---

[2] The calculation for this lost tax revenue is explained in my working paper, "Trade Settlement Failures in U.S. Bond Markets" (September 23, 2008). STP Working Paper No. STP2007_1, Available for free download at SSRN:
https://ssrn.com/abstract=1016873 or http://dx.doi.org/10.2139/ssrn.1016873

[3] It took more than fourteen years to wind down the Lehman Brothers bankruptcy. According to an article by FRB-NY (2019), Lehman's customers recovered 100% of their claims, although about half of those were resolved by transferring them to Barclays and others. It is unknown if Barclays and other brokers took on the IOUs. https://libertystreeteconomics.newyorkfed.org/2019/01/creditor-recovery-in-lehmans-bankruptcy/ . In contrast, the 2011 MF Global bankruptcy revealed a shortfall of $1.6 billion in funds available versus customer funds owed; that case involved illegal use of customer funds.

[4] Supra note 2. An updated paper was published by IUP *Journal of Financial Risk Management* (Hyderabad), Vol. 18, Iss. 4, pp: 7-22.

Despite this, rather than require that sold bonds be delivered to the buyer, the Treasury Market Practices Group at the Federal Reserve Bank of New York merely points out FTDs as "examples of strategies to avoid."

Now for the really bad news. The tolerance for unsettled trades and complete disregard for the effect of supply on setting true-market prices is also responsible for the "sub-prime crisis," which everyone seems to agree on as the root of the current global financial turmoil. You see, there are more credit default swaps — CDS — traded on mortgage bonds than there are mortgage bonds outstanding. A CDS is like insurance. The buyer of a mortgage bond pays a premium, and if the mortgage defaults then the CDS seller makes them whole. CDS are sold in multiples of the underlying assets.

A conservative estimate is that $9 worth of CDS "insurance" has been sold for every $1 in mortgage bond. Therefore, someone stands to gain $9 if the homeowner defaults, but only $1 if they pay. The economic incentives favor foreclosure, not mortgage work-outs or Main Street bailouts.

In the same process that is multiplying Treasury bonds, sellers are permitted to "deliver" CDS that were not created to correspond with actual mortgages; call them "phantom CDS". According to October 31, 2008 data on CDS registered in the Depository Trust & Clearing Corporation's (DTCC) Trade Information Warehouse, about $7 billion more CDS insurance was bought on Countrywide Home Loans than Countrywide sold in mortgage bonds.[5] That provides a terrific incentive to foreclose on mortgages.

Countrywide is the game's major player: The gross CDS contracts on Countrywide of $84.6 billion are equivalent to 82% of the $103.3 billion CDS sold on all mortgage-backed securities (including commercial mortgages) and 90% of the total $94.4 billion CDS registered at DTCC that were sold on residential mortgage-backed securities.

General Electric Capital Corporation is the fifth largest single name entity with more CDS bought on it than what it has sold; someone is in a position to benefit by $12 billion more from consumer default than from helping consumers to pay off their debt. Only Italy, Spain, Brazil and Deutsche Bank have more phantom CDS than GECC, according to the DTCC's data.

---

[5] When I wrote this article, I was able to access the DTCC's database of "Aggregated Transaction Data by Reference Entity of Single-Name CDS." Some data is still publicly available if you know where to look for it: https://www.dtcc.com/repository-otc-data

The US auto manufacturers also have net phantom CDS in circulation: $11 billion for Ford, $4 billion for General Motors, and $3.3 billion for DaimlerChrysler (plus an additional $3.5 billion at the parent Daimler). Of course, these numbers change from week to week and only represent CDS voluntarily registered with the DTCC, so the real numbers could be much greater.

Who stands to gain? There is no transparency for CDS trades, which means that we don't know who these buyers are. But in order to get paid on these CDS, the buyer must be a DTCC Participant… and that brings us to Citigroup, Goldman Sachs, JP Morgan and Morgan Stanley – all Participants at DTCC and instrumental in designing and developing CDS trading around the world. By the way, these firms are also in the group that reports FTDs in US Treasuries; the top four firms represent more than 50% of all trades. You can do the math from there.

The US government and regulators are in the best position to end these fiascos, turn us away from casino capitalism, and return our financial industry back into a market. It won't require any new rules, laws or regulations to fix the situation. If someone takes your money and doesn't give you what you bought, that's just plain stealin', and we already have laws against that.

The pleasure of their company

February 11, 2009

Executives from banks including Goldman Sachs, JP Morgan Chase, and Bank of America (who bought Merrill Lynch) have been called to Capitol Hill to explain what they did with their shares of the $750 billion bailout.

Here's a good question to put to those executives: how much did you spend on whores?

According to a story by *20/20*[6] aired on ABC on February 6, 2009, Wall Street executives and bankers used company credit cards to pay for prostitutes. When the head of the prostitution ring was arrested, her list of clients included bank executives who used company credit cards and disguised the charges as

---

[6] https://abcnews.go.com/Blotter/story?id=6813806&page=1

"computer consulting, construction expenses" and "roof repair on a warehouse".[7]

This raises their behavior to the level of a felony: committing fraud to hide a crime. Soliciting prostitutes is still a crime – even if it is rarely enforced. Disguising whoring as a tax-deductible business expense certainly qualifies as fraud. Making it even worse, if the ABC story is true, several of the bankers paid for their pleasure with our money. Included in the roster are:

- an investment banker at Goldman Sachs who spent $27,000
- an investment banker at JP Morgan Securities who spent $41,600
- a managing director from Merrill Lynch

Anyone who has spent time on Wall Street, as I did during the 1980s and 1990s, knows that paying prostitutes as entertainment goes on all the time. They fool themselves into thinking that they deserve it, or that everyone does it so it must be ok, or that no one is getting hurt.

Yet this is a pattern that goes well beyond buying women. I taught business ethics at New York University and the Stern School of Business for many years; ethics and economics is one of the field specializations in my PhD. Many people who paid for prostitutes with what amounts to the public's money already rationalized other unethical decisions, like, for example, misleading a client on a stock because it will inflate their bonus. Or giving a AAA-rating to a mortgage-backed security that looks dodgy but will earn a big fee.

So, if you have already taken the plunge in other areas, when you have a choice to spend $41,000 of the company's money on a prostitute, you don't consider the ethics. You have already made that decision before; you may have done it a thousand times before.

This is the kind of lapse that allows someone like John Thain to spend $1 million to redecorate his office while taking public funds. Or for a supposed public icon

---

[7] In 2023, former President Trump was indicted for fraudulently recording $130,000 paid as alleged hush money to Stormy Daniels (in exchange for not talking about an alleged sexual encounter). The money was entered in records kept by the Trump Organization as the cost of legal services from his former attorney, Michael Cohen. Falsifying business records is a violation of New York state law. The act rises to a felony when the falsified record is part of an effort to hide a different crime; for the Bailout Babies, the underlying crime is solicitation (or pandering). Most states charge solicitation as a misdemeanor, including Nevada where it is only legal in licensed brothels, which are only legal in ten of the 16 counties. You can read the indictment here:
https://www.scribd.com/document/636099588/Donald-J-Trump-Indictment#

like Robert Rubin to defend his role in the Citicorp destruction by saying he could have made even more money working somewhere else.

And believe it or not, it's still going on. Another bailout baby, JP Morgan Chase is still completing a renovation of its New York headquarters at a reported cost of $250 million.[8] They started their project in June 2007. Citigroup started their renovation of the executive offices in New York in September 2008, just as Congress was approving the first bailout package.

The good news is not everyone gives into the temptation. I know guys who walked away; guys who refused to take part in it even when their Wall Street boss offered to pass along the prostitute who was giving everyone in the office oral sex that afternoon. These guys wanted to wake up the next morning and look into their daughter's eyes without remorse. Guys who decided to create a business environment in which they would want those daughters to live and work.

These are the guys who would take responsibility for their misjudgments in business and say no to a bonus in a year when their clients have been devastated. Sadly, many of those guys left Wall Street a long time ago. They probably are not the guys who are lined up for bailout money. This is not the kind of problem where you stick around to fight for change. The problem with winning a gutter fight is that you are still in the gutter. Sometimes it's better to just walk away.

According to the Associated Press,[9] nine out of ten senior executives still at the banks that took federal bailout money were there to play a role in creating the crisis. Far too few have been thrown out for incompetence. So far none has been thrown in prison for fraud or theft. Most probably will take their nice vacations, count their sick days accumulated, and keep that vital company credit card for entertaining. This is not the case, of course, for the 100,000 bank employees who lost their jobs between 2006 and 2008.

As the newest shareholders in these banks, the US taxpayers should have some say in all this. Shareholders should be able to oust the Board and the executives who led their firms, and the country, into this morass. We have bailed these miscreants out but without exercising any control. So, we end up paying for the

---

[8] https://www.cnbc.com/id/28898461

[9] https://www.nbcnews.com/id/wbna28869701

pleasure of their company while they go out and use our money to pay for someone else's. On Wall Street, or here in Omaha, that's called getting screwed.

Story of the financial crisis: Burnin' down the house with good intentions and lots of greed

March 19, 2009

Last week, the Chairman of the Federal Reserve, Ben Bernanke, told Congress that he didn't know what to do about the economy and the repeated need for bailouts. This week, the Oracle of Omaha Warren Buffett, Chairman of Berkshire-Hathaway told the press that he couldn't understand the financial statements of the banks getting the bailout money.

This made it a daunting challenge the other day, when the Program Director for the Bellevue (Nebraska) Kiwanis Club asked me to talk to his group about the current state of the economy. Despite the many often outrageous examples of excessive greed and even criminality, the current debacle began with good intentions: provide opportunities for homeownership to a segment of the population that was historically left out.

New credit rating systems had to be developed to take into consideration the fact that some immigrant groups prefer to live in extended families (multiple generations in one household). The individual income of just one member of the household may not qualify for a loan. However, since they would all be paying the mortgage, the total household income could be considered when calculating mortgage qualification. Yet, their family patterns meant assets are only held by the male head of household. That's just one example, and there are many more. It's just that banks and others came to realize that the existing systems were excluding people who would actually be very good borrowers. The original "subprime" borrowers were like the original "junk bond" companies – they didn't fit the mold of a model credit customer. But among them were MCI and Turner Broadcasting – plus Enron and Worldcom, of course.

Like junk bonds,[10] the new mortgage product came to be abused by borrowers and lenders alike. This was made worse by developments that blurred the line between banks and brokers. Both parties participated in actions that allowed banks to have their in-house brokers sell off their mortgage loans to Wall Street in the form of bonds. This is called "originate and distribute". The same bank

---

[10] https://www.amazon.com/gp/product/0195149238?ie=UTF8&tag=newgeogrcom-20&linkCode=as2&camp=1789&creative=390957&creativeASIN=0195149238

wrote the mortgages, packaged the loans for sale and distributed the bonds to their clients – collecting fees at every stage.

And here's where greed entered the picture. The demand for these bonds completely outstripped the supply: senior management put pressure on the troops to write more mortgages and sell more bonds. The fees were pouring in from everywhere. The demand was so great that an average of 40% of the trades failed for lack of delivery – broker-dealers were selling more bonds than were issued.[11] Each bond trade, whether or not there was a failure to deliver, resulted in a commission for the buying and selling broker-dealers. They didn't have to tell the buyers that there was no delivery – the broker-dealers figured they could fix it later. This was the initial breakdown in regulatory oversight.

The next one came when no one was watching over the credit rating agencies. According to a story on PBS, managers at Standard & Poor's credit rating agency were pressured to give the bonds triple-A ratings in the pursuit of ever higher fees.[12] (We've yet to learn all the details of the potential collusion between banks, brokers, rating agencies, etc., but more news is coming out all the time – stay tuned!)

Along the way, it became clear that these investments in mortgage bonds were, in fact, risky – despite their triple-A credit ratings. That's where the credit default swaps came in – credit default swaps (or CDS) are simply contracts akin to insurance policies. The bond holder pays a small premium up-front and they get all their money back if the bond goes into default which could happen, for example, if the homeowner owing the mortgage in the mortgage bond ends up in foreclosure. This was another idea with good intentions – it made the bonds more popular and sent more money back to the bank for more mortgages.

The way the theory on structured securities was developed, if a bank can sell the mortgages they can use that cash to write more mortgages and so support local communities that need to expand housing opportunities. It should also disperse the risk, spread it around, so that some economic problem in one town, like a factory closing, won't cause the local bank to go out of business. Losses on local mortgages would be spread out geographically, spread out over a large number of investors and over different types of investors (individuals,

---

[11] https://papers.ssrn.com/sol3/papers.cfm?abstract_id=1016873
[12] Originally aired on 21 November 2008. NOW on PBS, Season 4, Episode 4, "Credit and Credibility." NOW last aired in April 2010.

companies, pension plans, etc.) so that no one of them should suffer all the damage.

Greed enters the picture again: instead of the CDS derivatives being sold only to the people who owned the bonds and only in a quantity equal to the value of the bonds that were issued, an unlimited number of swaps were sold.[13] This is as if you have a $1 million home and someone sold you $20 million worth of insurance. The temptation to burn down the house was just too much. What you see now is arson. They are burning down "the house" to collect on the insurance. Except if it were your typical insurance, it would be regulated, and you would have to have "an insurable interest" in hand to buy the policy at all. This ensures that there would be no more derivatives issued than there are assets to back them up. No, these CDS derivative contracts are completely unregulated and unmonitored.

Sadly, there were no video surveillance cameras in place when Wall Street was spreading around the gasoline and striking the match. Yet now we are stuck watching the house – and the economy – burn down.

Burnin' down the house! Part two: Wall Street has a weenie roast with your 401k

March 30, 2009

Last week I wrote about the first part of my talk to the Bellevue Kiwanis Club on why our economy is in the position it is today. It is a story about good intentioned policies – like modifying credit scoring for Americans working in a cash-economy – that were bastardized in the execution – like some Americans using modified credit scoring to lie about their income. Just like there were superstar firms among the original "junk bond"[14] companies, there were also firms like Enron and WorldCom.

In the first part of my story: banks wrote mortgages, their broker-arms sold them to the public in the form of bonds, they paid fees to Standard & Poor's and Moody's to get triple-A credit ratings, and they devised crazy default protection schemes which they also sold in the public capital markets. On top of all that,

---

[13] https://creditfixings.com/CreditEventAuctions/static/credit_event_auction/docs/credit_event_auction_primer.pdf

[14] https://www.amazon.com/gp/product/0195149238?ie=UTF8&tag=newgeogrcom-20&linkCode=as2&camp=1789&creative=390957&creativeASIN=0195149238

they screwed up the paper work so there was no relationship between houses and the ultimate financial paper[15] that could be used to cover potential losses.

That's when Wall Street staged a weenie-roast over the blazing fire of your 401k plan. They were making so much money in fees and trading profits that they decided to extend the scheme to car loans, credit card debt, and anything else they could package and sell off in capital markets around the world. When new money stopped flowing in and when the value of the underlying assets began to decline, the whole mess came falling down over their – and our – heads.

In case after case, there are more derivatives than there are underlying assets. Here's an example of just how absurd this is: The market value of Bank of America (BofA) is $32 billion; the derivatives that payoff if BofA fails are worth $119 billion. This isn't rocket science math. It's worth a lot more to someone to see BofA fail than it is to see them succeed. Here's a table (see Appendix 2) of some financial companies and home builders, alongside some countries, to give you an idea of what the potential cost would be of letting them collapse – because the derivatives would have to be paid off if they collapsed. Where the market value of a company's publicly traded shares (or the outstanding public debt of a nation) is less than the derivatives outstanding (a positive number in the difference column), the "market" is probably betting in favor of the company/country going bankrupt.

In other words, you could buy all the shares of Lennar for $1.2 billion. However, if they go bankrupt, the payoff will be $40 billion for the holders of the derivative contracts. And at this point, we – the US taxpayers – are in the position of paying off on these derivative contracts sold by banks and other "too big to fail" companies. The table also tells you that the "markets" think that Bank of America is significantly more likely to fail than, say, Brazil – which is probably true, if for no other reason than the fact that Brazil has an army and Bank of America doesn't!

The bottom line is that the government must continue to bailout these banks and large companies because many of them, including AIG which is now owned about 80% by us, are the same entities that will have to pay off the bets if the other companies fail. There's really no way out of it now. I remain opposed to the bailouts – they create "moral hazard," the scenario whereby there are no

---

[15] https://www.youtube.com/watch?v=8D8punVHdDk&ab_channel=EconLaw2009

consequences for failing and it can be more profitable to fail than to succeed. But: I understand why they are being done and why we must keep doing it.

The reason is: it matters to our 401k plans, the pension plans of teachers and firefighters, the retirement benefits of loyal, hard-working Americans. You see, the debt of insurance companies and other triple-A rated credits (AIG had a good credit rating less than 12 months ago) are required investments for money market funds, pension plans, etc. Take a look at the prospectus for any of these investments if you have them and you'll see what I mean. It is necessary for such funds to make triple-A investments because the funds need to be able to make payments and honor withdrawals, sometimes on short notice. That means they have to hold some very safe, very easily sold investments. Investments like those issued by AIG.

If the mutual funds holding your 401k and the pension fund supporting the schoolteachers and all that go broke – well, no one wants to imagine what that America would look like. Despite all the bad economic news, few Americans have run out in the streets in protest and even those who did didn't vandalize any property, public or private. Nor did we take our CEOs hostage. In fact, I think a little civil unrest may be called for: print this story, wrap it around a hotdog, mail it to the New York Stock Exchange and tell them to enjoy their weenie-roast!

Here's why: the time is coming very soon when Wall Street will need us again. Uncle Sam is doling out the bailout money to the financial institutions, but even now they are devising ways to get ordinary investors to come back to the markets – and to use our own money to do it.

TARP criminal charges possible

April 24, 2009

Of the three monitors established by the legislation that created the Troubled Asset Relief Program (TARP), only one has the authority to prosecute criminals. That is the Office of the Special Inspector General (SIGTARP[16]) whose motto is "Advancing Economic Stability through Transparency, Coordinated Oversight and Robust Enforcement." The Special Inspector General in charge, Neil Barofsky, told Congress before the recess that he was by-passing the Rogue Treasury to get answers directly from TARP recipients about what they are doing with the bailout money (see p75). Now, SIGTARP has set up a hotline

---

[16] https://www.sigtarp.gov/

(877-SIG-2009) for citizens to report fraud or "evidence of violations of criminal and civil laws in connection with TARP." To date, they have received 200 tips and launched 20 criminal investigations.[17]

What started out as a bailout costing $750 billion quickly turned into $3 trillion – an amount about equal to the US government's 2008 budget. This week, SIGTARP released a 250-page report in an attempt to place "the scope and scale [of TARP] into proper context" and to make the program understandable to "the American people." I can't recommend that you read a report of that length, or even that you download it[18] (more than 10 megabytes) unless you have broadband internet access. (In fact, I don't understand what makes them think that the American people are going to understand anything that takes 250 pages to explain… Isn't over-complicating one of the problems they want to solve?) You can get all the high points in Barofsky's statement to the Joint Economic Committee[19], which is only seven pages and a few hundred kilobytes. If you have more time than patience, you can watch the testimony on C-SPAN[20].

I applaud the hard work of the SIGTARP to provide oversight to Treasury even though they are "currently working out of the main Treasury compound." Let's hope they can break free of the hazards associated with the self-regulation that got us into this financial mess in the first place.

How soon we forget: Wall Street wages

April 26, 2009

It also wasn't that long ago that Congress held hearings on the bonuses paid to AIG employees after the bailout. Now, according to *New York Times* reporter Louise Story, Wall Street compensation is rising back to where it was in 2007[21] – the last year that these firms made oodles of money with investment strategies that turned toxic the next year.

---

[17] https://money.cnn.com/2009/04/21/news/economy/tarp_cop_barofsky/?postversion=2009042103

[18] https://www.sigtarp.gov/sites/sigtarp/files/Quarterly_Reports/April2009_Quarterly_Report_to_Congress.pdf

[19] https://www.govinfo.gov/content/pkg/CHRG-111shrg52273/pdf/CHRG-111shrg52273.pdf

[20] https://www.c-span.org/video/?285452-1/troubled-assets-relief-program-quarterly-report

[21] https://www.nytimes.com/2009/04/26/business/26pay.html?_r=1&th&emc=th [paywalled]

And, yeah, we get it – there is a theoretical connection between compensation and performance. But we also know that there's a difference between theory and practice. Too many of the same employees who either perpetrated the events leading to the meltdown or stood idly by while it happened are still in place.

When AIG finally revealed what they did with the bailout money, we found out that a big chunk of it went overseas. Now, *New York Post* reporter John Aidan Byrne tells us that the bailout recipients are bailing out[22] – on US workers! Ms. Story found that Bank of New York Mellon, Bank of America and Citigroup, all recipients of billions of bailout dollars, are shifting more jobs overseas. The explanation, that nothing in TARP prohibits them from moving jobs out of the US, is so lame I'm surprised Story even bothered to mention it.

The initial indicators of the current financial meltdown were visible in mid-2007. The deeper, underlying causes were recognized, talked about in Washington and then ignored as far back as 2004. The collective memory is short. Nobody wants to hear the bad news, especially when it's this bad and it goes on for this long. The morning you wake up and wish the financial meltdown would just go away is your most dangerous moment – wishing won't make it so.

Betting against the USA – told ya' so!

May 24, 2009

More than once in this space, I've said that derivative financial products set up a perverse incentive where investors have more to gain from the failure of companies and homeowners than their success. If you haven't seen it yet, take a look at the longer version of my description of the causes and consequences of the current crisis to understand how failed financial innovations, like credit default swaps, contributed to the meltdown of 2008. I wrote that article back in November (see p84).

Once again, only Bloomberg.com is out front on this story. More hedge funds are catching onto the casino-like qualities of betting against America's economic success. Reporters Salas, Harrington and Paulden could have quoted my *NewGeography* writings directly: "companies [have] more credit-default swaps outstanding than the bonds the contracts protected..." and, referring to Clear

---

[22] https://nypost.com/2009/04/26/bailing-on-us-workers/

Channel Communications, "some of its creditors stand to profit from its failure."

Told ya' so!

Brother rabbit's bonuses

August 3, 2009

On July 30, 2009, New York State Attorney General (AG) Andrew Cuomo delivered a report to Congress on the bonuses paid to the employees of nine recipients of the TARP bailout money. He called it "The 'Heads I Win, Tails You Lose' Bank Bonus Culture."[23] AG Cuomo concluded that even "in these challenging economic times, compensation for bank employees has become unmoored from the banks' financial performance." The report is only about banks, of course, since all the investment banks and brokerage firms changed their status to "bank" to become eligible for TARP bailout money last fall.

Some of the banks that took the TARP money, like JP Morgan (NYSE: JM), Morgan Stanley (NYSE: MS) and American Express (NYSE: AXP), did what they could to return it as quickly as possible,[24] including buying back the warrants.[25] It will be very hard, indeed, for the financial institutions to change the public perception now that we have seen their willingness to take any risk, to make money at any cost – only to take a handout from the public coffers when things go badly so they can continue to "make money" for themselves. The banks are entities, but they are run by people who have jobs and get bonuses and perks. Former-Treasury Secretary Hank Paulson's plan to plunder the US Treasury on behalf of his former Goldman Sachs (NYSE: GS) mates on Wall Street set these banks up as the target of public scorn.

Late Friday, July 31, the House of Representatives approved a bill that would allow regulators to limit executive compensation[26] at financial institutions with assets greater than $1 billion if they find that the programs would "induce excessive risk-taking" behavior among bank executives. This comes a full eight months after Bank of America (NYSE: BAC) was first subpoenaed by AG

---

[23] https://ag.ny.gov/sites/default/files/press-releases/archived/Bonus%20Report%20Final%207.30.09.pdf

[24] https://money.cnn.com/2009/04/22/news/tarp.babies.fortune/index.htm

[25] https://www.reuters.com/article/GCA-CreditCrisis/idUSTRE56L5UX20090722

[26] https://www.reuters.com/article/ousivMolt/idUSTRE56U5AL20090731 Section 956 of the Dodd-Frank Wall Street Reform and Consumer Protection Act of 2010 required banks and regulators to jointly issue guidelines that prohibit incentive-based pay arrangements that encourage inappropriate risk-taking by financial executives.

Cuomo about executive bonuses.[27] It is a far cry from anything that would create a sense of justice out of a system where two TARP recipients, Citigroup (NYSE: C) and Merrill Lynch, operated in a way that lost $54 billion in 2008, took $55 billion in TARP bailout money, and then paid $9 billion in employee bonuses.

Despite the hue and cry of the public, these bonuses have continued.[28] In my view they will continue into the future.[29] Although we may think that sticking labels on the banks' behavior, or asking Congress to legislate some discipline, will make a difference, it is unlikely to change anything. After the early 2009 bonuses were revealed, the banks claimed that the bonuses were required by contracts and could not be broken without violating the rule of law. They got away with this claim even as contracts with the United Auto Workers were being revised. It's like a modern version of "The Wonderful Tar-Baby Story," a folk story by Joel Chandler Harris. "Bred and born in a briar patch, Brother Fox, bred and born in a briar patch!" And with that Brother Banker skipped out just as lively as a cricket in the embers.

Thanks to David Friedman for bringing the FT article on the report[30] to our attention.

Honest services from bankers? Increasingly not likely
November 13, 2009

Once you understand what financial services are, you'll quickly come to realize that American consumers are not getting the honest services that they have come to expect from banks. A bank is a business. They offer financial services for profit. Their primary function is to keep money for individual people or companies and to make loans. Banks – and all the Wall Street firms are banks now – play an important role in the virtuous circle of savings and investment. When households have excess earnings – more money than they need for their expenses – they can make savings deposits at banks. Banks channel savings from households to entrepreneurs and businesses in the form of loans. Entrepreneurs can use the loans to create new businesses which will employee more labor, thus increasing the earnings that households have available to make more savings deposits – which brings the process fully circle.

---

[27] https://www.law.com/dailyreportonline/almID/1202551713336/

[28] https://www.reuters.com/article/reutersComService4/idUSTRE55N54D20090624

[29] According to a Reuters Senior Editor, as of July 21, 2022, rules for banker incentive compensation had not been finalized. https://tax.thomsonreuters.com/news/12-years-and-waiting-dodd-frank-banker-incentive-compensation-rules-remain-on-hold/

[30] https://www.ft.com/content/ff921710-7d2a-11de-b8ee-00144feabdc0 [paywalled]

As US households deal with unemployment above 10% as a direct result of the financial crises caused by excessive risk-taking at banks, one bank, Goldman Sachs, posted the biggest profit in its 140-year history. According to Nobel laureate economist Joseph Stiglitz at Columbia University, Goldman's 65% increase in profits is like gambling where they are the "house" whose favor the odds are always in[31] – the largest growth came from its own investments and not from providing financial services to households and businesses.

Under fraud statutes created in 1988, Congress criminalized actions that deprive us of the right to "honest services."[32] The law has been used generally to prosecute fraudsters and potential fraudsters – from Jack Abramoff to Rod Blagojevich[33] – whenever the public does not get the honest, faithful service we have a right to expect.

The theory of "honest services" was used in one of the best-known US cases of financial misbehavior – Jeff Skilling of Enron – who has been granted a hearing[34] early next year with the US Supreme Court on the subject. Prosecutors won the original 2006 conviction on the strategy "that Skilling robbed Enron of his 'honest services' by setting corporate goals that were met by fraudulent means amid a widespread conspiracy to lie to investors about the company's financial health." The US Attorney argued that CEO Skilling set the agenda[35] at Enron. In this case, the fraud and conspiracy were means by which corporate ends were met.[36]

---

[31] https://usatoday30.usatoday.com/money/industries/banking/2009-09-15-blankfein-goldman-sachs_N.htm

[32] 18 U.S. Code § 1345 - Injunctions against fraud. Available at
https://www.law.cornell.edu/uscode/text/18/1345

[33] https://www.wsj.com/public/resources/documents/WSJ-20081209-blagojevichcomplaint.pdf

[34] https://usatoday30.usatoday.com/money/companies/management/2009-10-13-skilling_N.htm

[35] https://www.chron.com/business/enron/article/Skilling-appeal-hinges-on-meaning-of-honest-1598669.php

[36] The US Supreme Court decided the case on 24 June 2010. In the opinion on this point, Supreme Court Justice Ruth Bader Ginsburg wrote: "…we disagree with the Fifth Circuit's honest-services ruling. In proscribing fraudulent deprivations of 'the intangible right of honest services,' §1346, Congress intended at least to reach schemes to defraud involving bribes and kickbacks." The law is too vague to be applied when a private employee engages in undisclosed self-dealing. *Jeffrey K. Skilling v. United States*, 561 U.S. 358 (2010). https://supreme.justia.com/cases/federal/us/561/358/

Skilling's defense attorney admitted in his appeal before the 5th Circuit in April that his client "might have only bent the rules for the company's benefit." The appeal was not granted – a move by the court that is viewed as an overwhelming success for the prosecution. The application of the theory of "honest services" to the Skilling case – targeting corporate CEOs[37] instead of elected officials – has been the subject of debate[38] which may explain why the Supreme Court agreed to hear the arguments.[39]

Regardless of the outcome of that or other cases on the subject, the fact remains that bankers are doing better for themselves than they are for American households. This is the number one complaint we have about banks today. If I had to summarize the rest of what bothers us about banks, I would start with the fact that they are secretive. They take advantage of a very common fear of finance to convince consumers that they know what's good for you better than you do.

Next in line is the fact that they have purchased Congress. Banks have access to the halls of power that – despite 234 years of egalitarian rhetoric – ordinary voters can never achieve. Finally, we resent banks because we are required to use their services,[40] like a utility, to gain access to the American Dream by building wealth.

Financial services contribute about 6 percent to the US economy. Manufacturing and information industries use financial services, but the industry increasingly depends on itself: recall the portion of Goldman's earnings growth coming from using its own investment services. According to the latest data from the Bureau of Economic Analysis, the financial services industry requires $1.27 of its own output to deliver a dollar of its final product to users. Despite the fact that our economic reliance on financial services has been creeping up steadily since 2001, they remain one of the least required inputs for US economic output – only wholesale and retail trade have less input to the output of other industries.

---

[37] https://www.wsj.com/public/resources/documents/20090511skillingcertp.pdf

[38] https://corporate.findlaw.com/litigation-disputes/circuit-grapples-with-honest-services-fraud.html

[39] See note 14. The Supreme Court unanimously nullified Skilling's honest services fraud conviction. Skilling appealed the remaining charges which were sent back to the lower court. In June 2013, Skilling reached a deal with the Justice Department to serve 14 years and pay $42 million to the victims of Enron's fraud. He was released from custody in February 2019, after 12 years in federal prison.

[40] https://usatoday30.usatoday.com/news/nation/2009-11-04-bank-on-side_N.htm

So, why did Congress vote them nearly a trillion dollars' worth of life-support bailout money at the expense of taxpayers? Why did Wall Street get swine flu vaccine ahead of rural hospitals and health care workers? Why did they get the bailout without accountability? By making banks account for what they did with the money, congress could have:

1. prohibited spending on bonuses and lavish retreats;
2. ensured improved access to credit for small and medium enterprises; and
3. provided transparency to taxpayers on who got how much and what they did with it.

Need more reasons to demand honest services from a banker? Try this list:

1. Congress raised the FDIC insurance to $200,000 to make depositors comfortable leaving money in banks; then the banks passed the insurance premium on to customers – including those that never had $200,000 cash in the bank in their lives and probably never will. Seriously, how much money do you have to have before it makes sense to have $200,000 in cash in a savings account earning 0.25%?
2. Banks can borrow at 0% from the Fed yet they raise the interest rates they charge even their best customers. The bank I use for my company willingly lent me $10,000 last year to open a new office and approved a $7,000 credit card limit. Last month they sent me a letter saying they are raising the interest rate by +1.9 percentage point – though I have never missed a payment deadline.

The banks can use our deposits to purchase securities issued by the Federal government, which are yielding better than 3 percent. They pay us about 0.25 percent yet still find it necessary to tack on a multitude of fees – which amount to 53 percent of banks' income today, up from 35 percent in 1995.

For now, Brother Banker skips along as lively as a cricket in the embers. But remember this: Marie Antoinette didn't know anything about the French revolution until they cut off her head. Matt Taibbi, in a recent *Rolling Stone* article called Goldman Sachs a "great vampire squid wrapped around the face of humanity, relentlessly jamming its blood funnel into anything that smells like money."[41] We are at risk for leaving the virtuous circle behind and entering a vicious circle of spiraling inflation.[42] A massive increase in government debt is being paid down by printing more money. Between July 2008 and November

---

[41] "Wall Street's Naked Swindle", 5 April 2010.
[42] https://asiasociety.org/video/nassim-nicholas-taleb-what-were-doing-wrong

2008, the Federal Reserve more than doubled its balance sheet from $0.9 trillion to $2.5 trillion. A year later, there is no evidence that they are trying to rein it in. As Brother Banker fails to provide honest services, a briar patch of a different kind may be waiting around the corner.

Goldman's gunslingers: 401k + 9mm = 666?

December 9, 2009

In the new Wall Street math of the post-9/2008 world, it seems that some people turn to humor and others to rage. First, they burned down our 401k plans: some people found this funny and made jokes about their "201k" plans.[43] The French got angry and took CEOs hostage.[44] Now, Goldman bankers are buying semi-automatic weapons to protect themselves from the angry mob. Matt Taibbi is desperately seeking humor in this, currently rating it a 7 on a scale of 1 to 10. Alice Schroeder, the story's originator, finds it humorless, suggesting there could (should?) be "proles...brandishing pitchforks at the doors of Park Avenue."

In true on-the-ground reporting, a Bloomberg reporter wrote a story after a friend told her that he had written a character reference so that a Goldman Sachs banker could get a gun permit. Alice Schroeder (author of *The Snowball: Warren Buffett and the Business of Life*, Bantam, 2009) also recounts a few examples of Goldman bankers using their other-worldly prescience to protect themselves: Goldman Sachs Chief Executive Officer Lloyd Blankfein – only too well known now for saying that Goldman is doing "God's work" – got a permit "to install a security gate at his house two months before Bear Stearns Cos. collapsed."[45]

All of this contributes to the view that Goldman Sachs is, indeed, "a great vampire squid[46] wrapped around the face of humanity, relentlessly jamming its blood funnel into anything that smells like money." I'm certain that *Rolling Stone* and *Bloomberg* have taken action to protect their right to be critical of Goldman. I've spent plenty of time on the phone with their fact checkers to know they put a lot of effort into being able to support every word they print.

---

[43] https://www.24-7pressrelease.com/press-release-rss/reviews-for-stock-shockthe-movie-110137.php

[44] https://abcnews.go.com/International/story?id=7170102&page=1

[45] These stories were later debunked by New York Magazine.
https://nymag.com/intelligencer/2009/12/are_goldman_sachs_bankers_real.html

[46] https://www.rollingstone.com/politics/politics-news/the-great-american-bubble-machine-195229/

Blogger Mike Morgan, who founded www.GoldmanSachs666.com[47], had to defend his right to be critical of Government Sachs by going to court last April when Goldman lawyers Chadbourne & Parke threatened him[48] with trademark infringement.

But it isn't just Goldman and it isn't just our 401k retirement plans that have been damaged. There are fundamental problems in the way our capital markets are being run. The people running the system have known about these problems since at least the Crash of 1987 – I warned the US central depository for all securities (Depository Trust Company) about it in 1993.[49] Brooksley Born warned[50] a presidential working group about it at a Treasury Department meeting in 1998 – and it contributed to the crash of 2008. As you read this today, nothing has been done to stop it from happening again. The real question is: which group will be the first to turn to action? Those with a sense of humor, those with a sense of security provided by a handgun[51] or those with the sense to make changes?[52]

Random Wall Street walking

April 14, 2010

There was a popular book in 1973 –*A Random Walk Down Wall Street* (by Burton Malkiel, W.W. Norton & Company, now in its 9th edition, 2007) – that pooh-pooh'ed the idea that one investor's stock picks could always be better than another investor's stock picks.[53] The punch line is that you could randomly throw darts at the Wall Street Journal financial pages and do just as well as anyone else investing in the stock market. I first read it in 1980, while taking Investment 101 in business school at night and editing economic research documents for the Federal Reserve Bank of San Francisco during the day. I had a very memorable argument with John P. Judd, then senior research economist and more recently special advisor to Bank president and CEO Janet Yellen.

John thought the Wall Street brokers were crazy for thinking they could make more than average returns on investment. I thought the Federal Reserve was

---

[47] http://www.goldmansachs666.com/

[48] https://www.theregister.com/2009/04/14/goldman_sachs_666_in_court

[49] For the whole story, see *Naked, Short and Greedy* (Spiramus 2019).

[50] https://en.wikipedia.org/wiki/Brooksley_Born

[51] https://nalert.blogspot.com/2009/12/goldman-sachs-employees-buys-guns-as.html

[52] https://www.washingtonpost.com/wp-dyn/content/article/2009/05/25/AR2009052502108.html

[53] As of 2023, there have been 13 editions, with over 1.5 million copies sold.

crazy for thinking they could control the money supply. John was already a PhD economist; I was still working on my Bachelor's degree in business administration.

Twenty years later I also have a PhD in economics, but there are still two camps pulling in different directions in their dangerous tug-of-war on the economy. There are the double-dip pessimists led by Yale Economist Bob Shiller and most recently discouraged by Paul Ferrell[54] of MarketWatch. And there are the "Mad Money" optimists who believe that Jim Cramer will tell them everything they need to know to get and stay rich, while Ben Bernanke consoles them with sound bites like "increased optimism among consumers … should aid the recovery."

At the heart of the problem is the same, original argument I had with John Judd – "is there a way to beat the averages" – except that this time around Wall Street is in bed with the Federal Reserve. You can no longer tell the crazies apart.

Which brings me back to the Random Walk. If Wall Street has their way, they will inflate the market just enough to induce you to put your money back in. Don't forget the Weenie Roast of 2008. If the government – either Congress or Treasury or the Federal Reserve – has their way, they will let it crash again, too. Don't forget that it was only Wall Street that got bailed out the last time. I think the chances are 50-50 either way.

Goldman's failure to disclose

April 21, 2010

The big news in finance this week is that Goldman Sachs got busted[55] – finally – for fraud related to those mortgage-backed bonds. At the heart of the Securities and Exchange Commission charges is the accusation that Goldman Sachs failed to disclose[56] conflicts of interest it had on some mortgage investments. One of the charges that Michael Milken pleaded guilty to in the 1980s was the failure to disclose. "This type of non-disclosure has [not since] been the subject of a *criminal* prosecution," according to his website.[57] The charges against Goldman are for civil fraud. The difference between civil and

---

[54] https://www.marketwatch.com/story/new-dow-high-ahead-happy-talk-feeds-sheep-2010-04-13

[55] https://money.cnn.com/2010/04/24/news/companies/Goldman_Senate_documents/index.htm

[56] https://www.huffingtonpost.co.uk/entry/what-did-tarp-accomplish_n_363423

[57] https://www.mikemilken.com/myths.taf

criminal cases is that civil cases are usually disagreements between private parties; criminal cases are considered to be harmful to society as a whole.[58] The judge in the Milken case found that his failure to disclose resulted in $318,082 of financial damage. The SEC is charging that Goldman's failure to disclose resulted in a $1 billion loss to investors. The former resulted in criminal charges, the later in civil. One has to wonder, given Milken's 10-year sentence for a relatively small dollar-valued infraction, what would be appropriate if the Goldman case was the subject of criminal prosecution.

The only criminal case related to the financial crisis that has been brought against any Wall Street executive so far was against two Bear Stearns hedge fund managers. They were found not guilty in November of "falsely inflating the value of their portfolios."[59] Theirs was a crime of commission not omission – they were charged with actively lying to investors and not with failing to disclose information. The closest situation that *might* result in criminal fraud charges for failure to disclose will be if the Justice Department pursues charges against Joseph Cassano, the AIG accountant who failed to disclose[60] information about the magnitude of the losses AIG had insured. Federal prosecutors have been investigating this since at least April 2009[61] – information about investigations is not made public, including if the investigation has been dropped, so we don't know for sure that there aren't charges in the pipeline.[62]

All this Wall Street activity that resulted in the US taxpayers forking over $3.8 trillion in bailout money – it's really hard to imagine that some good-guy-with-a-badge somewhere can't figure out who harmed our society as a whole.

---

[58] https://www.findlaw.com/litigation/filing-a-lawsuit/civil-cases-vs-criminal-cases-key-differences.html

[59]

https://money.cnn.com/2009/11/10/news/companies/bear_stearns_case/index.htm?post version=2009111108

[60] https://money.cnn.com/2010/04/19/news/companies/goldman_aig/index.htm

[61] https://wheelhouseadvisors.wordpress.com/2009/04/29/criminal-failure-to-disclose/

[62] The two-year investigation ended in May 2010 with no criminal charges brought against Cassano.
https://www.washingtonpost.com/wpdyn/content/article/2010/05/22/AR2010052200033.html

Goldman profited from crisis – shocking!

April 25, 2010

If someone is just finding out last week that Wall Street is profiting from the crisis it created, then I have only one question for them – "what rock have you been living under for the last two years?"

I've been shining a bright light on this since I first joined NewGeography.com to cover finance. From one of my first articles in November 2008, where I explained the nuances of financial innovations – "Who stands to gain? … Citigroup, Goldman Sachs, JP Morgan and Morgan Stanley …. You can do the math from there." (see p84) – to recent blogs on the impact of stimulus and bailout spending – "Goldman Sachs … even got transaction fees for managing the Treasury programs that funded the bailouts." (see p128) – I hope that it has been more obvious than painful that you have to take personal responsibility for your finances because you can't rely on Wall Street to do it for you.

Last week, the SEC charged Goldman Sachs with civil fraud. On Friday, a group of investors filed a lawsuit against Goldman's executives[63] for behaving in an "unlawful" manner and for "breaches of fiduciary duties" – meaning they were reckless with other people's money. Goldman is also being sued by the Public Employee's Retirement System of Mississippi for lying about the real value of $2.6 billion in mortgage-backed securities (MBS). I remind you that there's a good chance that Goldman (and other Wall Street banks) were and are selling MBS that don't have mortgages behind them – as I like to put it, there's no "M" in their "BS".

In a nauseating twist to the story, AIG (according to sources quoted in the press) insures Goldman's board against investor lawsuits – so AIG may be paying the costs of defending Goldman's executives in addition to any fines or settlements on the cases. AIG is still on bailout life support from US taxpayers.[64] In December 2009, the Federal Reserve Bank of New York took $25 billion worth of AIG preferred stock as partial payback for the $182.3 billion bailout.

Even less shocking to readers of NewGeography.com should be the story that the SEC lawyers were busy surfing the internet for pornography[65] when they should have been preventing this stuff from happening in the first place. I wrote an article last February about bailed-out Wall Street bankers spending taxpayer

---

[63] https://www.reuters.com/article/us-goldman-lawsuit-idUSTRE63P3XP20100426
[64] https://home.treasury.gov/data/troubled-assets-relief-program/aig
[65] http://edition.cnn.com/2010/POLITICS/04/23/sec.porn/

money on prostitutes (see p89). Those SEC staffers will need to be up to date on all things unholy when they head for the door that leads them to more lucrative jobs on Wall Street.

Like the arsonist who gets the insurance payoff after burning down his own house, the Wall Street bankers profited from transaction fees in creating the crisis, profited from the bailout payoffs funded by the US taxpayers and they continue to profit from their credit derivatives[66] as whatever was left standing begins to collapse around us. Like most Americans, I think I'd get some sense of satisfaction from seeing someone in handcuffs over what has been done to the value of our savings and the global reputation of our capitalist system.

---

[66] https://www.huffingtonpost.co.uk/entry/goldman-sachs-emails-big-short_n_550547

6. Systemic Issues

This chapter on Systemic Issues goes into detail about topics that are widely misunderstood by the non-financial public. For example, when I started covering financial topics for NewGeography, I took the time to describe the role of mortgage bonds in the financial crisis of 2008 in some detail. Much of the early coverage in the popular press directed the blame toward reckless homeowners. It wasn't until much later that they turned their attention to the role reckless Wall Street banks played in the years leading up to the collapse. The first article lays the foundation for what follows by explaining how mortgages came to be traded on Wall Street as bonds through a process known as "securitization". With securitization, some underlying assets – like mortgages, car loans, etc. – are bundled together to create a bond which the lender can sell to be traded in capital markets. Financial innovations like securitization were supposed to democratize capital by making it easier to fund less-popular projects, both public and private. Like many inventions, it was abused for the enrichment of a few.

Financial innovation: Wall Street's false utopia

October 3, 2008

In the popular media much of the blame for the current crisis lies with sub-prime mortgages. Yet the main culprit was not the gullible homebuyer in Stockton or the seedy mortgage company. The real problem lies on Wall Street, and its addiction to ever more arcane financial innovations. As we try to understand the current crisis, and figure ways out of it, we need to understand precisely what, in the main, went wrong.

I have studied financial innovation for years and worked with some of the best minds in that business. In 2003, I wrote in *Beyond Junk Bonds*[1] that financial innovation is the "engine driving the financial system toward improved performance in the real economy". Innovative debt securities, like collateralized mortgage obligations (CMOs),[2] I had hoped, would add value to the economy by reallocating risk, increasing liquidity, and reducing agency costs. Like the broken promises of communism, it turned out to be a utopia that was not achieved.

CMOs were designed to diversify risk by shifting it to larger, better capitalized and diverse institutions. Here's an example of how that is supposed to work. Traditionally, a bank in Riverside, California would write and hold the

---

[1] *Beyond Junk Bonds*, Susanne Trimbath and Glenn Yago, OUP, 2003

[2] This is the same as a mortgage-backed security or MBS.

mortgages for homes in the area. Then, if some negative shock impacted jobs and income in the area, that bank would have to absorb all the resulting defaults. This would put the local bank at an inordinate risk of failure. With CMOs, the risk would be spread out across banks and investors in a broader geographic area. Since CMOs could be held internationally, even a nationwide economic downturn might have little impact on any single mortgage holder.

Unfortunately, the dealmakers sold the riskiest pieces to a few hedge funds, thereby consolidating the risk rather than allocating it broadly. The result was the spectacular crash of Bear Stearns and the incendiary damage done to a slew of US and international financial institutions.

CMOs were supposed to make more money available for lending to homeowners than would otherwise have been the case. Instead, it produced more paper, that was more heavily leveraged and less secure. Securitized mortgages were misused to the extent that $45 trillion in bonds were issued on $5 trillion in assets; it's as if someone bought insurance for 9 times the value of the house.[3] By 2007, the market was over-sold: more bonds had been sold than could be delivered, possibly even more than had been issued. On average, nearly 20% of CMO trades have failed to settle since 2001, driving down the price of the bonds through the inflated appearance of supply.

CMOs should have been used to protect against conflicts of interest between managers, stockholders, and bond holders[4]. Instead, the same companies that issued the CMOs were buying large positions in the securities. Most CMOs are typically initiated by banks seeking to remove credit risk from their balance sheets while keeping the assets themselves. Normally, these securities are issued from a specially created company so that the payments from the riskiest borrowers, i.e. the sub-prime mortgagees, can be separated from the more credit-worthy payees. A trustee and a portfolio manager receive fees from the newly created company.

While CMOs reduced some of the risk to the local banks, it also led some of those banks to lend imprudently. With the cash flowing easily back to the banks after the CMOs were sold, some lenders became increasingly risk-seeking – the opposite of the intended purpose of CMOs. Companies like Bear Stearns, who

---

[3] In 2022, there were only $12.2 trillion mortgage-backed securities outstanding.

[4] In economics, we refer to these as "agency costs" because the managers act as agents for the stockholders.

acted as trustee and portfolio manager for the CMOs, also purchased the CMO securities (usually through a subsidiary hedge fund).

Critically missing from the market for CMOs was the lack of a standard for the issuance. In more than one case, when a CMO investor attempted to foreclose on a property for mortgage delinquency, courts found insufficient documentation to support the CMO's lien on the property. Without legally binding "receipts" of ownership, CMOs have had insufficient real backing – producing results we are still trying to cope with.

Sure, sub-prime mortgage defaults may have been the straw that broke the camel's back. But Bear Stearns was in financial difficulty three to six months before the sub-prime mortgage default rate spiked. The real fundamental problem lay in the multiple sales of mortgages through CMOs – the result of too much faith in financial innovation. Experts believe that, for every $1 of mortgage that defaulted, the investment banks fell behind as much as $15 in payments on the CMOs. These, not the actual mortgages of homeowners, represent the bulk of the securities that Treasury Secretary Paulson wants $700 billion to buy.

Solving the financial crisis: looking beyond simple solutions

January 17, 2009

When presented with complex ideas about complicated events, the human tendency is to think in terms of Jungian archetypes: good guys and bad guys, heroes and villains. The more complicated the events, the more the human mind seeks to limit the number of variables it considers in unison in order to make sense of what it sees. The result is a tendency to describe events in the simplest black and white terms, ignoring the spectrum of colors in between.

This principle can be seen in the current explanation of the financial crisis. University of West Virginia Professor of Sociology Lawrence Nichols has developed what he calls the "landmark narrative" shaping how the public reacts to dramatic swings in financial cycles.[5]

---

[5] For example, see the chapter "The Lesson of Lincoln: Regulation as Narrative in the Savings and Loan Crisis" in *The Savings and Loan Crisis: Lessons from a Regulatory Failure* https://www.amazon.com/gp/product/1402078714?ie=UTF8&tag=newgeogrcom-20&linkCode=as2&camp=1789&creative=390957&creativeASIN=1402078714

As Professor Nichols explains, the narrative described by the landmarks can be a contrived and even inaccurate version of history. By its nature, the shorthand narrative is often unable to describe the detailed reality of an occurrence. Much like an interstate highway, the landmark narrative takes the valley pass, avoiding the mountaintops from which the full view of history can be seen and understood. If we move away from the landmark narrative – beyond the highway for a view from the hilltop – we'll see more of the landscape: enough to make sense of the complicated events that make up our financial environment.

There is real danger in limiting our view of events to what can be described by the landmark narrative. It's like describing New Jersey from the I-95 Turnpike: funny enough for late night television but not particularly useful for problem solving. Basing our view of events on the landmark narrative can, and very well might, lead to "solutions" that could prove as dangerous – or worse – than doing nothing.

Specifically, reactions to the current financial crisis are making their way into popular consciousness, potentially becoming imbedded in unpredictable and usually indelible ways. In a democracy, our elected officials are bound to respond to these shifts in popular consciousness. The constant repetition of contrived and inaccurate versions of events eventually leads us to suffer what Nobel Laureate Merton Miller called "the unintended consequences [of] regulatory interventions." Austrian Economist Ludwig von Mises, in fact, warned decades earlier that market data could be "falsified by the interference of the government," with misleading results for businesses and consumers.

As Americans, we have repeatedly failed to learn this lesson. Throughout our history, Americans have had an irrational fear of finance. Deemed to be too complicated, the field of finance lends itself easily to description by landmark narrative. Quite possibly to our detriment, the rise of the financial sector has been tied to economic expansion throughout our modern business history. The more robust the flow of finance in capital markets, the more robust is economic activity. Our economy, our livelihood and our well-being are inextricably related to finance at home and around the world.

So, what are the assumptions about finance we see today? It turns out many of the assumptions are often erroneous and usually dangerous. The problems on Wall Street, for example, did not stem from too few laws; rather, it resulted from not enforcing the laws we already have. When I talk to regulators and industry participants about problems with failures-to-deliver in bond and equity markets, they often respond that there is no rule against it. Indeed, there is no specific law that says that the seller of stock cannot fail to deliver the shares on the settlement date (usually three days after the trade); there is no specific punishment in place. Yet it seems clear that if someone takes your money and doesn't give you what they promised, this is stealing and there are laws against it. Look at it this way: there is no specific law that says, "it is a crime to hit a person on the head with a hammer." Yet I assure you that if I hit you on the head with a hammer the police will arrest me for a crime. It will have some other name (like "assault with a deadly weapon") instead of "the crime of hitting a person on the head with a hammer." But I will be just as arrested. And it is just as much a crime.

So, the real problem here is not a lack of laws, but a lack of enforcement of what already exists on the books. Our reluctance to act on this reality has serious consequences. First, we don't focus on punishing the perpetrators. Our government says they don't have time for "finger pointing" because they are too busy rushing rapidly to fix the problem – a problem they have yet to define. Instead, they pour money into institutions, allow huge bonuses to be paid with public money, lavish retreats on insurance company executives – and then insist what we need is massive regulatory reform.

This has reached the level of absurdity. The House Financial Services Committee held hearings on January 5 to assess the alleged $50 billion investment fraud engineered by Mr. Bernard L. Madoff. The assumption is that somehow, we don't have the laws on the books to prevent Ponzi schemes; in fact those laws have been there for decades. A rash of new laws to prevent such occurrences is not necessary; we simply need to enforce what already exists.

Yet rewrite we will, and with what may well be reckless abandon. Opening the session, Congressman Paul E. Kanjorski (D-PA), the Chairman of the Subcommittee on Capital Markets, Insurance, and Government Sponsored Enterprises, called for Congress to "rebuild" the regulatory system and commence with "the most substantial rewrite of the laws governing the US financial markets since the Great Depression."

But this is the wrong approach. The real question isn't new laws – although that may make good headlines for vote-seeking congressmen. The more basic question should be: where has the lawman been?

Hearings like this are an integral part of the "landmark narrative." Unless we've learned our lesson, we will be in for a rash of new rules, regulations and legislation paving the path for a future round of financial turmoil while allowing the perpetrators who created the crisis to avoid prosecution. Remember Sarbanes-Oxley, the measure supposed to prevent ill-doing by Wall Street. Passed in 2002, it didn't seem to do anything except keep accountants and lawyers busy. In fact, it had the unintended consequence of discouraging small businesses from going public because of the extra cost for the reporting it required. Need more examples? Here's a speech by an SEC economist[6] that explains how regulations designed "to reduce executive compensation could actually increase expected compensation." I've written in the past about "regulatory chokeholds"[7] that make the failures of financial institutions almost inevitable.

In 2009, we are presented with a new opportunity to display our capacity to evolve beyond the same old pattern of reaction and spurious law-writing. When dealing with violations of the law by respectable and powerful groups (like bankers), we need to consider using the laws already there; it's simply time to find someone to enforce them.

Phantom bonds update: the new treasury bond owner's manual

December 24, 2008

Shortly after my piece on Phantom Bonds, "Blame Wall Street's Phantom Bonds For The Credit Crisis", posted in November (see p84), a friend called from New York to ask if I'd seen the latest news. Bloomberg News reported on December 10 that "...The three-year note auction drew a yield of 1.245 percent, the lowest on record... The three-month bill rate [fell] to minus 0.01 percent yesterday." The US Treasury is seeing interest rates on its notes that are "the lowest since it started auctioning them in 1929."

My friend is an intelligent person, a lawyer who managed to accumulate more than $1 million working a 9-to-5 job in a not-for-profit firm and retire in her 50s. Some of her portfolio is in Treasury bonds, so she had a lot of questions. In the course of our conversation, it became clear that I wasn't going to be able to explain all she needed to know on the phone, despite her background. I decided to write this short owner's manual.

---

[6] https://www.sec.gov/news/speech/spch031706css.htm

[7] *Beyond Junk Bonds* (Chapter 3)

https://www.amazon.com/gp/product/0195149238?ie=UTF8&tag=newgeogrcom-20&linkCode=as2&camp=1789&creative=390957&creativeASIN=0195149238

Here's how it works, and how it ties back to the problem of phantom bonds. When the US government needs to raise money it authorizes its agent, the Federal Reserve Bank (FRB), to sell securities. The different names for these securities are associated with how long they will remain outstanding, like the term of a loan: bills are up to one year, notes are up to seven years, and anything longer than that is a bond. We'll just call them bonds to make it easy.

The FRB has relationships with several primary dealers like Citigroup, Goldman Sachs, JP Morgan, and Morgan Stanley. When notifications are sent out that some bonds will be sold, these primary dealers submit bids in the form of prices. If a financial institution bids $99 for a $100 bond, then that bond will essentially pay - or 'yield' — roughly 1% from the US Treasury (UST) to its holder. If the investor bids $101 for the $100 bond, then it will pay 1% for the privilege of lending money to the UST; the bond's 'yield' would then be minus 1%. That's a very good thing if you happen to be the UST, which of course we all are because it's all taxpayer money.

So — as the prices of bonds rise, the yields fall, and these yields translate into the interest rate that the UST pays to the bondholders in order to borrow the money the next time it needs to fund the budget deficit (and to refinance the existing national debt).

This is all roughly speaking, of course. But the idea is that the interest rates are set based on the prices that are bid in something that's like a blind auction. The bidders don't see the other bids, but because there are more bids than there are bonds available, financial institutions will bid the highest prices they can to avoid being shut out altogether. (FRB usually gets bids for 2 to 3 times as many bonds as they have available to sell.) This is good for UST, with a heavy emphasis on the "us"! High bond prices translate into low interest rate loans for UST.

Bonds are funny that way: when a bond's price goes up, its interest rate goes down, and interest is the cost of borrowing money. So, we should like to see Treasury bonds selling at very high prices, and with very low costs to the UST. Unfortunately, all those fails-to-deliver — those phantom bonds — especially over the past few months, had the effect of pushing down the price of bonds by (artificially) increasing the supply. That was keeping the interest rate paid by UST higher than it needed to be over the last year or so.

When bond prices are high — or inching up, as they are now — we all benefit. UST sold $32 billion in 30-day Treasury bills on December 9th at a yield of 0%, meaning that investors are lending UST money for nothing except the promise to return their money without losing any of it. Investors bid for four times as many of these particular Treasury bills as were available for sale. This is as it should be.

As the primary brokers rush to cover their phantoms — those failed to deliver Treasuries of the past — in order to settle their transactions, we're seeing a surge in the price of treasury securities. The prices of bonds are rising, the yield is falling; the UST is paying lower rates on the money it borrows from investors.

An increase in the price of the new bonds can also mean that the price of existing bonds - those already outstanding - will also increase. The increase in the prices of outstanding bonds will help my friend in New York. A good part of her $1 million retirement portfolio is invested in Treasuries. Treasury bond funds, like those run by Merrill Lynch and Vanguard, are earning 11 to 12 percent for their investors.

These high rates of return in Treasury bond funds won't last forever, of course. The number of failures-to-deliver in Treasuries is falling quickly, now that the spotlight is on. When settlement is final and on time, then the usual rules of supply and demand will apply. Prices of new bonds and those bonds in the funds (the outstanding bonds) will even out. But the demand for UST bonds will likely stay strong as long as there is global financial turmoil. And that demand turns out to be good for the US (lower interest rates) and good for us (higher prices for the bonds in funds).

People like my friend in New York ask me if Treasury bonds are safe. I tell them: if the US Treasury fails to pay you back, you'll have bigger problems than a decrease in the value of your portfolio.

We sneezed, they got pneumonia

February 25, 2009

Don't worry about China taking over the US economy. Despite what all the talking heads on TV and the radio talk shows are saying, there isn't another country out there that hasn't been hammered at least as badly as we have by the financial meltdown. The problem with any other country attacking the US dollar, for example, is that they are all holding a lot of US dollars. You probably remember last year they were worried about the fact that we import so many goods that we have big "trade imbalances" – meaning that we buy more of their goods than they buy of ours.

Now remember this: we pay for those imports with dollars. So, again, if the dollar is worth less (or worthless) then they are not going to be getting as much for their imports. Raising the price of their goods, that is, simply charging more dollars won't do them any good either. We're in a recession, and Americans are tightening their belts. Demand for imported goods, like demand for all goods except luxury goods, is price sensitive. The more they charge, the less we buy. According to an article on CNN.com, our belt tightening has ended the "Road to riches for 20 million Chinese poor."[8]

Furthermore, it's in the best interest of countries around the world that the US dollar stays strong. The door does swing both ways. According to Jack Willoughby at Barrons.com, "European banks provided three-quarters of the $4.7 trillion in cross-border loans to the Baltic countries, Eastern Europe, Latin America and emerging Asia. Their emerging-markets exposure exceeds that of U.S lenders to all subprime loans."[9]

To support all that exposure, the European Central Bank has been obtaining dollars from the US Federal Reserve in currency swaps. The value of these swaps, where dollars are exchanged for other currencies at a fixed and renewable exchange rate, went from $0 to $560 billion this year.

And the Federal Reserve printing presses keep rolling along.

We need a new oracle

March 26, 2009

Warren Buffett was on CNBC for three hours on March 9, 2009, dishing out his wisdom.[10] All this fanfare despite having lost $24 billion in value last year, and handing the title of Richest Man in the World over to Bill Gates. Buffett made multiple references to "war" in describing the current financial crisis.

There are several problems with Buffett's comparison of the current state of the economy to war, as pointed out in a story that ran in the *Omaha World-Herald* the day after the interview: "While the situation is daunting by all accounts, some economic and military experts say comparing a deep recession to a world

---

[8] http://edition.cnn.com/2009/WORLD/asiapcf/02/20/china.economy.family/index.html
[9] Willoughby, Jack. "The Long View." *Barron's*, vol. 89, no. 17, 2009, pp. 26-28,32,34.
[10] http://fm.cnbc.com/applications/cnbc.com/resources/editorialfiles/2012/05/03/2226803
_Ask%20Warren%20-%20Complete%20Transcript%20-%202009-03-09.pdf

war takes things too far."[11] What we are seeing is less like war – in which an outside enemy attacks you – and more like arson. To make matters worse, the people who burned down the house are now collecting the insurance!

Warren Buffett – the widely revered Oracle of Omaha, where I live – is one of those who built the boom in the capital markets and are benefiting from the bust. No surprise then that Buffett whose primary business vehicle is Berkshire Hathaway, a financial holding company, supports the bailout of financial institutions. Their businesses include, among others, property and casualty insurance and a financial holding company. When Senator Ben Nelson (D-NE) told me that he talked with Warren before voting for the first bailout package, I button-holed him after lunch and gave him an ear full.

Of course, Buffett was in favor of the bailout – his companies directly benefited as did the investments made by his companies. He put $5 billion into Goldman Sachs preferred stock with a 10% dividend – a substantially better rate of return than the US government got on our $10 billion bailout, er, I mean "investment." Berkshire Hathaway was the largest shareholder in American Express Co. when they received $3.4 billion from Uncle Sam.

Buffett appeared on CNBC a year ago (March 3, 2008). At that time, he was forthcoming about the risks Berkshire Hathaway was taking. He told CNBC at the time that he had "written 206 transactions in the last three weeks" which were default swaps on municipal bonds – the financing used by cities and states to fund everything from building schools to general obligations.

Buffett bragged that "the municipality has to quit paying" before any losses would have to be covered. This gives him incentive for another payout from Uncle Sam in addition to the Wall Street bailout – he also has incentive to support the stimulus package. If the cities and states default on their debt, then Buffett (Berkshire Hathaway companies) would be on the hook to make good on the full value of the bonds. At that point in March 2008, after just three weeks of investing, Buffett said he made $69 million in premiums for guaranteeing payment on $2 billion of municipal bonds. The primary insurer received about $20 million, an amount significantly less but that carries more risk. If that doesn't seem to make sense, then you understand – the pricing of risk and

---

[11] Morton, Joseph. "The Economy may be Hell, but it's Not War." McClatchy - Tribune Business News, Mar 11, 2009. Now the Washington correspondent for the Dallas Morning News, Mr. Morton was then Bureau Chief for the Omaha World Herald.

premiums did not make sense. This systematic irrationality was also a contributing factor to the current financial mess.

The scheme of buying and selling bond payment guarantees is very much dependent on rising asset prices (and no recession), just like any Ponzi scheme. Describing his investment strategy in March 2008, Buffett clearly said that what he and the other insurers in this market are "hoping for is new money." He even admitted that getting new money was preventing him and others in the market from having to "totally face(d) up to the mistakes that they've made."

By now, Bernie Madoff has shown you how a Ponzi Scheme falls apart in a down market. In the 2008 interview, Buffett gave us a preview of what keeps him awake at night. Cities and states don't go broke very often, but when they do "it could be contagious." Luckily for Buffett, the Congress – "the best Congress that money can buy", according to Sen. Kennedy – voted to send "stimulus" money to the cities and states.

In fact, Buffett wouldn't have to pay on any of those bonds unless the primary bond insurer went broke, too. That primary bond insurer is Ambac Financial Group, Inc. Ambac is the first to pay in the event of default on the municipal bonds that Buffett is guaranteeing. If any of the bonds go bad, Ambac has to pay the bondholders. If Ambac got into financial trouble Buffett said he would "be out trying to help them raise money" – otherwise Berkshire Hathaway would have to pay off the bonds. Now, in March 2009, Buffett talks about the economy going over a cliff while Ambac teeters on the edge of junk bond status.[12] When it falls, it could take Berkshire Hathaway with it.[13] The table below shows what happened to Ambac's credit rating between Buffett's two appearances on CNBC.

---

[12] https://www.forbes.com/2009/09/22/ambac-municipal-bonds-business-ratings.html?sh=22cb2aaf5c70

[13] Update: 25 March 2010 S&P downgraded Ambac to 'R' (non-investment grade). 1 November 2010 Ambac missed a debt interest payment 1 and filed for Chapter 11 bankruptcy the following week. In 2008, Berkshire Hathaway reported $7,461 million "investment and derivative" losses.

Timeline of Ambac Credit Rating Slide

Date (M/D/Y)	Event
3/3/2008	Buffett appears on CNBC discussing investment scheme relative to Ambac
3/12/2008	Moody's confirms Ambac's AAA rating; changes outlook to negative
4/24/2008	Moody's reiterates negative outlook on Ambac's AAA rating following earnings announcement
5/13/2008	Moody's says worsening second lien RMBS could impact financial guarantor ratings
6/4/2008	Moody's reviews Ambac's AAA rating for possible downgrade
6/19/2008	Moody's downgrades Ambac to Aa3; outlook is negative
9/18/2008	Moody's places ratings of Ambac on review for possible downgrade
11/5/2008	Moody's downgrades Ambac to Baa1; outlook is developing
3/3/2009	Moody's reviews Ambac's ratings for possible downgrade
3/9/2009	Buffett appears on CNBC; no discussion of Ambac

Acting selfish and self-serving is what got us into this mess in the first place. We've been witnesses to bloated executive compensation in the face of lousy corporate performance. We've seen mega-billionaires living lavish lifestyles for years on the proceeds of Ponzi schemes and fraud. Maybe it's time for a new Oracle, in Omaha or elsewhere, because this one has been giving us bad advice.

US Buffett update: downgrade from oracle to seer?

March 16, 2009

A day or so after he was on CNBC, Warren Buffett went on Bloomberg Television and told them that he'll continue to sell derivatives contracts. He's getting deeper into investments that he has called "financial weapons of mass destruction." Apparently, he's betting that there will not be a crash (which would require a payout) in corporate junk bonds, municipal bonds or stock markets in the UK, Europe and Japan. Here's the punch line: his stock is up 17.2% since he started talking!

Berkshire Hathaway shares peaked last year at $147,000 each when Buffett was buying energy companies. The price is so very high because they have a policy of never paying dividends. Therefore, all the company's earnings are put back into investments. If you tried to use a standard finance model to determine the appropriate price for these shares, the answer would be "infinity" because you can't divide by $0 dividends. Anyway, two months after the peak, the shares were in the tank – relatively speaking – at $77,500 per share. By the end of the week before his TV appearances, the shares were even lower, at $72,400. The day of the CNBC interview: Berkshire Hathaway shares closed at $84,844 – a cool 17.2% gain. Remember, this is the man who said he is fearful when people are greedy and greedy when people are fearful.

On March 12, Berkshire Hathaway lost its triple-A credit rating from Fitch Ratings because of potential losses from those derivatives.[14] Not that we should believe everything Fitch says – Fitch is among the credit rating agencies that gave triple-A ratings to subprime mortgage bonds, and look what happened to those investments! For what it's worth, Fitch gives Berkshire a "negative" outlook, meaning another cut is possible within a couple of years.[15] The two other big ratings agencies, Moody's Investors Service and Standard & Poor's, still rate Berkshire triple-A.

Buffett's partner agrees with us

May 1, 2009

Billionaire investor, Warren Buffett, is hosting the Berkshire Hathaway shareholder meeting "Capitalist Woodstock"[16] in Omaha this weekend. Every news truck this side of Kansas City has been moved into town to cover the event.

While using words like "evil", "folly" and "demented" to describe the activities that generated the global financial meltdown, Buffett's partner, Charlie Munger, told CNBC in an interview that credit default swaps (CDS) should be outlawed completely.[17] I have said clearly that Buffett's strategy on CDS has gotten him in too deep. His strategy requires "new money" coming into the system regularly at a time when investors are pulling back.

Munger also says that "the people who make a lot of money out of the system as it is have a lot of political power and they don't want it changed." We think he must be speaking about Buffett here, too. Berkshire Hathaway is a financial company that benefits from the bailout of financial companies. Buffett must also

---

[14] Berkshire Hathaway's Long Term Issuer Default Rating was downgraded to AA+ on 12 March 2009.

[15] In fact, Berkshire Hathaway was downgraded again on 10 Feb 2010, to AA- where it remains.

[16] https://money.cnn.com/2009/05/01/news/newsmakers/buffett.preview.fortune/index.htm

[17] https://www.cnbc.com/id/30520826

be aware that the government will continue to make bailout payments, that will be passed along to CDS holders, just like the approximately $50 billion Uncle Sam passed out through AIG during the fall of 2008.

According to a report from Reuters,[18] Berkshire Hathaway will not report their 1st quarter financial results on Friday and no new date or reason for the delay has been given.[19] According to Bloomberg, the results will be delayed until six days after the meeting. There is some speculation at CNBC that Buffett may want to avoid some "terrifically worried" investors[20] at the meetings this weekend. The stock price closed down $1,995 per share[21] on Friday, May 1.

Oh, Canada? A safe-haven for banking investments
February 26, 2009

Looking for a safe haven for your banking investments? The Royal Bank of Canada (RBC) is about three times the size of Citigroup, Royal Bank of Scotland or Deutsche Bank – and RBC hasn't cut their dividend in more than 70 years. Although Canadian banking profits declined double-digits last year, they actually had profits. Pretty much the rest of the world's banks are reporting massive losses.

It seems the folks above the 49th parallel have been fiscally responsible. According to a story on Bloomberg.com "not one government penny" has been needed to support any Canadian bank "from British Columbia to Quebec" since the financial meltdown began in 2007. Not that the Canadian government left them out in the cold, either. A $C218 billion fund was set up last October – ostensibly to be sure Canadian banks could compete in international markets with all the government-backed banks in the rest of the world – but none of the banks took any of it.

According to Bloomberg, European governments "committed more than €1.2 trillion ($US1.5 trillion) to save their banking systems from collapse." As close as I can tell, between the Federal Reserve and Treasury, the US has poured over $3 trillion down the drain of financial institutions.

---

[18] https://www.reuters.com/article/earningsSeason/idUSN2943070120090429
[19] Berkshire's 10k filed with the SEC 8 May 2009 shows a $2,543 million loss (before taxes) for the first quarter 2009, including a $1,517 million loss from derivatives. https://www.sec.gov/Archives/edgar/data/1067983/000119312509105560/d10q.htm
[20] https://www.cnbc.com/id/30519695
[21] https://www.bloomberg.com/quote/BRK%2FA%3AUS

Only seven banks in the world have triple-A credit ratings – two of them are Canadian. While the rest of the developed, industrial nations are pouring hundreds of billions each down the black hole that is their financial systems, our Neighbors to the North were engaging in "solid funding and conservative consumer lending."

Canada is the only member of the G-7 to have balanced their budget 11 years in a row. Immigrating to Canada is looking like a better idea all the time.

The next global financial crisis: public debt

July 15, 2009

The cloud of the global financial meltdown has not even cleared up, yet another crisis of massive proportions looms on the horizon: global sovereign (public) debt.

This crisis, like so many others, has its roots in the free flow of credit from the preceding economic boom years. The market prices of assets were rising steadily. Rising valuations, especially where they were based on improving revenues from robust economic activity, led to rising income streams for governments. This encouraged governments to borrow more, perhaps often to expand services – and the bureaucracy required to offer services – although sometimes to improve infrastructure.

At the same time, rising market prices for financial assets encouraged more savers and investors into the market. That led to an increasing supply of investable funds, which drove demand for sovereign and municipal debt (in addition to the mortgage-backed securities). This process, driven by the financial services industry instead of the real economy, is eerily similar to the driving forces behind the "subprime crisis." The demand for public offerings pulled more debt issuance out of borrowers with seemingly little concern for repayment: the financial sector gains its profits from issuance fees, trading fees, underwriting fees, etc. As in the case of mortgages, it will be those who buy and hold the debt, along with the borrowers, who will suffer the consequences.[22]

Certainly, emerging nations took advantage of the depth of rich nation capital markets to increase their debt through public offerings. At the end of June 2009, only Italy, Turkey and Brazil were covered by more credit default swap contracts than JP Morgan Chase and Bank of America. In addition to those two

---

[22] The number and percent of sovereign bond defaults spiked in 2008, 2010, 2012 and 2013.

global banks, Goldman Sachs, Morgan Stanley, Deutsche Telekom AG, France Telecom and Wells Fargo Bank all have more credit derivate coverage than the Philippines.

Yet there is clearly a potential default problem here. Gross credit default swaps outstanding for the debt of Iceland are equal to 66 percent of GDP, about 20 percent of GDP for Hungary and the Philippines and around 18 percent for Latvia, Portugal, Panama and Bulgaria. If these countries default on their debt, those global banks who sell credit derivatives will be making enormous payments – whether or not the defaulting countries receive any support or bailouts from international donor organizations (like World Bank or International Monetary Fund).

The table in Appendix 3 shows the GDP for the countries named in the most credit default swap contracts (as most recently reported to Depository Trust and Clearing Corporation). For each sovereign (country, state or city), we show the value of their public debt both as a figure and as a percent of GDP. The telling factor here is that the "financial markets," if they are to be believed, judge these entities as more likely to experience "a credit event" than others. A credit event, as we learned when the AIG saga unraveled can be anything from a decline in the market price of debt to an outright default on payments.[23] (See Appendix 3 - Sovereigns named in most credit default protection.)

The obvious consequence is that a crisis in sovereign debt would cause problems not just within those nations, states or cities – but also among their trading and economic partners, among their lenders (banks, other sovereigns or international donor organizations) as well as the global financial institutions who sold default protection through the credit derivatives markets. The financial impact would be more than anything we have seen so far: most global financial institutions received bailouts from their sovereign governments to soften or at least delay the impact of the September 2008 financial crisis. Yet, I believe the more dire consequence of a widespread sovereign debt crisis, if there is one, will be civil unrest fomented by the deterioration in governments' critical functions that will result from their weakened financial positions.[24]

---

[23] After the Great Financial Crisis, the amount of outstanding credit default swaps fell dramatically, from $61.2 trillion at the end of 2007 to just $9.4 trillion in 2017. https://www.bis.org/publ/qtrpdf/r_qt1806b.htm

[24] Venezuela offers a case study. Public debt increased in the years leading up to 2008. By 2014 there were signs of economic collapse and by 2016 default seemed likely. On 13

Policy makers will have few options available across the globe to combat this crisis. The rich world's governments have not been able to contain their debt burdens through budgetary discipline alone. Between Federal Reserve Chairman Ben Bernanke[25] and Treasury Secretary Tim Geithner, they've done everything except load the helicopter with dollar bills to finance the bailout with freshly-minted US dollars.

Policymakers are just as likely to precipitate a financial crisis as any other investor or borrower – they seem to have no prescient knowledge of the dangers associated with over-speculation, lack of solid accounting practices, balancing a budget, etc. How else do we explain their dependence on borrowing? Basic accounting principles – not to mention ideas going back at least to the biblical story of Joseph and the Pharoah – would guide users to monitor income and spending; actuarial analysis directs us to save during times of "feast" and spend the surplus during times of "famine."

Yet the United States government and others have already decided to monetize their financial problems at levels not seen before. I shudder to even think what sovereign default would mean to a large-country (a G8 member, for example); however, I deem such a scenario as highly unlikely. A quick look at the table indicates the countries that have never defaulted or even rescheduled a debt payment in their history (see Appendix 3). The defaults will more likely come from spendthrift small countries, or big states like California.[26]

The world economy has encountered these debt situations before. But in this environment, a sovereign debt crisis would be unlike anything we have experienced in the past. Not only have financial markets become more globally integrated – with countries borrowing and lending across national borders with ease – but the use of credit derivate products has increased the chance of a default turning into a global catastrophe. These derivatives will have a multiplier effect on every sovereign debt default. We know for a fact that credit

---

November 2017, S&P declared Venezuela in selective default. Despite a change in political regime in 2019, all debt restructuring strategies were abandoned in early 2022. After the National Assembly disbanded the interim presidency 3 January 2023, the US has not legally recognized any Venezuelan government. (Source: Center for Strategic & International Studies.) After a wave of anti-government protests in 2014 and 2017 were defeated by a police crackdown, millions of Venezuelans left the country to escape economic hardship. UN data in 2022 suggested that more than seven million people had left since 2015.

[25] https://www.federalreserve.gov/boarddocs/speeches/2002/20021121/default.htm
[26] http://www.newgeography.com/content/00896-who-killed-californias-economy

default swap contracts are written without being limited to the total value of the underlying assets. Therefore, there could be nine to fifteen times as many credit default contracts to be paid by global banks as there is sovereign debt in default.

Today there are outstanding about $2 trillion of credit default swaps contracts on just fifty of the world's 200 nations. These contracts could become payable under even the most modest credit event, spreading the damage globally even before debt-service payments are missed. For example, it is now known that AIG's Financial Products Division wrote contracts that became payable when the market price of debt decreased, regardless of whether or not the borrower had missed a payment. These circumstances did not exist during any previous debt crisis, including the most recent default cycle, the crises in emerging market debt of the 1980s and the 1990s. If widespread sovereign defaults happen, we can expect to see something new and potentially much more damaging.

Dubai debt debacle

December 1, 2009

When a bunch of American bankers woke up last Thursday, I hope they found more to be thankful for than just a traditional turkey dinner. It's thought that the American banks will have less exposure[27] to Dubai World (an investment company that managed and supervised a portfolio of businesses and projects for the Government of Dubai) than most European or Asian banks – although the American banking industry is known to hide a thing or two up their sleeves. Dubai World is asking creditors for a "standstill" – meaning they want the interest to stop accumulating on their debt. It's a polite way of saying they can't afford the interest payments anymore.

Dubai is one of the seven states that make up the United Arab Emirates (UAE). Dubai borrowed heavily to finance a building boom supported by high oil prices. They now lay claim to the world's tallest building and an island in the shape of a palm tree – at least General Motors went broke building cars. The capital of the UAE is Abu Dhabi. It's unlikely that Abu Dhabi can come to the rescue. Just last February Abu Dhabi injected $4.5 billion into five banks that were coming under financial pressure when the real estate market shifted.

---

[27] https://www.marketwatch.com/story/us-banks-less-exposed-to-dubai-than-europe-2009-11-27

Bailing out banks seemed to stop the US government from bailing out General Motors.

Dubai World is said to be in debt for $60 billion, although some reports put the figure much higher at about $90 billion. Even at the low end, that figure is equal to all the foreign direct investment in the UAE. (Foreign direct investment is all the money that foreigners invested in UAE.) By comparison, the direct investment of all UAE residents in other countries is less than one half that amount (about $29 billion at the end of December 2008). But don't think that means that Dubai World's investments are of little consequence outside the Gulf region. Recent projects include ports in London and Vancouver. DP World (Dubai Ports World, a holding-company owned by the government of Dubai in the United Arab Emirates) was at the center of a controversy in February 2006[28] when they announced the purchase of a firm that oversees operations at six US ports – DP World subsequently sold them off.[29]

Dubai World is the UAE government's investment conglomerate. That makes this a crisis in sovereign (public) debt – possibly only the first shoe to drop in the coming crisis I warned about back in July. Hope you don't get tired of hearing me say "told ya' so" – I suspect it will happen with increasing frequency during the next twelve months. The real problem with defaulting sovereigns is that there is no Chapter 11 bankruptcy process for them, like there was for General Motors. When a country defaults on their debt, they just stop paying – governments can change the rules on a whim.

Over-charged and under-stimulated

March 4, 2010

As we reported in July of last year, Goldman Sachs and other US bank bailout success stories are reaping big dollar benefits from the nebulous world of public-private interactions. Goldman Sachs – somehow always first in line for these things – even got transaction fees for managing the Treasury programs that funded the bailouts.

Now, the senator in my neighboring state of Iowa is once again trying to wake up Congress to the facts. You may recall that Senator Chuck Grassley (D-IA) admitted almost a year ago that he and the other members of Congress were fooled into voting for the bailout because they thought former-Treasury

---

[28] https://www.washingtonpost.com/wp-dyn/content/article/2006/02/11/AR2006021101112.html

[29] https://www.cbc.ca/news/world/debt-crisis-puts-spotlight-on-dubai-world-1.832960

Secretary Paulson actually knew what the hell he was doing when he asked for $750 billion in the fall of 2008. "When it's all said and done, you realize he didn't know anything more about it than you did."

Late last week, the Huffington Post[30] called our attention to a letter that Senator Grassley sent to Goldman Sachs[31] about the fees they will collect on the next bit of federal stimulus – bonds that are used to underwrite the latest jobs bill. Grassley points to a November 27 report from Bloomberg News for some evidence that Goldman may be over-charging local governments by more than 30 percent above what is normally charged for bond underwritings (i.e., handling the paperwork and rounding up some buyers).

In Grassley's letter, he includes a quote in the article to the effect that the local governments don't care about the fees since there is a "large subsidy." However, according to the *Financial Times* – and we agree with their assessment – Goldman and others are able to charge excessive fees because the financial crisis reduced their competition. When banks were required to raise more capital before they could pay back their bailout money, they did – and earned record fees for themselves in the process!

It is eerily similar to the driving forces behind the "subprime crisis" that was repeatedly blamed for the financial crisis. The financial sector gains its profits from fees – issuance fees, trading fees, underwriting fees, etc. – unheeding of the impact on the real economy, taxpayers and the cost to the nation as a whole.

Financial crisis: too late to change?

April 2, 2010

A travelling salesman is driving down a country road when he runs over a cat. Seeing a farmhouse nearby, he approaches to confess this unfortunate situation to the pet's owner. When a woman answers the door, he says, "I'm sorry, but I think I just ran over your cat." She asks him, "Well, what did it look like?" "Oh, m'am," he replies, "I completely ran over it, so it was very awful, just a smear on the road…" "Oh, no," she interrupts, "I mean, what did it look like *before* you ran over it."

Congress and the Administration are trying to find ways to spend more money in their quest to stimulate the economy. But just like that travelling salesman, they are working with the picture after the wreck – and they can't seem to focus

---

[30] https://www.huffingtonpost.co.uk/entry/sen-grassley-grills-goldm_n_478526
[31] https://www.grassley.senate.gov/news/news-releases/grassley-asks-goldman-sachs-about-underwriting-fees-build-america-bonds

on what things looked like before it happened. In other words, they are so happy to be spending money without restraint that they have neglected to figure out how we got into this mess in the first place. We all know that the problem started in the financial sector – I don't know anyone who would disagree with that. In fact, the banks were the first to get money from the federal government – the October 3, 2008 act of Congress that will forever be known as The Bank Bailout.

Sadly, nothing is different today than it was on September 17, 2008 – the day that your 401k turned into a 201F. The now officially "to big to fail" banks are no more restrained in their activities today than they were in the days, weeks, months, and years leading up to the crisis. If anything, they are a little freer because now they are all "banks" with a federal guarantee to enjoy ever more risk-taking behavior without consequences.

Becoming a bank means that the money they hold can be protected by the Federal Deposit Insurance Corporation (FDIC). The FDIC has been so depleted by the epidemic[32] of collapsing financial institutions that analysts thought it would be forced to borrow money from the Treasury before the end of 2009.[33] Since January 1, 2010, another 41 banks have failed.[34] To hold the wolves at bay, the FDIC Board eased the rules on buyers of failing banks, opening the door for hedge funds and private investors to gain access to "bank" status – and the protections that go with it. At the end of the third quarter of 2009, the FDIC's fund was already negative by $8.2 billion, a decrease of 180 percent in just three months (from July to September 2009). According to the Chief Financial Officer's report,[35] the FDIC projects that the fund "will remain negative over the next several years" as they absorb some $75 billion in failure costs through the end of 2013. Taking their lead from Congress – that has a policy of robbing the future to pay off the past – the FDIC is proposing that banks pre-pay their insurance fees for the next three years.

---

[32] https://www.fdic.gov/about/financial-reports/report/2009annualreport/financial.html
[33] FDIC can borrow up to $100 billion from the US Treasury. At the end of 2022, they could cover a maximum of $222.5 billion with $128 billion in assets plus borrowing authority. In March 2023, the Federal Reserve borrowed an additional $143 billion to fund the FDIC's bailout of Silicon Valley Bank. This prevented FDIC from having to borrow from the Treasury, which was already struggling to fund the government while staying under the debt limit set by Congress.
[34] https://www.reuters.com/article/idUSTRE62Q02J20100327
[35] https://www.fdic.gov/about/financial-reports/corporate/cfo_report_3rdqtr_09/0909_CFO_Report.pdf

There is no relief in sight, either. Just this week, a case of "insider trading" in New York was dismissed [36] because the deal involved credit default swaps which – as I explained here last March – pay off losses "like" insurance but are not regulated like insurance; and which are bought and sold "like" securities but not regulated like securities. Although they are at the root of the causes of the financial crisis, not one new rule, regulation or law has been implemented to stop this nonsense from continuing. If you look at who's in charge of figuring out what went wrong – and making recommendations on how to prevent it from happening again – you will find the Financial Crisis Inquiry Commission [37] consists of political appointees who "have consulted for legal firms involved in lawsuits over the crisis." [38]

That's not reassuring. A Commission composed of members who earn their livelihood from financial institutions – including those that precipitated the crisis – is unlikely to solve or have any incentive to discover the mystery of the causes of the greatest financial collapse in the history of the world. This group is part of the problem – not the solution.

Eighteen months after Wall Street roasted weenies on the bonfire of your 401k, the one noticeable difference is that the stock market is higher than it was on that fateful day in 2008. Unfortunately, this version of "economic recovery" is being driven by the financial services industry instead of the real economy. As rising stock prices encourage more savers and investors into the stock market, they create an increasing supply of investable funds in the hands of the banks – who remain as free to speed down our financial highways today as they were when they ran over the economy like that poor cat on a country road, leaving nothing but a stain on the pavement.

The financial crisis continues to be an inside job

December 6, 2010

Over the weekend I saw the documentary movie *Inside Job* [39] with a friend who is not a financial markets expert. After the show, I told her I was relieved to see that the movie covered the majority of the causes of the collapse of financial markets in 2008. Part of my relief was from thinking that everything would be better now that "everyone" knows the facts. Then my friend pointed out that

---

[36] https://seekingalpha.com/article/196488-cds-gaming-continues-unfortunately

[37] https://cybercemetery.unt.edu/archive/fcic/20110310172443/http://fcic.gov/

[38] https://usatoday30.usatoday.com/news/washington/2010-01-31-conflict_N.htm

[39] https://www.sonyclassics.com/insidejob/

there were only six people in the audience – obviously "everyone" wasn't seeing this movie!

The movie did a good job of covering virtually everything I've been writing about at *NewGeography* since 2008. They did leave out the part where Goldman Sachs and other Wall Street banks were issuing mortgage-backed bonds without writing mortgages. This is totally understandable. It's very difficult to show what doesn't exist in video. It's easy enough to show homes in foreclosure – but what pictures and videos can you use to show that there aren't any mortgages behind bonds, especially when the bonds aren't even printed on paper? The pictures of hookers, strippers and cocaine use make the movie ominous enough and have a certain visual appeal that producers look for in a story.

Inside Job included lots of stuff on who is funding the academic studies being used to justify wrecking the financial markets. They present more on the serious academic fraud in the crisis than I was aware of. I first posted Tweets[40] about Duke University back in June 2009. A couple of Duke University professors published a research report about a model they developed that justifies manipulating stock prices and corporate votes.[41] What I Tweeted was: "It should be illegal to write this crap." Duke University's research center is funded by a wide selection of the bailed out financial institutions.[42] Your tax dollars at work!

The point I try to raise – perhaps loudly because it's a little self-interested coming from me – is that the perpetrators of the financial crisis are funneling billions of dollars to the academics who will write anything they are told for the sake of continued funding. In the meantime, those who are willing to take the adverse position are relegated to the Daily Show (no offense, Jon).

Then I sat through *Inside Job* and I saw this segment on former Federal Reserve Board of Governors member, and current professor at Columbia University Business School, Frederic Mishkin. Before the crisis, Mishkin took money from the Chamber of Commerce in Iceland to write a report about the "*Stability*" of their banking system. The source of the funding was not disclosed in the published report (an academic no-no). Then, after Iceland's banks completely

---

[40] https://twitter.com/susannetrimbath
[41] https://papers.ssrn.com/sol3/papers.cfm?abstract_id=1108632
[42] In 2010, the Founding Sponsors included Goldman Sachs, Banc of America Securities, Merrill Lynch, Wachovia, AIG, Lehman Brothers, and UBS Warburg.

collapsed, Mishkin changed the name of the paper on his resume to the *"Instability"* of Iceland's banking system. This was shocking to me, as I didn't realize how deeply the desire to deceive ran among these guys. Mishkin resigned from the Federal Reserve Board in the middle of the crisis – yes, even the rats will abandon a sinking ship.

Last week, Mishkin was on CNBC's Squawk Box (a chuckle-head fest about how to make money on the day's stock trades) pontificating about Fed monetary policy. CNBC is no stranger to corrupting academics to support their bad habits. *Inside Job* included examples of a slew of academic economists taking money from Wall Street to write papers justifying the systemic failures. Here's an example they didn't have. Someone recently sent me a study penned by professors at the University of Oklahoma Price Business School. The study[43] concluded that naked short selling (the practice of selling shares you don't own and can't borrow) is beneficial for making financial markets more efficient. Insane, right? No reasonable person would agree that it is good for markets if you can sell things that don't exist – yet it happens every day, even in the market for US government securities. It takes fewer than six degrees to connect the dots. The University of Oklahoma's Price College of Business is named for major donor Michael Price. Price is a "personal friend"[44] of CNBC personality Jim Cramer. For more on Jim Cramer's ties to Naked Short Selling check out the March 12, 2009 episode of the Daily Show.[45]

I was getting very discouraged about continuing to write about the causes of the crisis, since no corrective actions are being taken. A lot of work remains to educate the public about the issues and to come up with solutions. The old political ways are too corrupt to work anymore. It seems like we keep covering the same territory without progress, but I'm inspired by the closing line of *Inside Job*: "Some things are worth fighting for."

---

[43] https://www.cfr-cologne.de/download/workingpaper/cfr-09-09.pdf
[44] https://www.ou.edu/content/dam/price/News_room/Publications/2010/Mad_money.pdf
[45] https://www.cc.com/video/iinzrx/the-daily-show-with-jon-stewart-jim-cramer-pt-2

The next public debt crisis has arrived

March 20, 2012

In July of 2009, while the smoke from the global financial bonfire was still thick in the air, I wrote for *NewGeography* about another crisis of massive proportions just looming on the horizon: the Global Crisis in Public Debt (see p124).

Three years later, the news of defaults, bankruptcies, debt forgiveness requests, receiverships, and bailouts are in the news every day. Across the globe, sovereign entities – from US cities to European nations – are suffering under staggering debt loads, decimated revenues, and intense pressure from the very capital markets that they should be able to turn to for refuge. Last month, Jefferson County, the largest in Alabama, moved forward with their bankruptcy proceedings over the objections of the Wall Street banks. Suffolk County in New York declared a financial emergency.[46] The *Financial Times* had an interactive map showing all but twelve US states with budget shortfalls[47] for 2012. Eleven US cities, counties and villages have filed bankruptcy since 2008, plus 21 municipal non-government entities (e.g., utilities, hospitals, schools, etc.), according to the Pew Center on the States.[48]

This crisis for cities, states and nations, like so many other financial crises, has its root in the free flow of credit that existed during the preceding economic boom years. The market prices of assets rose steadily. Rising valuations, especially based on improving revenues from robust economic activity, led to rising income streams for governments. This encouraged governments to borrow more, perhaps often to expand services – and the bureaucracy required to deliver them – and sometimes to improve infrastructure and make capital investments.

At the same time, rising market prices for financial assets encouraged more savers and investors into the market. In the US, the flow of cash to Wall Street was further encouraged by favorable tax treatment for the earnings on retirement savings and municipal bonds. The steady influx of new money produced an increasing supply of investable funds, which drove demand for sovereign and municipal debt (in addition to the mortgage-backed securities).

---

[46] https://www.ft.com/content/f51e5e4a-67df-11e1-978e-00144feabdc0#axzz1os2mAnUJ
[47] The webpage is no longer available.
[48] The Pew Center on the States was a research program of Pew Charitable Trusts from 2007 until 2012.

This process was driven more by the financial services industry than the real economy. As of March 5, 2012, the Federal Reserve Bank of New York reported more than $5,000,000,000,000 ($5 trillion) in overnight securities financing – that's money that makes money but nothing else – that's more than 20% of US GDP sitting around, not creating jobs, not building infrastructure, just sitting. Since the investment of securities financing is virtually all done electronically, it creates very few jobs. What it does produce is a boost in revenues for bankers – which they can translate into often lavish bonuses.

The financial sector also adds to its profits from issuance fees, trading fees, underwriting fees, etc. Then there's "Market Risk Trading," a euphemism for letting anyone buy a contract to gamble on the probability that Greece won't be able to repay their debt or that you will miss a mortgage payment. Anyone can buy that contract, even the arsonist next door who has a say in whether or not you will be able to refinance your mortgage. In the end it is the borrowers who will suffer the consequences because they will be unable to refinance their debt and the gamblers who will win by withholding financing in anticipation of the insurance payout.

At the end of June 2009, only Italy, Turkey and Brazil were covered by more credit default swap contracts than JP Morgan Chase and Bank of America. Goldman Sachs, Morgan Stanley, and Wells Fargo Bank all had more credit derivate coverage than the Philippines.

Entered the Top 1,000 for credit default swaps after 2009:

Reference Entity	Debt as %GDP	CDS* as %Debt
Australia	30.3%	11.2%
New Jersey	7.8%	11.2%
New Zealand	33.7%	8.6%
Illinois	6.8%	8.2%
Texas	3.4%	6.6%
Kingdom of Saudi Arabia	9.4%	3.8%
Lebanese Republic	137.1%	2.4%
Arab Republic of Egypt	85.7%	1.0%

*CDS are credit default swaps, financial contracts that pay off if the named (reference) entity experiences a credit event like a ratings downgrade or a missed payment.

[Abu Dhabi also appears in the 2012 list of the top 1,000 entities named in credit default swaps at DTCC, but debt and GDP data are not available.]

Source: DTCC Trade Information Warehouse.

What was a potential default problem in 2009 has become reality in 2012. In 2009, gross credit default swaps outstanding for the debt of Iceland were equal to 66 percent of GDP, and around 18 percent for Portugal. As these countries struggle with their debt, the global banks – primarily the US banks – sell credit derivatives and stand to collect enormous payments – whether or not the defaulting countries receive any support or bailouts from international donor organizations. The reason is that most credit derivatives contracts pay out on "credit events." A "credit event" can be something as simple as a downgrade from Moody's or Standard and Poor's – whose managers testified before Congress that credit rating changes can be bought.[49] Standard & Poor's executives admitted in 2008 that they were being forced to relax rating requirements to improve revenues.[50] If, for example, $69 billion worth of credit derivative payoffs are available on a Greek default then how much could the owner of a credit swap afford to pay for a rating change?

The absurdity of rating Egypt more credit worthy than Australia is only part of the story. The sad fact is that Wall Street banks can sell more credit risk protection than there is credit at risk. If all the public debt of a country is $1 billion, it means that country has borrowed $1 billion in public capital markets. But Wall Street banks are buying and selling more credit risk insurance than there is credit risk. This is the same problem I wrote about in 2008 that we saw in the Treasury bond market – when you sell more bonds than exist these trades are called "naked" sales or "phantoms".[51] A similar problem in stocks[52] contributed to the 2008 crash.

There are more cities, counties, states, and nations in financial trouble. According to the Bank for International Settlements,[53] there were *$615 trillion* in Over-The-Counter (OTC) derivatives contracts outstanding worldwide at the end of 2009. That's about *9 x global GDP*. In other words, the entire world would have to work for 9 years just to produce enough to pay off the derivatives – before we had a dime left over to pay off the original debts.

---

[49] https://www.nytimes.com/2010/04/24/business/24testify.html
[50] According to statement made in a program originally aired on 21 November 2008. NOW on PBS, Season 4, Episode 4, "Credit and Credibility." NOW last aired in April 2010.
[51] https://www.youtube.com/watch?v=FzEhOly-QvQ&ab_channel=GaryMatsumoto
[52] https://www.youtube.com/watch?v=gHsxLhY-EvE&ab_channel=KristinaLeighCopeland
[53] https://www.bis.org/publ/otc_hy1005.htm

In this environment, the sovereign debt crises may produce something scarier than anything we have experienced in the past. The use of credit derivatives products has increased the chance of a default turning into a global catastrophe. It won't be enough to pay off the debt owed by one of these sovereigns. That payoff will be magnified by the value of the derivatives. These derivatives will have a multiplier effect on every sovereign debt default or "credit event." The table in appendix 4 only includes the credit derivatives warehoused with the Depository Trust and Clearing Corporation in the US – there is no source of information on the real global magnitude.

A crisis in sovereign debt would cause problems not just within those nations, states, or cities but also for the global financial institutions who sell default protection through the credit derivatives markets. The bankruptcy of Jefferson County (AL) threatens to take down muni-bond insurer Syncora Guarantee[54] (who, by the way, is suing JPMorgan Chase over losses in mortgage-backed securities saying that JPMorgan Chase misrepresented the loans to obtain the insurance). Another such institution was Ambac Financial Group, Inc.,[55] which I described in an article published months before the original prediction of the global crisis in public debt (see p118). Ambac – like Berkshire Hathaway – was in the business of guaranteeing the payments of public debt (and mortgage-backed securities). Ambac filed for bankruptcy in November 2010.[56] With Ambac gone, Berkshire is next in line to pay because of Warren Buffett's credit default swaps.[57]

Policy makers have had few options available across the globe to combat this crisis. The European Union Commission is attempting to control the amount of credit insurance being sold by limiting the sale of "naked" credit default swaps. A proposal was approved by the European Parliament on November 15, 2011 to restrict the sale of credit insurance to any buyer who "does not have ownership of the underlying government debt." The limited regulation passed by the EU Parliament allows the sale if the buyer has ownership in something

---

[54] https://www.wsj.com/articles/SB10001424052970204880404577225280156326416
Syncora Guarantee was a US subsidiary of Syncora Holdings Ltd., a Bermuda-based company, last reported financials in 2018: a loss before taxes of $106 million on revenue of $108 million. Syncora Holdings sold its interest in Syncora Guarantee effective 30 December 2019.

[55] https://www.ambac.com/home/default.aspx

[56] https://www.wsj.com/articles/SB10001424052748703514904575602911478916800

[57] Berkshire Hathaway recorded pre-tax losses of $251 million on credit default contracts in 2011. They terminated their last credit default contract in July 2016.

vaguely related to the sovereign debt – like allowing the purchase of swaps on Italian government debt if the buyer owns shares of an Italian bank. French President Sarkozy said in January that he would propose special levies on naked credit default swaps.[58] The imposition of fines or taxes (levies) has not eliminated similar activity in stock and bond markets in the US. Actions taken in Europe at least are a start which is more than US regulators have done.

Meanwhile, Federal Reserve Chairman Ben Bernanke and Treasury Secretary Timothy Geithner continue to load the helicopter with dollar bills to finance the payouts with freshly minted US dollars. They sell us the fantasy of free-market capitalism while laying down a labyrinth of financial rules and regulations allowing a dozen or so politically connected banks to reap the rewards while avoiding the risk of failing. US financial institutions have been placing losing bets through unregulated derivatives markets only to be bailed out as "systemically important" – a euphemism for "too politically connected to fail." The rest of the world is taking steps to stop the damage. When will the US government step up to the plate? (See Appendix 4 - Sovereigns named in most credit default protection.)

The swaps of Damocles

October 23, 2012

"Privileged people don't march and protest; their world is safe and clean and governed by laws designed to keep them happy...."

Michael Brock in John Grisham's *The Street Lawyer* (Doubleday, 1998).

"There can be nothing happy for the person over whom some fear always looms..."

Cicero, Tusculan Disputations 5.62, via Wikipedia.com

If you were fearful after Wall Street decimated your life-savings in September 2008 then you should know that the sword of Damocles remains above your head.

Absolutely nothing of any significance has changed. Not rules, laws or regulations. Not government oversight or external auditing. Nothing. What happened to our financial well-being in the Fall of 2008 can happen again tomorrow. If anything is being done, it is being expertly designed to make

---

[58] A Naked Credit Default Swap is a credit default swap holding that is not backed by enough of the underlying asset. It is comparable to getting automobile insurance without owning a car or taking fire insurance on someone else's house.

A DECADE OF ARMAGEDDON

things worse for Main Street and better for Wall Street. When the tech bubble burst in March 2000, the Federal Reserve dropped dollar bills from helicopters and inflated the housing market. At least that time around, it was obvious where the next bubble would come. In an effort to hide the inflation this time around, the Fed is pumping money into dark corners of finance where it will eventually impact everything everywhere.

First, a quick recap: During 2007, payments on mortgage-backed bonds began failing faster than actual mortgages. Wall Street wrote bonds faster than Main Street needed mortgages – two bankruptcy judges estimated that one-third of the bonds didn't have mortgages backing them.

Meanwhile, insurance companies like AIG were writing credit default swaps even faster – some say there were as many as 15 swaps for every bond (by value). In 2008, AIG was unable to pay off on the credit default swaps (like insurance contracts) they wrote for the Wall Street bankers. The bankers had named themselves beneficiaries and they began cashing in – again – when the whole thing went up in flames.

Then-Secretary of the Treasury Hank Paulson went to Congress and said the world would end if taxpayers did not give him $750 billion to bailout the banks. Congress said, "Sure, why not, you seem like a nice guy" and the Wall Street Bailout was signed into law by George W. Bush on October 1, 2008. In the months that followed, we learned that the Federal Reserve topped off the Wall Street tanks with trillions more dollars – a lot of which went to foreigners and private companies not under their regulatory purview. Since then, Federal Reserve Chairman Ben Bernanke has been dropping dollar bills out of helicopters by buying more and more mortgage un-backed bonds from Wall Street because – well, no one is quite sure why he is doing this.

Eventually, Senator Chris Dodd (D-CT) and Representative Barney Frank (D-MA) got their names attached to a new public law, which President Obama signed on July 21, 2010 – about two years after the bailout – that was supposed to reform Wall Street and protect consumers. Five months after the signing, Sen. Dodd announced his retirement (not long after it was made public that he and several Senators received very friendly terms on a mortgage from sub-prime mortgage bond King Angelo Mozilo of Countrywide). Rep. Frank will not seek reelection in November 2012. Neither Dodd nor Frank planned to be around when the bill was actually effective. You see, a lot of Dodd-Frank was only to require that someone else do studies, write reports and propose rules.[59] Less than half of the rules were required to be written before Rep. Frank leaves office – Dodd left office before any action was required under the public law with his name on it.

Both Dodd and Frank are retiring with full pensions, but the same cannot be said about the public law with their names on it. As of September 21, 2012, about as many Dodd-Frank rules have been proposed as there are mortgages backing those mortgage-bonds the Fed is buying. According to a review by New York law firm Davis Polk[60] (as of September 4, 2012):

Of the 398 total Dodd-Frank rulemaking requirements:
- 131 (32.9%) have final rules
- 135 (33.9%) have proposed rules
- 132 (33.2%) have not yet been proposed

Of the 247 rulemaking deadlines that have passed:
- 145 (61.2%) have been missed
- 31 (13%) have not even had proposals

So far as I was concerned, the only actual success of Dodd-Frank came from an amendment which required the Federal Reserve to disclose exactly to whom they gave the bailout money – information on 21,000 transactions valued at $16 trillion[61] that *Fox News*, *Bloomberg* and *Rolling Stone* Magazine sued to get after the Chairman and Vice Chairman of the Fed refused to reply to questions from Congress. Turns out the Fed officials went from sins of omission to sins of commission – Bloomberg reported in December that they hid billions of dollars in loans[62] from the mandated reports. Despite now knowing that the Federal Reserve is giving money to unregulated companies with no means of retrieving it, the US public – outside of a faithful few Occupy Wall Street protestors still out there – have failed to notice or react. Hence, nothing has changed that would prevent a repeat of the events that precipitated the 2008 bailouts from occurring again tomorrow.

"But wait! That's not all!" as they say in late-night TV infomercials. More than ignoring the law, more than delaying the reforms, Wall Street is now actively

---

[59] For more on this, see *LNL*, especially Appendix 5.
[60] https://www.davispolk.com/insights/resource-centers/dodd-frank-resource-center
[61] https://www.federalreserve.gov/newsevents/reform_transaction.htm
[62] https://www.bloomberg.com/news/articles/2011-11-28/secret-fed-loans-undisclosed-to-congress-gave-banks-13-billion-in-income

working to get new laws written to exempt themselves from Dodd-Frank – which, we thought, was specifically written to reform their activities. On September 19, H.R. 2827 was passed by Congress to exempt[63] from any Dodd–Frank rulemaking the very activity that is bankrupting some US cities and states and counties.[64]

The law they are now exempted from is the one that would require them to accept legal responsibility for putting the best interests of the municipalities and taxpayers first – a blanket requirement for fiduciary duty that already exists but is consistently ignored by the "Wall Street survivors of the financial crisis"[65] as they are called by William D. Cohan, author of the *New York Times* bestseller *House of Cards: A Tale of Hubris and Wretched Excess on Wall Street* (Doubleday, 2009). Cohan emphasizes that bribing clients like Jefferson County is not new – although it seems evident that the problem may be more widespread now than ever before in US history. Jefferson County (AL) may be the best known – their bankruptcy followed on the heels of bribes and billions of dollars' worth of toxic swap deals. The Wall Street banks not only bribe officials to commit municipal taxpayers to financial obligations they can never repay, but they also pay competing banks so they can charge higher fees and interest rates. This breaches the simple trust you are entitled to expect even from used car salesmen (in states with "Lemon Laws") – but no such protection is afforded anyone who must deal with Wall Street.

In the end, we are all required to deal with Wall Street. This is a danger more real, and more imminent, than anything the world may ever have faced. It is as if we have been told that an asteroid the size of Texas is barreling toward Earth and Ben Bernanke hit the button that launched the nuke – that missed. It's still coming[66]. Wall Street remains unreformed, and consumers of financial services remain unprotected.

---

[63] https://www.rollingstone.com/politics/politics-news/wall-street-rolling-back-another-key-piece-of-financial-reform-244669/

[64] Update: H.R. 2827 was not passed by the Senate.

[65] https://www.bloomberg.com/opinion/articles/2012-07-01/how-wall-street-scams-counties-into-bankruptcy

[66] https://finance.yahoo.com/blogs/daily-ticker/roubini-says-perfect-storm-may-clobber-global-economy-143152963.html

High frequency trading is not fast enough

April 4, 2014

A new book by the original yellow journalist of Wall Street, Michael Lewis, initiated global coverage about the flaws of American capitalism. The culprit in Lewis' new book is High Frequency Trading or "HFT." There is no doubt that US capital markets are imperfect. *New York Times* DealBook writer Andrew Sorkin lays the blame at the feet of the stock exchanges[67] of which there are so few remaining that the Federal Trade Commission could label them a monopoly.

Even defenders of HFT, like Tim Worstall at *Forbes*,[68] have to admit that it has risks and problems. It pushes volatility when markets are under stress; programming errors and misuse of software packages have been known to bankrupt the trading companies. The argument in favor of HFT fails when its proponents bring in "free market" economic theories – primarily because the stock market is not "free" in any economic sense. There are a limited number of big players – five banks in the US control 85-95% of trading depending on which market you measure. That is still more like an oligopoly than a competitive market. There are barriers to entry set up by the SEC, the FRB, and state banking and securities commissions. Finally, the transaction costs are enormous. Anyone active in the market knows about trading commissions and management fees. DTCC took in over $1 billion in revenue in 2012 (latest available) and still lost over $25 million. You get the picture – there is no free market argument.

The programs used for high frequency trading are bastardizations of heat transfer dynamic equations. Those underlying equations are based on assumptions. First, they only hold true when time goes to infinity – but trades are executed in finite time. Next, they assume linear behavior – but markets are more like waves than straight lines. Finally, those equations require simultaneity of action. No matter how close the servers are located to the exchange, the computers are not fast enough to read the prices in one market and execute a trade in the next without some lag which violates the assumption.

---

[67] https://archive.nytimes.com/dealbook.nytimes.com/2014/03/31/fault-runs-deep-in-ultrafast-trading/?_php=true&_type=blogs&_php=true&_type=blogs&_php=true&_type=blogs&_r=2

[68] https://www.forbes.com/sites/timworstall/2014/03/31/michael-lewis-is-entirely-wrong-about-high-frequency-trading-hitting-the-little-guy/?sh=7fd1f37b6e04

Richard Bookstaber called it *A Demon of Our Own Design* (Wiley, 2007). The university whiz-kids who built the programs knew they were violating the assumptions, but they were under pressure from their Wall Street bosses so they decided to take the money and run the programs – warts and all.

Trading programs treat capital markets as if one security is indistinguishable from the next – and that defeats the purpose of having capital markets at all. The reason we have these markets is so that entrepreneurs can access capital to fund new opportunities. Instead of letting computer programs decide which stock has the best opportunity for a price change, investors should be deciding which business has the best opportunity for success. The funded opportunities create jobs that pay income to households who turn around and put some of those earnings into savings. Lots of little savings accumulate into a pool of loanable funds that become available to other businesses to fund other opportunities to create more jobs, etc., etc. The goal of high frequency trading is to make money – at any cost. And the cost is the ability of capital markets to serve their primary purpose.

10 steps to financial system stability: lessons not learned

November 20, 2014

Recently, *BloombergView* writer Michael Lewis[69] called attention to tape recordings made by a Federal Reserve Bank of New York bank examiner who was stationed inside Goldman Sachs' offices for several months during 2011-2012. She released the tapes to *This American Life*[70] who aired her story on September 26, 2014. Every media article I've seen on this topic begins with a prelude warning how complicated and hard to follow the story will be. If you picked up this book to read, you are probably several steps ahead in your understanding of the causes and consequences of the Great Financial Crisis.

Central to the theme of the *American Life* story is the release of a 2009 report by Columbia University[71] professor David Beim on why the Federal Reserve – especially the New York office which was supposed to be watching the banks – failed to act to prevent the crisis. Beim listed about a dozen "Lessons Learned"

---

[69] https://www.bloomberg.com/opinion/articles/2014-09-26/the-secret-goldman-sachs-tapes
[70] https://www.thisamericanlife.org/536/the-secret-recordings-of-carmen-segarra
[71] https://www.documentcloud.org/documents/1303305-2009-08-18-frbny-report-on-systemic-risk-and.html

by bank supervisors *after* the financial crisis. In this article, we list the Lessons *not* Learned *before* the financial crisis.[72] These lessons come from decades-old studies of financial regulation from around the world. If any US policy makers had paid attention in school, we would have avoided the global financial collapse of 2008. The United States – which was at the center of that storm – had been preaching these steps to emerging market nations for decades. Unfortunately, they just were not following them for us. In the fall of 1998, those emerging market economies seriously threatened the financial stability of the West. In the fall of 2008, it was the West that brought the threat upon itself and the rest of the world.

Four Policies, Five Tasks and One Idea

Policies not implemented

1. Have private, independent rating agencies: US rating agencies were technically independent because they were not owned by the government. However, with the creation by the Securities and Exchange Commission (SEC) of the "Nationally Recognized Statistical Rating Organization" or NRSRO designation, three big credit rating agencies were the only ones accepted for use to meet regulatory requirements – they were issuing 98% of all credit ratings. This NRSRO designation gave a government imprimatur to selected businesses, creating undue reliance on them by financial markets globally. By 2008, the "NRSRO" term appeared in more than 15 SEC rules and forms (not including those directly used for NRSROs), plus rules in all 50 states. NRSROs are also referenced in 46 Federal Reserve rules and regulations. Even though the SEC sanctioned and required the use of the NRSROs they had no say in the process used to establish the ratings.

Despite even pseudo-independence from the government, the NRSROs were not independent of the financial institutions that paid them to issue credit ratings. The government sanction gave them more power to wield against – or in favor of – the banks and companies they rated. They made money consulting for the same firms, resulting in pressure to rate bonds higher than they should have been rated.

2. Provide some government safety net but not so much that banks are not held accountable: Many banks – and all of the New York Feds "primary dealers" – achieved "too big to fail" status through the Wall Street Bailout Act (Dodd-Frank 2010). A few were allowed to fail in the months leading up to the

---

[72] A more in-depth discussion is available in *LNL*.

passage of the Bailout – most notably Lehman Brothers – in what amounted to the federal government picking winners and losers without accountability. The Federal Deposit Insurance Corporation (FDIC) was nearly bankrupt in late 2009, removing the safety net that protected depositors. The FDIC was so depleted by the epidemic[73] of collapsing banks, they eased the rules on buyers of failing banks, opening the door for hedge funds and private investors to gain access to "bank" status – and the protections that go with it. At the end of September 2009, the FDIC's fund was already negative by $8.2 billion, a decrease of 180% in just three months. FDIC is projected to remain negative over the next several years as they absorb some $75 billion in failure costs just through the end of last year.[74]

At the same time, bailed-out banks, brokers and private corporations received additional financial support from the Federal Reserve in a move unprecedented in US history. Billions of dollars in loans were made to the banks without proper documentation. The lack of transparency in the process used by the Treasury to decide who would receive bailout funds and what the recipients have done with the hundreds of billions of dollars was the subject of a GAO audit we wrote about in 2011 (see p23).

3. Allow very little government ownership and control of national financial assets: Four years after the crisis, the US Treasury still owned more than half of American International Group, Inc., (AIG). AIG was the world's largest insurance company – giving the government ownership of international financial assets, too. The US government took ownership positions in virtually every major financial institution during the bailout, plus some non-banks that had lending arms (like General Motors Acceptance Corporation). The GAO audit of the Fed shows we loaned money to and took ownership stakes in a slew of non-regulated, non-financial businesses like Target and Harley Davidson. The lack of transparency in these transactions is dangerous. Austrian Economist Ludwig von Mises warned decades earlier that market data could be "falsified by the interference of the government," with misleading results for businesses and consumers.

---

[73] https://www.fdic.gov/about/financial-reports/report/2009annualreport/financial.html
[74] See footnote 33 in "Financial Crisis: Too Late to Change?" above for an update on the FDIC's fund.

4. Allow banks to reduce the volatility of returns by offering a wide-range of services: Until the passage of the Dodd-Frank Wall Street Reform and Consumer Protection Act in 2010, banks were restricted to buying securities defined as investment grade by the NRSROs. Given what we now know about these ratings and the actual riskiness of some AAA-rated investments, the requirement actually made bank investments more dangerous. The process followed in the years (even decades) leading up to the collapse of credit markets was not one that would meet the definition of "unrestricted." Although there appeared to be a wide range of activities available to US banks, the restriction on credit ratings would eventually increase volatility by concentrating risk instead of dispersing it. Just because a bank can trade in a particular investment does not mean that they should.

The steps outlined here are a comprehensive program, not a menu of options. There is no sense allowing banks wide latitude to make risky investments if proper supervision and enforcement is not in place. That leads us to the next steps: the necessary tasks for prudent regulation.

Tasks Not Taken
Ten years before the most recent financial crisis (1998), the international financial system had already entered a new era. Speaking at the Western Economics International Association in 2001, Lord John Eatwell said, "The potential economy-wide inefficiency of liberalised financial markets was indisputable." Eatwell had been writing about these problems for decades.

5. Require financial market players to register and be authorized: US regulators failed to act on establishing registration for hedge funds, failed to establish requirements for registering who can issue collateralized mortgage obligations (mortgage-backed securities), and failed to act on loopholes in regulations prohibiting insurance companies like AIG from issuing credit default swaps through subsidiaries – the list goes on. Dodd-Frank established the Financial Stability Oversight Council to designate "Systemically Important Nonbanks" – yet another government imprimatur for unregulated entities. Instead of making sure only authorized businesses perform financial activity they are only making sure those big financial firms are bailed out faster in the future.

6. Provide information, including setting standards, to enhance market transparency: There were no standards for issuing derivatives. Nor for collateralized debt like the mortgage-backed bonds where there was no link back to the homes/real estate that were mortgaged. Because the financial issuers had no standard for reporting changes in ownership to land offices who keep track of liens on homes (usually a county-level property office), probably one-third of the bonds the Fed is buying in their monthly "quantitative easing" purchases are truly worthless.

7. Routinely examine financial institutions to ensure that the regulatory code is obeyed: Without registration and standards, of course, there can be no surveillance by any regulator. Congress admitted that while "most of the largest, most interconnected, and most highly leveraged financial firms in the country were subject to some form of supervision" it proved to be "inadequate and inconsistent." The story described to *This American Life* by Carmen Segarra is not news – it is only one more in a long history of problems.

8. Enforce the code and discipline transgressors: Despite existing rules allowing regulators to prohibit offenders from engaging in future financial activity, only minimal fines have been issued. "Too big to fail" practices allow regulators to "look the other way" on money laundering and other issues that put our national security at risk. According to the Special Inspector General's Quarterly Report (September 2012), the "Treasury [is] selling its investment in banks at a loss, sometimes back to the bank itself" allowing even banks who have the ability to pay to get out of the program for less than they owe. Those responsible for creating the situation that required the Bailout have not been called to discipline. Quite the contrary, many were paid elaborate bonuses at the same time their financial institutions were receiving bailout funds.

9. Develop policies that keep the regulatory code up to date: More than a decade before the crisis, Brooksley Born raised enormous concerns over derivatives in the US – including credit default swaps – during her tenure as chair of the Commodity Futures Trading Commission (1996-1999). Both the SEC and the Federal Reserve Board objected to her ideas. On June 1, 1999, Congress passed legislation prohibiting such regulation, ushering in a long period of growth in the unregulated market. Five years after the financial crisis began, rules are still not implemented. AIG became subject to Federal Reserve supervision only in September 2012 when they bought a savings and loan holding company. By October 2, 2012, AIG had been notified that it is being considered for the "systemically important" designation – the "too big to fail" stamp of approval for everything they do.

One Way Out

Which leads us to one old idea that every student who ever took economics 101 should remember:

10. Create specialized financial institutions: In the context of what we know about the policies and tasks that support financial stability, only one additional factor needs to be considered, and that is an old theory on the economic gains from specialization. In *The Wealth of Nations*, Adam Smith told us that the bigger the market the greater the potential gains from specialization. With equity markets alone reaching a global value of $46 trillion, the potential gains are enormous.

Peter Drucker made this point on specialization in 1993 in his prophetic book *Post-Capitalist Society* (HarperCollins, 2009). While diversification is good for a portfolio of financial investments, in large systems it means "splintering." In a system as large as financial markets, diversification "destroys the performance capacity" of the system. If financial institutions are tools to be used in furthering the efforts of the broad economy, then as Drucker writes "the more specialized its given task, the greater its performance capacity" and therefore the greater the need for specialization.

The rise of the financial sector has been tied to economic expansion throughout our modern business history. The more robust the flow of finance, the more robust the potential for economic activity. Greater efficiency in capital markets can lead directly to greater efficiency in industry.[75] Our economy, our livelihood and our well-being are inextricably related to finance at home and around the world. It is now necessary to return to the basics and recognize the long run value of economically efficient specialization. We are living in the post-capitalist society described by Drucker. US regulators have been overly focused on the financial theory of portfolio diversification, ignoring the economic importance of gains through specialization. Drucker's forecast was accurate:

---

[75] https://www.amazon.com/Mergers-Efficiency-Institute-Financial-Innovation/dp/1402070152/ref=sr_1_2?ie=UTF8&qid=1412003097&sr=8-2&keywords=susanne+trimbath

"Organizations can only do damage to themselves and to society if they tackle tasks that are beyond their specialized competence."

None of this is to say that our long-term failure is guaranteed. What happens next will be an experiment on a grand scale. The Financial Crisis Inquiry Commission concluded: "The captains of finance and the public stewards of our financial system ignored warnings and failed to question, understand, and manage evolving risks within a system essential to the well-being of the American public." Carmen Segarra did not tell us anything new: hopefully what she told us – and what ProPublica[76] and others are writing about it – will help a wider public to understand the problem.

A leaky economy

June 4, 2015

Real gross domestic product is growing at an anemic pace of just 0.2% in the first quarter. (Compare that to the 2.2% increase in the fourth quarter of 2014.) Exports are down, and state and local governments are spending less. The consumer price index is falling in a condition known as *deflation*. Even national defense spending is down. Despite the bad news, consumer spending and home building are rising. Real disposable personal income is roaring ahead at growth rates of 6.2 percent in the first quarter of 2015 and 3.6 percent at the end of 2014. Even the personal savings rate is up (5.5 percent so far this year and 6.2 percent at the end of 2014). These consumer factors are attributed to an increase in government social benefits, though, and not to jobs and economic prosperity. Social Security makes payments[77] to more than 64 million Americans and nearly 3 million more receive federal government retirement checks. More than 20 percent of the US population is basically living on fixed incomes.

The banks also continue to benefit from government largess. The Federal Reserve's Open Market Committee has been holding onto the view[78] "that the current 0 to 1/4 percent target range for the federal funds rate remains appropriate" for more than five years. The stated purpose of offering this free money to banks is to maintain high employment. Although the Fed declines to set a specific goal, they generally believe that the unemployment rate should be around "5.2 percent to 6.0 percent." For perspective, the US unemployment rate averaged 6.15 percent last year (2014); compare that to an average

---

[76] https://www.propublica.org/article/ny-fed-fired-examiner-who-took-on-goldman
[77] https://www.ssa.gov/policy/docs/quickfacts/stat_snapshot/index.html
[78] https://www.federalreserve.gov/newsevents/pressreleases/monetary20150318a.htm

unemployment rate of 4.62 percent in 2007, the year before the financial crisis that was the reason for dropping the federal funds rate to zero.

The offsetting condition that could thwart the Fed's efforts to bolster the economy is high inflation – too much money chasing too few goods. The Fed has a stated goal of keeping inflation at or below 2%. As long as there are enough people working, producing plenty of goods and having money to spend on those goods, inflation should not be a problem. In the 12 months just ended, consumer prices *fell* 0.1 percent. In 2007, prices rose about 2.1 percent. The most recent peak inflation was nearly 6 percent in 2008 and the peak deflation was about -2.4 percent in 2009.

As long as there is some unemployment, wages and prices will not rise too rapidly – if we had more jobs than workers there would be a tendency for employers to bid up wages in trying to attract the best workers. But we are facing the opposite situation. Despite so much Federal Reserve money pouring into banks, the economy is slowing and deflating.[79]

There is worse news. Corporate fixed investment is running higher than the cash being generated by businesses. This was true in 2007 right before the crash and also in 1977 when Hyman Minsky[80] wrote about "the era of the post-World War II financial crunches, squeezes, and debacles." Corporations investing more than they are earning is the kind of event the Fed means when they write: "The Committee currently anticipates that, even after employment and inflation are near mandate-consistent levels, economic conditions may, for some time, warrant" continuing their loose-money policy. They are referring to exactly this condition where an incipient financial crisis can be triggered by increases in interest rates.

Borrowing to Make Ends Meet: Then

$ Billions	2003	2004	2005	2006Q4	2007Q3
Internal funds (US)	732.0	850.7	1061.3	747.2	782.4
Internal funds (total)	831.3	928.4	995.0	935.8	912.3
Fixed investment	747.5	788.3	889.7	1000.6	1057.0

Source: Flow of Funds, Table F.102 Nonfarm Nonfinancial Corporate Business March 6, 2008 (Federal Reserve System, Washington, D.C.)

---

[79] https://www.bea.gov/data/gdp/gross-domestic-product
[80] https://www.levyinstitute.org/about/minsky/

Borrowing to Make Ends Meet: Now

$ Billions	2010	2011	2012	2013Q4	2014Q4
Internal funds (US)	1520.4	1575.2	1569.2	1607.2	1590.2
Internal funds (total)	1676.7	1728.5	1761.0	1844.6	1782.6
Fixed investment	1178.6	1297.4	1415.2	1512.9	1681.0

Source: Flow of Funds, Table F.103 Nonfinancial Corporate business March 12, 2015 (Federal Reserve System, Washington, D.C.)

The reasoning is quite simple: if businesses are investing more than they are making, they must be borrowing to do it. Fixed investment – the construction of things like buildings, plants and factories – has to be paid for before it produces income. That means taking a lot of short-term loans, refinancing them when they come due and sometimes borrowing a little more to cover the interest due on the last loan. If interest rates rise between the planning phase and when the completed project starts generating revenue, that is what triggers Minsky's "incipient" financial crisis. The only difference between the gap in 2007 and the gap in 2014 is that some of it is being made up by foreign earnings – a source that may not hold up[81] as Europe teeters on its third recession in six years, China's growth slows and Japan continues to struggle. The possibility of the Fed raising interest rates is receding further and further into the future.

Falling prices and low interest rates might sound like "good" things. They are not. Low interest rates favor borrowers (and speculators) but it harms the elderly and baby-boomers going onto pensions because it reduces the rate of return they can earn on their safe-harbor investments like savings accounts and government bonds. Speculators in stocks, real estate, collectibles, etc. make out in a low-interest rate environment with deflation. Safe-and-sound investors are more likely to lose because they are more likely to depend on interest for income. This is especially true for households living on fixed incomes who have a low tolerance for investment risk.

This is another *Lesson Not Learned*[82] by US policymakers: Banks and businesses find a way around Fed policy while consumers take it on the chin. We will all be better off when businesses depart from the crony-capitalist cycle of dependency on Federal Reserve handouts. The business and consumer winners

---

[81] https://www.economist.com/leaders/2014/10/23/the-worlds-biggest-economic-problem
[82] See *LNL*

in the post-Capitalist society[83] will be the ones who learn to accumulate human-capital knowledge instead of staking the health of the economy on financial capital. Capital flows are characterized by panics and manias.[84] It will take human knowledge to resolve the financial crises that follow.

The incompetence hypothesis to explain the great recession

July 31, 2015

Seeking an understanding of the Great Recession, I am finding that most of the 2008 financial crisis and its aftermath can be explained by incompetence. In the final weeks of writing a book on the systemic failure in US capital markets,[85] I had to re-read the Securities and Exchange Commission (SEC) Inspector General's 2009 report on their failure to stop Bernard Madoff despite having received credible evidence of a Ponzi scheme. The inspector concluded that it did not have anything to do with the fact that an SEC assistant director was dating (and later married) Madoff's niece; or that Madoff had held Board seats at important financial regulators.[86] Despite eight substantive complaints and two academic journal research reports over 16.5 years about problems with Madoff's investments, Madoff was never caught. In the end he turned himself in, admitting to a $64 billion Ponzi scheme. The inspector's conclusion: incompetence.

In economics, 'interest' – whether it be self-interest or interest group pressure – is the 'safe' explanation for outcomes that are detrimental to the public. If interest group pressure (or even populism) is behind a bad policy decision, then it is not a 'mistake.' Rather, it is an intentional, rational decision as described by Chicago School economist and Nobel laureate George Stigler.[87] However, if a policy decision is the result of bad judgment, then Stigler cannot explain it.

---

[83] Peter F. Drucker, *Post Capitalist Society*, 1993, Hapercollins. Available at https://www.thriftbooks.com/w/post-capitalist-society_peter-f-drucker/279673/#edition=1746168&idiq=1121942

[84] https://en.wikipedia.org/wiki/Charles_P._Kindleberger

[85] See *LNL*

[86] Madoff had a seat on the Board of the International Securities Clearing Corporation, one of the predecessor organizations to the Depository Trust and Clearing Corporation, the world's largest post-trade processing centre. Madoff was also Chairman of the NASDAQ and had seats on the Boards at the National Association of Securities Dealers (now the Financial Industry Regulatory Authority – the same organization that failed to act on a referral letter from the SEC to stop R. Allen Stanford's Ponzi scheme).

[87] https://wiki.mises.org/wiki/Regulatory_capture

Brazilian economist Luiz Carlos Bresser-Pereira[88] suggests that the relevant variable in this case is incompetence. Incompetence is an independent explanatory variable; it cannot be explained in rational or historical terms.

Incompetence arises from three sources: 1) ignorance, 2) arrogance, or 3) fear. Policy advisors and regulators may be guilty of applying theories second-hand but with great authority and self-confidence. They may be ignorant of the complexities of economic theory, and they may apply abstract economic theories inappropriately to specific policy problems. For example, they allowed banks to engage in a wide range of investments under the financial theory of 'diversification.' That theory works for portfolios but not for businesses, which need to specialize to realize the gains from their comparative advantage. Financially derived theories like this were applied automatically, transformed into a series of clichés.

'Diversification' in a portfolio of financial investments lets you increase the returns while reducing the risk. But in business it means 'splintering' which destroys performance capacity and increases risk. Financial institutions are tools to be used in furthering the efforts of the broad economy: the more specialized financial institutions become, the greater their performance capacity. Increased productivity from specialization comes with better quality as businesses become more adept at their specific products and services. The differences in natural aptitudes and abilities produce economic benefits when tasks are matched to capabilities. The more experience a worker has at performing a task, the more efficient they become in doing their work. As management guru Peter Drucker wrote: 'Organizations can only do damage to themselves and to society if they tackle tasks that are beyond their specialized competence.'

An example of an economic theory applied arrogantly is Washington's constant fawning over 'free market solutions' when the rules, regulations and court decisions covering capital markets fill the bookshelves of law offices around the world. There is no such thing as a free market – no economist of value believes that a perfectly competitive market exists. The Wall Street Bailout is a good example of the third source of incompetence – fear. Consider this description of the exchange between Treasury Secretary Henry Paulson, Federal Reserve

---

[88] https://www.bresserpereira.org.br/index.php/academic-papers/7615-988

Chairman Ben Bernanke and the senior legislators from the House and Senate on Thursday, September 18, 2008: [89]

> **Sen. CHRISTOPHER DODD:** Sitting in that room with Hank Paulson saying to us in very measured tones, no hyperbole, no excessive adjectives, that, "Unless you act, the financial system of this country and the world will melt down in a matter of days."

> **JOE NOCERA:** Bernanke said, "If we don't do this tomorrow, we won't have an economy on Monday."

> **Sen. CHRISTOPHER DODD:** There was literally a pause in that room where the oxygen left.

Regardless of the source of the incompetence, the visible results are 1) failure to take correct strategic policy decisions, and 2) failure to adopt well-designed reforms.

Policy decisions are the day-to-day management decisions that usually produce immediate results. In monetary policy, for example, these would be interest rate decisions. Interest rate policy decisions need to be made at the right time and to move rates in the right direction.

Reforms produce medium-term outcomes that may or may not require legislative approval. The Dodd-Frank Act, which was supposed to reform Wall Street and protect Main Street, in reality created very little change but suggested that financial regulators reform their own rules. Poor reforms may be the result of incompetent designs and not just pressure from interest groups, although this also happens.

Bresser-Pereira's analysis offers one more alternative explanation for the cause of bad policy and reforms. Between interest and incompetence lies 'confidence building.' It is simply doing what is expected in an effort to gain the confidence of financial supporters. If we substitute "Goldman Sachs" for "United States" and "Wall Street" for "developed countries" in this quote from Bresser-Pereira, then his description of 'confidence building' is as true of Washington, D.C. as it is of Brazil:

> 'They do not limit themselves to seeing the United States and, more broadly, the developed countries, as richer and more powerful nations, whose political institutions and scientific and

---

[89] Source: Inside the Meltdown, *Frontline*, February 17, 2009, WGBH Educational Foundation, Boston.
https://www.pbs.org/wgbh/pages/frontline/meltdown/etc/script.html

technological development should be imitated. No, they see the elites in the developed countries both as the source of truth and as natural leaders to be followed. This subordinate internationalism ideology, already called 'colonial inferiority complex' and *entreguismo*[90], is as detrimental to a country as old-time nationalism. What I am singling out as a major source of incompetent macroeconomic policies is the uncritical adoption of developed countries' recommendations.'

If we say that bad policy decisions are always rational, motivated by interest, then we must conclude that policymakers are 'dishonest, protecting their own interest or those of their constituencies rather than the public interest' (Bresser-Pereira). If this view were always true, then the world would look more like communist Russia in 1980 than the way it does today. How would entrepreneurs and consumers have financed not only the invention but the proliferation of microchips, cell phones, and personal computers that have made the world safer and easier to navigate; how would they have discovered and made widely available artificial hearts, HIV medications and targeted cancer therapies? Since 1981, the number of poor people in the world declined for the first time in history, by 375 million. Global life expectancy was 68 in 2014, up from 61 in 1980; infant mortality is down to 49.4 per 1,000 live births in 2014 from 80 in 1980. Yet as a result of the havoc wrecked upon the global economy in 2008 by incompetent regulators, policy makers and bankers, global unemployment grew from 20 to 50 million while falling incomes combined with rising food prices to raise the number of undernourished people[91] in the world by 11 percent.

A solution, from this perspective, lies in cleaning house of the incompetent staff from Washington to Wall Street and improving recruiting methods to build competence for the future.

For more information:
Luiz Carlos Bresser-Pereira, Latin America's quasi-stagnation, in A *Post Keynesian Perspective on 21st Century Economic Problems* (2002), Elgar, UK.

The World Factbook 2013-14. Washington, DC: Central Intelligence Agency, 2013. https://www.cia.gov/the-world-factbook/[92]

---

[90] Brazilian Portuguese roughly translated as 'appeasement' or 'submission.'
[91] http://www.ilo.org/global/statistics-and-databases/lang--en/index.htm
[92] https://www.cia.gov/the-world-factbook/

7. Public Reaction

Public reaction in the United States to the revelations of the Wall Street bailout were subdued compared to other countries. The Landmark Narrative[1] that developed and was generally accepted by Americans went something like this: people bought houses they couldn't afford by using adjustable-rate mortgages, no-money-down and other schemes offered by banks. When the favorable terms ran out – as they always did because they came with one time limit or another – those homebuyers couldn't afford to keep up their mortgage payments. As they stopped paying their mortgages, they not only caused their mortgage bank to slide toward bankruptcy, but they also caused all those "sliced-and-diced" mortgage-backed bonds to fail, too. To this day, I continue to hear people talk about the cause of the Financial Crisis as the failure of homeowners to pay their mortgages. If that was your thought when you started reading this collection of essays, my wish is that I have opened your eyes to the false utopia being offered by Wall Street and the businesses and governments they support.

McClatchy Medill: real $timulating news

August 23, 2010

I saw a story in the *Omaha World Herald* last week with the title: "Benefits of stimulus bill spread unevenly over US". As I read through it, I became increasingly impressed. The journalists start off by laying out who said what about the benefits of stimulus spending. They provide quotes and facts from the White House, the Congressional Budget Office, and Joe Biden's spokesperson. They include viewpoints and analysis from professors at Berkeley, Harvard, George Mason and the editor of the *Journal of Economic Perspectives*. They even talked it over with the National Association of State Auditors, Comptrollers and Treasurers – the people in charge of receiving and accounting for the billions of dollars represented by the American Recovery and Reinvestment Act. What impressed me most, though, was that they did their own research – not just reporting what the Administration or Congress told them was happening or was supposed to be happening.

"Spending the Stimulus" was a website put together by McClatchy Newspapers and the Medill News Service to track what was promised and what was done, how much was actually spent and where and on what the stimulus billions were spent.[2] I was intrigued by their finding that "much of the stimulus money has

---

[1] *LNL*, p125

[2] The McClatchy-Medill website is no longer available. The Congressional Budget Office provides a summary through 2011: https://www.cbo.gov/publication/42682

yet to go out the door" eighteen months after the emergency, gotta-fix-it-now legislation was passed. After Congress approved $750 billion for the Wall Street Bailout in October 2008, I'm pretty sure all *that* money was out the door before December!

Even more intriguing is the finding that the money was spread around rather unevenly. Beyond the infantile "Why Did North Dakota got More Than Me?" rhetoric going around among the states (by the way, the McClatchy-Medill per-capita graphic shows that most of New England got more than North Dakota), is the more interesting discussion of where would the spending be most stimulating. Transportation money was directed to the states under the "usual formula" despite the fact that the Great Recession didn't follow a formula as it spread throughout the economy. The result: "researchers were unable to find any relationship between unemployment in a given area and the amount of stimulus dollars spent there." If unemployment is higher in some areas than in others, it wasn't for lack of stimulus spending.

Maybe this is a good thing. Instead of focusing on the political necessity of justifying billions of dollars to pull the country out of the Great Recession (unlike the complete lack of justification for bailing out Wall Street), the McClatchy-Medill report raises more interesting points. Is it "rewarding failure" to send more money to the states that most failed to develop diversified economies that are resilient to downturns? Would we be throwing good money after bad to provide more spending for states that didn't manage the cash inflow from the rapid rise in property taxes that came with rapidly rising home prices? Finally, did we really want a central government to make every decision – county by county – about where and on what the money would be spent?

Occupy Wall Street: about d@%& time!

November 6, 2011

"Privileged people don't march and protest; their world is safe and clean and governed by laws designed to keep them happy. I had never taken to the streets before; why bother? And for the first block or two I felt odd, walking in a mass of people, holding a stick with a placard..."

Michael Brock in John Grisham's *The Street Lawyer* (Doubleday, 1998).

I've been waiting for three years for Americans to get out in the street and protest the actions that created the Financial Crisis that sparked the Great Contraction. As ng.com frequent commenter Richard Reep[3] put it back at the beginning: "What happened to people's outrage? Where are the torch-bearing citizens marching on Washington?" If some third-world leader had pillaged the national treasury on their way out of town the way Hank Paulson did when he convinced Congress to spend $750 billion to bailout the Wall Street banks – with the full and enthusiastic support of New York Fed chief and now Treasury Secretary Timothy Geithner – there would be angry mobs, riots and possibly UN Peacekeepers.

Three years later, all we can muster is a sort of hippy sit-in – but I'll take it! It's better than letting it run over us, drip-by-drip, until there is no middle in our increasingly bifurcated economy.

Let me summarize what 99% of Americans should protest. It started in the early 2000s with good intentioned policies directed toward leveling the playing field by re-designing consumer credit ratings to allow more Americans to own homes. The move was embraced by Mike Milken and his followers as a way to further the cause of The Democratization of Capital[4] – oddly enough, an idea born out of the outrage of the Watts Riots of August 1965.

Republicans and Democrats alike joined in the movement and a great boom in home prices was born. Expanding homeownership opportunities, especially for minorities, was a fundamental aim of the Bush Administration's housing policy, one strongly supported by Democrats in Congress. Then everyone got greedy,[5]

---

[3] http://www.newgeography.com/users/rreep

[4] https://www.mikemilken.com/articles.taf?page=9

[5] https://www.rollingstone.com/politics/politics-news/mike-bloombergs-marie-antoinette-moment-100988/

including wanna-be real estate moguls who started flipping houses instead of working for their living.

Banks that were writing mortgages soon turned to securitization – bundling mortgages into bonds called mortgage-backed securities – so they could use the proceeds to lend more money to subprime borrowers. The banks were collecting fees at every step. They charged fees for making the mortgage loan and for putting together the bond deal; then they charged commissions for trading the bonds. The interest paid on the bonds was high because the interest charged on the mortgages was high – after all, these were less-than-credit worthy borrowers by traditional standards. The banks wanted to be compensated for taking the risk – even though they were selling the risk to someone else. It was all about making money on money and eventually demand overtook supply. But that didn't stop Brother Banker!

According to a story on PBS,[6] managers at Standard & Poor's credit rating agency were pressured to give mortgage bonds triple-A ratings in the pursuit of ever higher fees. In essence, the banks paid credit rating agencies to get triple-A ratings for their mortgage bonds so that insurance company and pension fund money could be added to the scheme. Insurance companies and pension funds are highly regulated in order to protect investors who rely on them for compensation in disasters and retirement.

If the bank couldn't get the top credit rating for some mortgage bonds, they turned to selling an unregulated kind of insurance called Credit Default Swaps. The swaps became so popular that people who didn't even own the bonds were buying the swaps. Eventually, there were more credit default swaps than there were bonds – and the banks were making fees on top of fees with no incentive to stop.[7] In the end, there was more money to be made in mortgage defaults than mortgage payoffs and some banks even stopped taking mortgage payments[8] to force the defaults. It was a little like the failing businessman who

---

[6] Originally aired on 21 November 2008. *NOW* on PBS, Season 4, Episode 4, "Credit and Credibility." *NOW* last aired in April 2010.

[7] According to the Bank of International Settlement, as of 30 June 2021, there were $610 trillion OTC credit derivatives outstanding with less than $3 trillion of credit exposure. It is difficult to compare recent numbers to 2008 because today's credit derivatives market includes foreign exchange, interest rate, equity-linked and commodity derivatives. Credit default swaps make up just 4 percent of the market.

[8] https://vvstaging.villagevoice.com/2008/11/05/wall-streetwalkers-the-sleazy-lehman-brothers-subsidiary/

burns down his own shop because he can make more on the insurance than he can trying to sell it.

When the swaps came due, companies like AIG collapsed under the pressure of the payments – and American taxpayers were left holding the bag. Using your insurance and pension benefits to create their bonfire,[9] Wall Street staged a weenie-roast! Two years ago, you could have purchased all the common stock of Lennar Homebuilders for $1.2 billion – but if they went bankrupt you could collect $40 billion on the swaps. (The European Union fixed this problem[10] in their sovereign debt markets – the US did not.) Like any Ponzi scheme, this one also required that "new money" continue to flow in so that the early investors could receive payouts – hence the need for Wall Street to get your retirement benefit money invested in these things. When Uncle Sam took 80% ownership of AIG in Hank Paulson's bailout scheme, again approved by our current administration's financial geniuses, the US Treasury in combination with the Federal Reserve provided an unlimited source of new money. *THAT* is what you should be protesting about today because it can – and probably will – happen again.[11]

Critics of the protesters like to equate Wall Street with all the companies that create jobs. This ignores how the stock market works. The only time that a company gets money from its stock is in the initial public offering. Those shares are mostly sold to syndicates, underwriters, and primary dealers, not the general public. What happens day in and day out on Wall Street is simply stirring the pot. When the company's stock goes up, it is the next seller and his broker that make money, not the company. The stock market should have everything to do with jobs. When households have excess earnings – more money than they need for their expenses – they make savings deposits or investments in the stock market through banks. Banks channel savings from households to entrepreneurs and businesses. Entrepreneurs use the money to create new businesses which employ more people, thus increasing the earnings that households have available for savings and investment, which would bring

---

[9] Referring to Tom Wolfe, *Bonfire of Vanities (Bantom, 1988).*

[10] https://www.reuters.com/article/uk-eu-cds-agreement-idUKTRE79H5ZV20111018

[11] In 2023, the Federal Reserve loaned money to the Federal Deposit Insurance Corporation (FDIC) to pay off insured and uninsured deposits when Silicon Valley Bank and Signature Bank failed. Legally, the FDIC should have gone to the Treasury for that loan but the Treasury was up against the debt limit and did not have the money.

the process fully around the virtuous circle. But Wall Street doesn't exactly do that anymore. It just makes jobs for Wall Street.

The other argument is that the problem isn't Wall Street, it's the government. Anyone who thinks that only one or the other is to blame doesn't understand how politics is financed.[12] According to the MAPLight.org's analysis, Senator Barack Obama's presidential campaign received more money in 2007-2008 from Wall Street than anyone else, but it was only $2 million more than the $22,108,926 that went to Senator John McCain's presidential campaign.

Blame the government and blame the Wall Street banks that sponsor their political campaigns – they are blaming each other anyway.[13] The occupy protestors - with the possible exception of the violent black band anarchists - are not the perpetrators we need to put in handcuffs.

The sad fact is that nothing in Washington, D.C. or Wall Street, NYC has changed since that day in September 2008 when Hank Paulson told Congress that the world would end if they didn't give him $750 billion to spread around Wall Street. For many people, like Michael Brock, it takes a life-changing event to make you look at the truth all around you. Fixing our broken financial markets requires systemic reform on a grand scale.

I think a lot of people who joined the 2008 tea parties – me included – thought we were mounting a petition against bank bailouts and the misuse of public funds. The US Government Accountability Office audit of the Federal Reserve, released in July 2011,[14] proves that the petition failed. Call your Representative, write to your Senator, and show up for the #Occupy or Tea Party events in your city. Like Michael Brock, you may find yourself savoring the exercise of civil protest.

---

[12] "MAPLight.org's research department revealed that each House member voting 'Yes' on the Financial Bailout received, on average, 41% more money, or $213,766, from Banks and Securities Firms than those voting 'No, $152,125." Financial Bailout Bill Friday, October 3, House Vote by Pamela Behrsin, 7 October 2008.

[13] https://news.yahoo.com/bloomberg-tells-occupy-wall-streeters-blame-congress-173212510.html

[14] https://www.gao.gov/products/gao-11-696

Epilogue

At the end of the Introduction, I suggested an equivalence between the global "Occupy" movements of 2008 and the meme-stock movements of 2020. What started in Reddit chat rooms eventually became the subject of Congressional Hearings and SEC regulatory action. The Occupy movements protested against "the 1%"; the Reddit users claimed, "We are the 99%." They called themselves "Apes". It was explained to me in 2021 as a way to connect the common denominator among all the Reddit investors. Since then, I've read and heard multiple versions of how the moniker got started and what it means. It turns out there is no hive-mind on Reddit. With or without their approval, the "Ape" moniker stuck. Media stories often refer to the moniker as an homage to the movie *Planet of the Apes*. They equate the revenge the movie Apes took against humans with the revenge the investor Apes wanted to take against Wall Street.

The reason I shook my head and muttered "here we go again" when I heard news about GameStop in early 2021 is because the idea that a household investor could buy one stock, hold it for a short time, and then retire on the earning was exactly what I saw happen over and over again in the early 2000s. The idea spreading on social media of a "Mother of All Short Squeezes" (MOASS) is exactly what investors in companies like Overstock and Taser expected would happen for them. When their dream retirement didn't come true, in the years leading up to the GFC, I was approached by many investors, companies and their lawyers asking that same question: "What the heck just happened to us?!?" I quickly realized that many of the meme-stock Apes were heading in the same direction. I posted on social media: "If I had a nickel for every time I heard an investor say they were going to stick it to the short sellers, I could buy Cher's house in Malibu, plus a helicopter and hire a full-time pilot to fly me out for grocery shopping!"

Back in the early 2000s they all had theories about "naked short selling"; some were disappointed when I told them that settlement failures (fails-to-deliver or FTDs) were their real problem – and that the regulators knew about it, did little or nothing to stop it and even thought it was "good for market liquidity". Most decided to go on believing what they believed by ignoring the facts I presented. The same thing happened with many of the Apes in 2021.

In the 2000s, I appeared in documentaries and news programs in the years around the GFC, including Bloomberg's 2007 Emmy® Award-nominated special report "Phantom Shares", *Stock Shock: The Short Selling of the American Dream* (2009, Mohr productions) and *The Wall Street Conspiracy* (2012, Brown Saddle Films and Hop On Films). In his 2008 pamphlet on the creation of the Depository Trust Company (DTC), William "Bill" Dentzer called the trade settlement system "the unglamourous 'plumbing' that links Wall Street back offices and the events that occur after the securities trade – the process known as trade clearance and settlement through which buyers gain ownership of securities and sellers receive payments" (YBK Publishers, New York).[1] In *Stock Shock* I used Bill's terminology to help the producer understand why no one had heard about my work in this area until after the price of their favorite stock collapsed: "We're the plumbers of Wall Street. And nobody wants to hear what the plumber has to say until the sh#! backs up in the living room!"

Well, in January 2021, the GameStop sh#! backed up into the living rooms of household investors and suddenly hundreds of thousands of them wanted to hear what this plumber had to say. Thanks to a review by investigative journalist Lucy Komisar, the meme-stock Reddit users found my book *Naked, Short and Greedy: Wall Street's Failure to Deliver* ("NSG", 2020, Spiramus Press). I was invited to do a few of the Ask-Me-Anything ("AMA") podcasts. My first experience turned out to be more "ask me anything about what the host wrote" – the host ignored hundreds of questions submitted by Reddit users and focused only on what he had written and posted. After that, I turned down most podcast invitations. I participated in the documentary *Apes Together Strong* (2023, Finley and Quinn Mulligan), and one episode of the HBO series *Gaming Wall Street* (2022, Tobias Deml). I did on-camera interviews for a few other documentaries but, as is often the case, ended up on the cutting room floor.

I found more in common about the two movements – Occupy and Ape, separated by more than a decade – than I found differences. Some of the same lawyers and industry service providers resurfaced to collect fees from the CEOs of more public companies. Those CEOs cried "naked short sellers" in 2021 just the same as the CEOs did in the early 2000s, just the same as the CEO of Lehman Brothers did when called before Congress in 2009. My response was the same all three times: short sales, stock lending and fails-to-deliver (called "settlement failures" in Europe) were their real problems.

---

[1] Bill was still Chair and CEO when I was hired at DTC in 1987. I got to sit in meetings and work with him several times. Shortly after I arrived, he gave a sort of pep talk to the operations staff. I will always remember his remark: "at DTC 'trust' is our middle name."

When investors and CEOs decried "naked short sellers" as the villains in the early 2000s, they got Regulation SHO (RegSHO) from the Securities and Exchange Commission. RegSHO explicitly made it illegal to naked short sell any stock – and then promptly added multiple exceptions. It didn't really matter – the regulation had no teeth for enforcement anyway. If it had, maybe the Apes wouldn't have seen the same problems recur in 2021.

Wall Street continues to devise new strategies to reap rewards on the backs of middle-income Americans. After the housing market collapsed in 2008, the private equity funds went into action. In some areas, they bought entire neighborhoods of single-family homes and turned them into rentals. There was a resurgence of "Contract-for-Deed," a predatory financial arrangement that puts all the usual homeowner responsibilities on the occupant but does not come with a build-up in home equity value. Its use in predominantly black neighborhoods in 1960s Chicago laid the groundwork for the Home Mortgage Disclosure Act of 1975 and the Community Reinvestment Act of 1977.

In Oakland (CA), between January 2007 and October 2011, over 40 percent of the more than 10,000 homes that went into foreclosure were purchased – with cash – by private real estate investors. The list goes on and on. For Wall Street, the coronavirus pandemic was just another money-making opportunity. Large, well-capitalized private-equity firms outbid individual buyers for single-family homes – pushing prices up and owner-occupied housing rates down. By 2022, twenty corporate landlords owned more than 40,000 single-family homes in North Carolina, including 25,000 just in the Charlotte area. Around Phoenix, Arizona, a company owned by private equity firm Blackstone Group went on a $10 billion buying spree in 2020, sucking up $150 million worth of houses every week, sparking bidding wars as they purchased entire blocks of homes. Jacksonville and Miami, Florida, were also targets for private equity firms' home buying sprees. The American Dream of homeownership took another hit in the post-GFC world as corporations turned whole neighborhoods into rentals. As usual, Congress held hearings and drafted legislation that died a quiet death in Committee: H.R.9246 *Stop Wall Street Landlords Act of 2022* was introduced by Representative Ro Khanna (D-CA) on October 28, 2022 and referred to committee the same day. Too little too late: the industry lobbyist National Rental Home Council was formed in 2014. Single family home rentals grew 30 percent from 2007 to 2015.

The 2021 GameStop (GME) saga presents a recent example of more Congressional hearings designed to close the barn door after the horses have bolted. GME is an international retailer of video games, consumer electronics and gaming merchandise, based in Texas. As the price of its stock rose rapidly, in January 2021 several brokers refused to let household investors buy more shares through their online accounts. It was obvious to the informed observer that they did this because they had already sold more shares than they could deliver. That triggered a call from DTCC for additional cash deposits to cover the mounting risk created by their failure-to-deliver shares for settlement. Rather than enforce the existing rules, which required additional cash deposits to offset the potential risk, DTCC waived the rule for Robinhood Securities, LLC. The US House Committee on Financial Services held hearings and issued a report Game Stopped: How the Meme Stock Market Event Exposed Troubling Business Practices, Inadequate Risk Management, and the Need for Legislative and Regulatory Reform. The report listed six bills drafted for discussion; only three were introduced for consideration by the 117th Congress. All were promptly referred to committee ... & never returned.

Importantly, the Committee found that "DTCC lacks detailed, written policies and procedures for waiver or modification of a 'disincentive' charge it calculates for brokers that are deemed to be undercapitalized and has regularly waived such charges during periods of acute volatility". In other words, DTCC picked winners and losers without consideration for limiting the adverse incentive effects. It was a replay of what the government did in 2008.

We saw US Treasury and Federal Reserve bend the rules again to bailout *all* the depositors at Silicon Valley Bank (SVB) and Signature Bank in 2023. The Federal Deposit Insurance Corporation (FDIC) is required to make good on deposits up to a limit (about $250,000 per account). In 2023, Washington decided to make good on ALL deposits, but the FDIC didn't have enough money to cover them all. FDIC should have gone to Treasury for a loan. However, Treasury was having its own problems – Congress was debating whether to lift the debt ceiling or default on paying the federal government's bills (including interest payments on outstanding debt). So, FDIC got the money from the Federal Reserve: bending the rules.

As I wrote in the Introduction: "Regulators failed to learn the lessons of previous crises, lessons about prudent regulation, strict enforcement and the disciplinary actions that remove the incentive for Wall Street to do it all again." *Lessons Not Learned* – and here we go again!

Appendix 1: Percentage Change in Total Workforce and Number of Unemployed, by State

Table for "Why homeownership is falling – despite lower prices: look to the job market" page 57

State	% change in total workforce	% change in number of unemployed	Unemployment rate as of Dec. 2008
Michigan	-1.9%	39.7%	10.6%
Rhode Island	-1.8%	88.1%	10.0%
Alabama	-1.8%	75.3%	6.7%
Illinois	-1.5%	40.3%	7.6%
West Virginia	-1.3%	4.6%	4.9%
Mississippi	-1.1%	25.6%	8.0%
Missouri	-0.8%	37.6%	7.3%
Tennessee	-0.4%	59.4%	7.9%
Ohio	-0.3%	33.8%	7.8%
Arkansas	-0.1%	12.7%	6.2%
New Hampshire	-0.1%	33.6%	4.6%
Utah	-0.1%	51.8%	4.3%
Delaware	0.0%	75.3%	6.2%
Wisconsin	0.1%	27.8%	6.2%
Maryland	0.1%	63.4%	5.8%
Kentucky	0.3%	48.4%	7.8%
Iowa	0.3%	20.7%	4.6%
Massachusetts	0.4%	61.1%	6.9%
Idaho	0.4%	142.6%	6.4%
Colorado	0.4%	53.8%	6.1%
Georgia	0.5%	78.3%	8.1%
Montana	0.5%	68.9%	5.4%
Maine	0.6%	44.5%	7.0%
Minnesota	0.6%	47.6%	6.9%
South Dakota	0.6%	35.4%	3.9%
North Carolina	0.7%	87.4%	8.7%
Indiana	0.7%	86.0%	8.2%
Connecticut	0.7%	48.0%	7.1%

State	% change in total workforce	% change in number of unemployed	Unemployment rate as of Dec. 2008
Florida	0.8%	80.9%	8.1%
New York	1.0%	51.9%	7.0%
North Dakota	1.0%	8.5%	3.5%
Vermont	1.1%	66.9%	6.4%
Nebraska	1.2%	46.0%	4.0%
Wyoming	1.3%	12.4%	3.4%
New York City	1.4%	47.2%	7.4%
Kansas	1.5%	27.4%	5.2%
South Carolina	1.6%	55.3%	9.5%
California	1.8%	60.4%	9.3%
Virginia	1.8%	69.2%	5.4%
New Jersey	1.9%	72.8%	7.1%
Hawaii	2.0%	82.9%	5.5%
Oklahoma	2.1%	21.7%	4.9%
Louisiana	2.2%	52.6%	5.9%
New Mexico	2.2%	56.2%	4.9%
Alaska	2.4%	22.4%	7.5%
Pennsylvania	2.4%	55.7%	6.7%
Washington	2.6%	60.0%	7.1%
Texas	2.6%	45.9%	6.0%
Oregon	2.8%	70.4%	9.0%
Arizona	3.4%	72.0%	6.9%
Nevada	4.9%	84.6%	9.1%
Average	**0.8%**	**53.2%**	**6.7%**
Median	**0.7%**	**52.6%**	**6.9%**

Source: US Bureau of Labor Statistics.

Appendix 2: Potential Derivatives Pay-Off

Table for "Burnin' down the house! Part Two: Wall Street has a weenie roast with your 401k", page 94

Entity	Derivatives Outstanding	Market Value or Public Debt	Difference
Bank of America Corporation	118,689,745,334	31,558,840,000	87,130,905,334
GMAC Llc	83,556,419,908	4,690,000	83,551,729,908
Morgan Stanley	84,271,180,804	24,186,940,000	60,084,240,804
Deutsche Bank Aktiengesellschaft	71,011,177,628	18,510,000,000	52,501,177,628
Citigroup Inc.	61,875,137,002	12,760,000,000	49,115,137,002
American International Group (AIG)	47,393,950,401	2,230,000,000	45,163,950,401
General Motors Corporation	43,373,996,836	1,540,000,000	41,833,996,836
Centex Corporation	41,027,349,092	856,760,000	40,170,589,092
Lennar Corporation	40,426,782,677	1,260,000,000	39,166,782,677
Ambac Assurance Corporation	36,835,358,941	189,580,000	36,645,778,941
Pulte Homes, Inc.	38,364,111,999	2,460,000,000	35,904,111,999
Ford Motor Company	39,618,004,718	5,030,000,000	34,588,004,718
The Goldman Sachs Group, Inc.	80,849,691,288	46,624,340,000	34,225,351,288
Barclays Bank Plc	44,579,007,183	11,160,000,000	33,419,007,183
Whirlpool Corporation	32,665,900,751	1,850,000,000	30,815,900,751
CBS Corporation	32,484,932,800	2,600,000,000	29,884,932,800
Southwest Airlines Co.	33,766,673,423	4,090,000,000	29,676,673,423
Toll Brothers, Inc.	27,532,256,817	2,590,000,000	24,942,256,817
Sprint Nextel Corporation	33,852,494,934	10,230,000,000	23,622,494,934
Autozone, Inc.	31,489,303,582	8,700,000,000	22,789,303,582
D.R. Horton, Inc.	19,889,587,401	2,540,000,000	17,349,587,401
Alcoa Inc.	20,554,123,223	4,620,000,000	15,934,123,223
American Express Company	28,098,626,953	13,970,000,000	14,128,626,953
K. Hovnanian Enterprises, Inc.	9,458,710,459	70,220,000	9,388,490,459
Aetna Inc.	15,056,041,259	9,720,000,000	5,336,041,259
Time Warner Inc.	33,530,285,093	29,240,000,000	4,290,285,093

Entity	Derivatives Outstanding	Market Value or Public Debt	Difference
Wells Fargo & Company	47,902,948,043	58,060,000,000	-10,157,051,957
JP Morgan Chase &Co.	61,250,536,812	86,770,000,000	-25,519,463,188
Russian Federation	102,631,256,656	151,000,000,000	-48,368,743,344
Abbott Laboratories	5,273,779,532	68,720,000,000	-63,446,220,468
Republic of Turkey	169,668,377,905	243,747,000,000	-74,078,622,095
Republic of Italy	157,609,796,730	248,773,000,000	-91,163,203,270
Berkshire Hathaway Inc.	18,409,990,929	126,860,000,000	-108,450,009,071
United Mexican States	76,677,172,011	320,334,000,000	-243,656,827,989
Federative Republic of Brazil	113,249,393,554	814,000,000,000	-700,750,606,446

Derivatives outstanding are data made available by the Depository Trust and Clearing Corporation for publicly traded credit default contracts deposited with them. Market value is for public companies generally in early March 2009; public debt is for countries generally from year-end 2008. Difference is author's calculation. The average derivatives outstanding for entities with positive differences are 22 times the value of the entity (excluding GMAC as an outlier with a multiplier of 17,816).

Appendix 3: Sovereigns named in most credit default protection*

Table for "The next global financial crisis: public debt", page 124

Sovereign Entity	GDP (2008)	Share World GDP (est)	Public Debt (current)	Debt % GDP
Japan	$ 4,348,000,000,000	8.6%	$ 7,408,992,000,000	170.4%
Republic of Italy	$ 1,821,000,000,000	3.4%	$ 1,888,377,000,000	103.7%
Hellenic Republic (Greece)	$ 343,600,000,000	0.4%	$ 309,583,600,000	90.1%
Kingdom of Belgium	$ 390,500,000,000	0.6%	$ 315,524,000,000	80.8%
State of Israel	$ 200,700,000,000	0.4%	$ 151,929,900,000	75.7%
Republic of Hungary	$ 205,700,000,000	0.3%	$ 151,806,600,000	73.8%
French Republic	$ 2,097,000,000,000	3.8%	$ 1,404,990,000,000	67.0%
Portuguese Republic	$ 237,300,000,000	0.4%	$ 152,346,600,000	64.2%
Federal Republic of Germany	$ 2,863,000,000,000	4.7%	$ 1,792,238,000,000	62.6%
United States of America	$ 14,290,000,000,000	21.4%	$ 8,688,320,000,000	60.8%
Republic of Austria	$ 325,000,000,000	0.5%	$ 191,100,000,000	58.8%
Republic of The Philippines	$ 320,600,000,000	0.5%	$ 181,139,000,000	56.5%
Kingdom of Norway	$ 256,500,000,000	0.3%	$ 133,380,000,000	52.0%
Argentine Republic	$ 575,600,000,000	0.8%	$ 293,556,000,000	51.0%
Republic of Croatia	$ 73,360,000,000	0.1%	$ 35,873,040,000	48.9%
Republic of Colombia	$ 399,400,000,000	0.6%	$ 191,712,000,000	48.0%
United Kingdom of Great Britain	$ 2,231,000,000,000	3.5%	$ 1,053,032,000,000	47.2%

Sovereign Entity	GDP (2008)	Share World GDP (est)	Public Debt (current)	Debt % GDP
and Northern Ireland				
Republic of Panama	$ 38,490,000,000	0.0%	$ 17,859,360,000	46.4%
Kingdom of The Netherlands	$ 670,200,000,000	0.3%	$ 288,186,000,000	43.0%
Malaysia	$ 386,600,000,000	0.3%	$ 165,078,200,000	42.7%
Kingdom of Thailand	$ 553,400,000,000	0.9%	$ 232,428,000,000	42.0%
Republic of Poland	$ 667,400,000,000	0.7%	$ 277,638,400,000	41.6%
Federative Republic of Brazil	$ 1,990,000,000,000	2.7%	$ 809,930,000,000	40.7%
Socialist Republic of Vietnam	$ 241,800,000,000	0.5%	$ 93,334,800,000	38.6%
Kingdom of Spain	$ 1,378,000,000,000	1.8%	$ 516,750,000,000	37.5%
Republic of Turkey	$ 906,500,000,000	1.1%	$ 336,311,500,000	37.1%
Kingdom of Sweden	$ 348,600,000,000	0.6%	$ 127,239,000,000	36.5%
Slovak Republic	$ 119,500,000,000	0.2%	$ 41,825,000,000	35.0%
Republic of Finland	$ 195,200,000,000	0.3%	$ 64,416,000,000	33.0%
Republic of Korea	$ 1,278,000,000,000	1.4%	$ 417,906,000,000	32.7%
Ireland	$ 191,900,000,000	0.4%	$ 60,448,500,000	31.5%
Republic of Indonesia	$ 915,900,000,000	1.7%	$ 275,685,900,000	30.1%
Republic of South Africa	$ 489,700,000,000	0.5%	$ 146,420,300,000	29.9%
Czech Republic	$ 266,300,000,000	0.5%	$ 78,292,200,000	29.4%
Republic of Peru	$ 238,900,000,000	0.2%	$ 57,574,900,000	24.1%
Republic of Iceland	$ 12,150,000,000	0.0%	$ 2,794,500,000	23.0%
Republic of Slovenia	$ 59,140,000,000	0.1%	$ 13,010,800,000	22.0%
Kingdom of Denmark	$ 204,900,000,000	0.4%	$ 44,668,200,000	21.8%

Sovereign Entity	GDP (2008)	Share World GDP (est)	Public Debt (current)	Debt % GDP
United Mexican States	$ 1,559,000,000,000	1.9%	$ 316,477,000,000	20.3%
Bolivarian Republic of Venezuela	$ 357,900,000,000	0.6%	$ 62,274,600,000	17.4%
Republic of Latvia	$ 39,980,000,000	0.1%	$ 6,796,600,000	17.0%
Republic of Bulgaria	$ 93,780,000,000	0.2%	$ 15,661,260,000	16.7%
People's Republic of China	$ 7,800,000,000,000	7.7%	$ 1,224,600,000,000	15.7%
Romania	$ 271,200,000,000	0.3%	$ 38,239,200,000	14.1%
Republic of Lithuania	$ 63,250,000,000	0.1%	$ 7,526,750,000	11.9%
Ukraine	$ 337,000,000,000	0.6%	$ 33,700,000,000	10.0%
Republic of Kazakhstan	$ 176,900,000,000	0.3%	$ 16,097,900,000	9.1%
Russian Federation	$ 2,225,000,000,000	4.3%	$ 151,300,000,000	6.8%
State of Qatar	$ 85,350,000,000	0.2%	$ 5,121,000,000	6.0%
State of New York	$ 1,144,481,000,000	2.1%	$ 48,500,000,000	4.2%
State of California	$ 1,801,762,000,000	3.4%	$ 69,400,000,000	3.9%
Republic of Chile	$ 245,300,000,000	0.3%	$ 9,321,400,000	3.8%
Republic of Estonia	$ 27,720,000,000	0.1%	$ 1,053,360,000	3.8%
State of Florida	$ 744,120,000,000	1.4%	$ 24,100,000,000	3.2%
The City of New York	$ 1,123,532,000,000	2.1%	$ 55,823,000,000	**

*List from Depository Trust and Clearing Corporation. [www.dtcc.com] Dubai was also on this list, but debt and GDP data were not available.

**NYC GDP includes entire NY-NJ-PA metropolitan statistical area; debt is for City of NY only.

Countries in Italics have never failed to meet their debt repayment schedules (Reinhart and Rogoff, *This Time is Different: Eight Centuries of Financial Folly* (Princeton University Press, 2009); Thailand and Korea received IMF assistance to avoid default in the 1990s.

Appendix 4: Sovereigns named in most credit default protection*

Table for "The next public debt crisis has arrived", page 134

Sovereign Entity	2009 Debt % GDP	2012 Debt % GDP	2009 CDS % Debt	2012 CDS % Debt	CDS change 2008 to 2012***	Region
Republic of Iceland	23.0%	130.1%	315.2%	40.4%	-2,322,155,904	Europe
Republic of Estonia	3.8%	5.8%	206.7%	193.4%	844,012,716	Europe
Ukraine	10.0%	44.8%	194.5%	28.9%	-23,102,981,592	Europe
Republic of Kazakhstan	9.1%	16.0%	144.0%	57.5%	-3,440,253,859	Europe
Republic of Bulgaria	16.7%	17.5%	100.6%	112.5%	4,163,215,975	Europe
Republic of Latvia	17.0%	44.8%	92.4%	62.3%	3,369,945,521	Europe
Bolivarian Republic of Venezuela	17.4%	38.0%	80.7%	45.9%	5,646,959,440	Americas
State of Qatar	6.0%	8.9%	76.4%	55.4%	5,040,787,988	Europe
Russian Federation	6.8%	8.7%	72.7%	55.7%	4,966,368,803	Europe
Republic of Turkey	37.1%	42.4%	56.1%	32.5%	-43,726,859,566	Europe
Republic of Lithuania	11.9%	37.7%	42.7%	28.8%	3,438,691,822	Europe
Republic of Panama	46.4%	41.7%	36.7%	37.1%	989,207,525	Americas
Republic of The Philippines	56.5%	49.4%	36.6%	28.8%	-10,157,402,334	Asia Ex-Japan
Republic of Peru	24.1%	21.9%	34.1%	41.1%	7,324,285,482	Americas
Romania	14.1%	34.0%	31.2%	20.6%	6,566,917,982	Europe
Republic of Chile	3.8%	9.4%	30.9%	21.2%	2,719,694,915	Americas
Ireland	31.5%	209.2%	28.2%	22.5%	27,767,560,886	Europe
United Mexican States	20.3%	37.5%	23.7%	20.2%	50,658,161,703	Americas
Republic of Slovenia	22.0%	45.5%	22.5%	23.0%	3,206,639,043	Europe
Republic of Hungary	73.8%	76.0%	21.6%	47.1%	37,403,179,311	Europe
Republic of South Africa	29.9%	35.6%	21.5%	24.6%	17,010,145,334	Europe
Argentine Republic	51.0%	42.9%	18.7%	17.2%	-2,448,737,614	Americas

Sovereign Entity	2009 Debt % GDP	2012 Debt % GDP	2009 CDS % Debt	2012 CDS % Debt	CDS change 2008 to 2012***	Region
Federative Republic of Brazil	40.7%	54.4%	18.2%	13.0%	14,703,918,548	Americas
Portuguese Republic	64.2%	72.1%	15.9%	25.2%	39,897,746,989	Europe
Republic of Colombia	48.0%	45.6%	15.9%	14.9%	1,221,052,625	Americas
Slovak Republic	35.0%	44.5%	12.8%	19.3%	5,533,166,393	Europe
Kingdom of Spain	37.5%	68.2%	11.9%	16.9%	101,554,412,387	Europe
Republic of Korea	32.7%	22.9%	11.8%	20.0%	22,088,912,724	Asia Ex-Japan
Republic of Croatia	48.9%	60.5%	11.5%	19.9%	5,612,474,098	Europe
Hellenic Republic (Greece)	90.1%	165.4%	11.1%	13.6%	34,488,989,840	Europe
Republic of Indonesia	30.1%	24.5%	11.0%	16.1%	13,723,880,843	Asia Ex-Japan
Malaysia	42.7%	57.9%	9.7%	7.8%	4,044,633,137	Asia Ex-Japan
Kingdom of Denmark	21.8%	46.9%	9.3%	17.2%	12,665,229,924	Europe
State of Florida	3.2%	17.9%	8.1%	16.8%	2,787,096,121	Americas
Republic of Austria	58.8%	103.3%	7.9%	21.3%	38,904,764,846	Europe
Republic of Italy	103.7%	120.1%	7.9%	14.6%	171,818,588,038	Europe
Kingdom of Thailand	42.0%	45.6%	7.1%	6.5%	1,675,447,429	Asia Ex-Japan
Socialist Republic of Vietnam	38.6%	54.5%	6.4%	5.9%	3,717,696,305	Asia Ex-Japan
Czech Republic	29.4%	39.9%	6.0%	11.5%	7,793,110,452	Europe
Republic of Poland	41.6%	56.7%	5.9%	9.7%	25,523,188,448	Europe
Republic of Finland	33.0%	49.0%	5.7%	17.3%	12,868,084,419	Europe
The City of New York	**	7.5%	4.3%	8.4%	3,555,950,000	Americas
State of New York	4.2%	24.8%	4.3%	5.3%	1,215,398,707	Americas
Kingdom of Sweden	36.5%	36.8%	4.1%	15.0%	15,665,446,384	Europe
Kingdom of Belgium	80.8%	99.7%	3.9%	15.1%	49,607,728,521	Europe
State of Israel	75.7%	74.0%	3.4%	7.0%	7,093,224,168	Europe
State of California	3.9%	18.3%	3.2%	12.7%	8,068,160,000	Americas

A DECADE OF ARMAGEDDON

Sovereign Entity	2009 Debt % GDP	2012 Debt % GDP	2009 CDS % Debt	2012 CDS % Debt	CDS change 2008 to 2012***	Region
Federal Republic of Germany	62.6%	81.5%	2.1%	4.5%	75,770,481,300	Europe
Kingdom of Norway	52.0%	48.4%	1.6%	6.3%	5,953,647,323	Europe
Kingdom of The Netherlands	43.0%	64.4%	1.6%	5.3%	19,494,129,128	Europe
People's Republic of China	15.7%	16.3%	1.5%	3.7%	49,294,027,432	Asia Ex-Japan
French Republic	67.0%	85.5%	1.5%	6.8%	108,226,300,245	Europe
United Kingdom of Great Britain & Northern Ireland	47.2%	79.5%	1.2%	3.6%	51,470,774,560	Europe
Japan	170.4%	208.2%	0.1%	0.8%	67,160,972,268	Japan
United States of America	60.8%	69.4%	0.1%	0.2%	19,471,174,892	Americas

*List from Depository Trust and Clearing Corporation. [www.dtcc.com]. Dubai was also on this list, but debt and GDP data were not available.

**2012 GDP for City of NY was calculated by subtracting all other MSA output from state GDP.

***Lower totals may indicate that some credit default swap contracts have been paid off.

Countries in *Italics* had not failed to meet their debt repayment schedules before 2008 (Reinhart and Rogoff, This Time is Different: Eight Centuries of Financial Folly (Princeton University Press, 2009); Thailand and Korea received IMF assistance to avoid default in the 1990s.

Appendix 5: MBS Explanation and Diagram

Mortgage-Backed Security (MBS Structure)

Excerpt from Beyond Junk: Expanding High Yield Markets, Susanne Trimbath and Glenn Yago, Oxford University Press (2002). Chapter 5. Extended Markets and Innovative Extensions.

> "Clearly, the traditional bond investment is evolving into new forms as investors try to improve their relative performance. The menu is larger than it has ever been, and there is something for everyone willing to break the old habit of buying fixed-rate, investment grade securities of companies whose best years often are behind them."

> The Case for High Yield Bonds,

> Drexel Burnham Lambert, 1984.

Structured Finance: Collateralized Debt Obligations

Collateralized debt obligations are relatively recent financial innovations that take assets subject to credit risk and restructure them into new debt securities issued in a number of separate tranches with different levels of creditworthiness. A special purpose vehicle (SPV) is created to buy risky assets and then re-issue them chiefly as high-grade bonds with a subordinated or equity tranche containing the great majority of the original assets' credit risk.

In a world of complete and perfect capital markets there would be no need for CDOs, but in incomplete or imperfect markets or in the presence of capital requirements, such structured products add value by increasing the liquidity of, usually high yield, debt offerings, allowing investors to gain access to high yield securities they would otherwise be unable to hold and reducing the amount of regulatory capital a bank is compelled to hold.

One important use of CDOs is to pool together a group of smaller issues. Individual bond issues may be a too small in size to attract sufficient trading volume or may be otherwise illiquid. Securitization though the creation of a CDO commonly increases liquidity and thus both reduces the liquidity risk of firms trading them and decreases bid-ask spreads on the securities. CDOs can also be used by institutions to gain access to the higher rates of return offered by either credit risk or correlation risk that they would be prevented from investing in by regulations. The collateralization of high yield bonds allowed institutions barred by law from holding these issues to gain access to their attractive yields.

A third use of CDOs involves the use of an SPV to shift part or all of a loan portfolio off a commercial bank's balance sheet into a collateralized loan obligation (CLO). Removing loans has the beneficial effect of allowing the bank to free up expensive regulatory capital that it would otherwise be compelled by regulation to hold. Finally, the value of CDOs stems from investors' seeming taste for vehicles at the extremes of the spectrum of risk – equity and high grade debt.

One broad type of CDO is the Mortgage-Backed Security (MBS), based on mortgages issued by banks or government sponsored housing finance institutions (Freddie Mac and Fannie Mae). Developments in the mortgage bond market began in 1983 with vehicles structured only with Freddie Mac assets to relieve problems of mortgage prepayment risk. Prepayment risk can be concentrated in the equity tranche of an MBS just as credit risk is compartmentalized in other structured securities. An MBS also allows investors to gain access to the mortgage-backed market without purchasing securities with maturities as long as the typical mortgage.

In the basic structure of an MBS the portfolio purchased by the Special Purpose Vehicle (SPV) is made up of mortgages. As the payments on the mortgages are collected, the MBS provides for interest and principal payments to the bondholders.

Mortgage-Backed Security (MBS Structure)

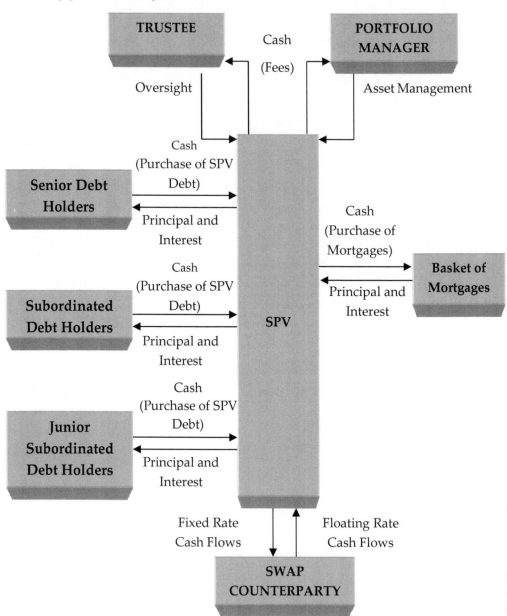

A DECADE OF ARMAGEDDON

Table of figures

Index of names

Also by Susanne Trimbath:

Naked, Short and Greedy - Wall Street's Failure to Deliver

Rigged financial markets and hopeless under-regulation on Wall Street are not new problems. In this book, Susanne Trimbath gives a sobering account of naked short selling, the failure to settle, and her efforts over decades, trying to get this fixed.

Spiramus Press, 2019

Lessons Not Learned - 10 Steps to Stable Financial Markets

Much has been written and spoken about the lessons learned from the financial crisis of 2009. In this book, we list the lessons not learned before the financial crisis. The purpose of this book is to demonstrate that the theoretical and intellectual frameworks for regulating financial systems that had been available since at least 2001 could have prevented the systemic failure in the United States that led to the collapse of global credit markets in 2008.

Spiramus Press, 2015

Scan for PDF of links and references:

https://spiramus.com/decade-of-armageddon-links-and-references